Exploring the Basic Income Guarantee

Series Editor

Karl Widerquist, Georgetown University in Qatar, Doha, Qatar

Basic income is one of the most innovative, powerful, straightforward, and controversial proposals for addressing poverty and growing inequalities. A Basic Income Guarantee (BIG) is designed to be an unconditional, government-insured guarantee that all citizens will have enough income to meet their basic needs. The concept of basic, or guaranteed, income is a form of social provision and this series examines the arguments for and against it from an interdisciplinary perspective with special focus on the economic and social factors. By systematically connecting abstract philosophical debates over competing principles of BIG to the empirical analysis of concrete policy proposals, this series contributes to the fields of economics, politics, social policy, and philosophy and establishes a theoretical framework for interdisciplinary research. It will bring together international and national scholars and activists to provide a comparative look at the main efforts to date to pass unconditional BIG legislation across regions of the globe and will identify commonalities and differences across countries drawing lessons for advancing social policies in general and BIG policies in particular.

Malcolm Torry

Basic Income—What, Why, and How?

Aspects of the Global Basic Income Debate

palgrave
macmillan

Malcolm Torry
Institute for Policy Research
University of Bath
Bath, UK

ISSN 2662-3803 ISSN 2662-3811 (electronic)
Exploring the Basic Income Guarantee
ISBN 978-3-031-14247-5 ISBN 978-3-031-14248-2 (eBook)
https://doi.org/10.1007/978-3-031-14248-2

This Palgrave Macmillan imprint is published by the registered company Springer Nature Switzerland AG
The registered company address is: Gewerbestrasse 11, 6330 Cham, Switzerland

Preface

From 1976 to 1978 I worked as a Clerical Officer administering means-tested benefits in the Department for Health and Social Security (DHSS) local office in Brixton, in South London. For the whole of those two years, I sat behind the public counter, increasingly aware of the damage that means-testing was doing to both claimants and staff. A somewhat ill-defined understanding that additional unconditional benefits, such as the UK's Child Benefit, were what was required, began to take shape. Training for ordination as a priest in the Church of England intervened, followed by a curacy in the parish in which the DHSS had its headquarters: and then in 1982 I found myself invited to the Department's summer school at which one of the lecturers was Hermione (Mimi) Parker, who had provided costings for a submission on Basic Income presented to a parliamentary committee by Brandon Rhys Williams MP. Two years later, by which time I was working for the South London Industrial Mission, I was invited to join a group that Mimi and others had gathered to research the desirability and feasibility of providing every individual with an unconditional income. That group became the Basic Income Research Group—subsequently the Citizen's Income Trust, and then the Citizen's Basic Income Trust—of which I was Director in a voluntary capacity for twenty years. Until 2014 I served full time in South London parishes, and successive Bishops of Woolwich kindly gave me permission to spend half a day a week working on Basic Income: permission for which I continue to be grateful. However, by 2014 the demands of the global Basic Income debate had become difficult to manage alongside full-time pastoral work on the Greenwich Peninsula and beyond, so I retired early in order to give the debate the time that it needed, and subsequently served as almost full-time voluntary Director of the Citizen's Basic Income Trust until 2020; as General Manager of the Basic Income Earth Network (BIEN) from 2016 to 2021, again in a voluntary capacity; as author of a variety of books: *101 Reasons for a Citizen's Income* (2015); *The Feasibility of Citizen's Income* (2016); *Citizen's Basic Income: A Christian social* policy (2016); *Why we need a Citizen's Basic Income* (2018: an almost entirely rewritten second edition of *Money for Everyone*, published in 2013); *A Modern Guide to Citizen's Basic Income: A multidisciplinary approach* (2020); and *Basic Income: A history* (2021); and as editor of *The Palgrave International Handbook of Basic Income* (2019).

For the past thirty years or so I have presented papers at various conferences, including BIEN's congresses. These have often been quoted and referenced in my books, but they have never been published as originally presented. I have also written chapters for edited collections, and articles for journals, and the subject matter of these has been less well represented in the books that I have authored or edited. I am grateful to Karl Widerquist, the editor of the series to which this volume belongs, for the insight that some of these chapters, articles, and conference papers would form a coherent book if brought together. This is that book.

Those chapters that have been published previously are reproduced as originally published, with only minor revisions; and conference papers have been reproduced as originally submitted, again with only minor revisions. The only amendments that have been made are that throughout the book formatting and referencing have been made consistent; an unconditional income for every individual has been called a Basic Income, rather than a Citizen's Income or a Universal Basic Income, as in some of the original chapters, articles, and conference papers; and some of the references and statistics have been updated. Occasionally the text has been amended where previous speculation or discussion of proposals can now be replaced by factual information. Unless they are constituted purely by changes in tense, such amendments have been identified by square brackets.

No attempt has been made to remove repetitions, so at the beginning of many of the articles, chapters, and papers, the reader will find an introduction to the concept of a Basic Income, and readers will also find other similar or identical material in two or more chapters where the arguments of the different chapters require that. Retaining such repetition should enable each chapter to be read on its own without reference to other chapters. Any reader wishing to read the book as a whole will be able to develop the habit of skimming material that is clearly similar to passages that they have already read.

The articles, papers, and chapters reproduced here were all written as contributions to the rationality and evidence base of the Basic Income debate. My hope is that this book will inspire its readers to make their own contributions to the rationality and evidence base that the increasingly lively and diverse global Basic Income debate will continue to need.

Detailed acknowledgements appear at the end of each of the chapters, but I would like here to express general gratitude to the publishers of previously published material for permissions to republish; to all those—reviewers, seminar and conference participants, and those whom I have consulted—who have contributed to the writing of the papers, articles, and chapters to be found here; and to those many people who have contributed to my understanding and exploration of the desirability and feasibility of a Basic Income.

Bath, UK Malcolm Torry

Contents

List of Figures

List of Tables

PART I

Introduction

CHAPTER 1

Basic Income: What, Why, and How?

Introduction

The book of which this is the first brief chapter is a collection of chapters previously published in edited collections, articles published in peer-reviewed journals, previously unpublished conference papers, and working papers previously published on a research institute website. All of these have been referenced at various times in the books that I have written, and most of them have been accessible in one way or another, but some are more accessible than others, and some are not accessible at all, apart from by application to the author. Realising that this scattered material might be more useful to individuals and organisations involved in the increasingly lively global debate on Basic Income if it was brought together, I suggested as much to Karl Widerquist, editor of the series in which this book appears, who suggested that it would form not simply a collection, but rather a coherent book: so this first chapter not only summarises the content of the other chapters but also explains how the collection fits together.

Each chapter reproduces the original article, paper, or chapter in the form in which it was first published. No attempt has been made to remove repetitions: and so, for instance, readers will find that several of the chapters begin with a brief explanation of what a Basic Income is. This ensures

M. Torry, *Basic Income—What, Why, and How?*,
Exploring the Basic Income Guarantee,
https://doi.org/10.1007/978-3-031-14248-2_1

that each chapter retains the integrity of the original paper or publication, and it enables a reader to read each chapter without referring to any other.

A few minor changes have been made. A variety of terms for Basic Income have been in use in the United Kingdom and globally during the past forty years, and particularly Basic Income, Universal Basic Income, Citizen's Income, and Citizen's Basic Income. The original publications and papers employed a variety of these. For the sake of consistency, 'Basic Income' has been used throughout the book. Similarly, referencing was in a variety of styles in the original publications and papers, and this too has been made consistent. Only where a statement made in the original paper or publication is no longer true is any correction made: for instance, where an experiment had not reported findings and now has; and occasionally tenses have been changed in order to aid comprehension. No attempt has been made to complete incomplete history. Any reader wishing to update their knowledge of the history of Basic Income can now refer to a comprehensive treatment of the subject (Torry, 2021).

The only chapter to which the above does not apply is Chapter 16. This contains material drawn from three working papers that report the results of microsimulation research on illustrative Basic Income schemes and a variety of other illustrative tax and benefits reforms. Here a paper written in 2019 forms the basis of the chapter, and material written in 2020 and 2021 is used to update and extend it. Because of the length of the working papers some of the material has been summarised. So in relation to this chapter, and only in relation to this chapter, any reader wishing to study all of the detail of the original research results will need to refer to the original working papers, which are easily accessible and are referenced at the end of the chapter in the usual way.

The Plan of the Book

The book is in five parts. First of all this brief introductory chapter also summarises the overall argument of the book; secondly, chapters about definitions of terms central to the Basic Income debate; thirdly, two discussions of reasons for the importance of Basic Income; fourthly, material on feasibility and implementation; and finally, a focus on the United Kingdom.

The first substantive part of the book, part II, is about definitions. The widespread nature of the Basic Income debate means that clear and agreed definitions of significant terms are now more necessary than ever and also more difficult to achieve than ever before. The first chapter in the section, Chapter 2, discusses the definition of Basic Income itself, with a view to constructing a categorisation of definitions.

Chapter 3 asks about the definitions of 'unconditional' and 'universal'—two terms frequently encountered in the Basic Income debate—and offers a categorisation of conditionalities that reveals a person's age to be the only conditionality permitted in relation to the definition of Basic Income, with the consequence that the amount of the Basic Income can vary with an individual's age but not in relation to any other conditionality.

Chapter 4 distinguishes between a Basic Income and a Basic Income scheme, with the former always being an unconditional income for every individual, and the latter specifying the amounts of the Basic Income for each age group, the funding method, and any accompanying changes to existing tax and benefits systems. A Basic Income will always have the same effects, but different schemes can have very different effects. Important conclusions are that to prove infeasible a particular Basic Income scheme does not prove Basic Income to be infeasible, and that only one scheme has to be proved to be feasible in a particular jurisdiction for Basic Income to be feasible in that jurisdiction. Similarly, arguments for or against a Minimum Income Guarantee, or any other mechanism that is not a Basic Income, are not arguments for or against Basic Income.

What this section of the book shows is how important the matter of definitions is to the global debate on Basic Income.

Part III of the book contains two chapters on reasons for a Basic Income. There are now numerous books on why Basic Income would be a good idea. My own first book on the subject, *Money for everyone*, published in 2013, was largely about this, as was its largely rewritten second edition in 2018, *Why we need a Citizen's Basic Income*: and between those two, *101 reasons for a Citizen's Income*, published in 2015, was what it said it was: simply a list of reasons for implementing a Basic Income. While the debate since then has turned more towards questions of feasibility and implementation, there is still plenty of debate about whether a Basic Income would be a good idea. The two chapters in this section of the book offer material on two reasons for Basic Income that might have been less discussed than some others.

Chapter 5 finds that Basic Income could both preserve and transform capitalism. First of all, a variety of definitions of capitalism are discussed, and then Basic Income is related to each of those definitions. The chapter concludes that it would be essential only to implement Basic Income schemes that reduce inequality; that Basic Income should not be used as an excuse to abolish services best organised in the public sector; that Basic Income could make the employment market more like the free market envisaged by capitalism; that Basic Income would enable workers to be less dominated by capital; and that Basic Income could help to transform a capitalist economy into an economy founded on the gift relationship.

Chapter 6 studies the resources needed to achieve an acceptable social minimum, the characteristics that those resources require, and their mode of delivery. The conclusion is drawn that in order to provide for a minimally decent life it is to the mode of delivery of resources, and particularly to that of income, that attention must be paid.

We can conclude from this section of the book that a Basic Income would both serve and transform the private capitalist sector, and enable the public sector to provide incomes in a way most conducive to the living of a minimally decent life.

Feasibility and implementation have been elements of the modern debate since its beginning, but about ten years ago they began to take on increasing importance. Part IV of the book contains articles, chapters, and conference papers that responded to the greater prominence of issues relating to feasibility and implementation.

Chapter 7, although being about the United Kingdom, is included in this section of the book because of the general lessons that it offers in relation to the political feasibility of Basic Income. It traces the history of unconditional incomes for children and of a variety of other policy proposals, and by asking why things happened as they did it draws conclusions as to the factors that might make a policy proposal more or less likely to be implemented. Particular lessons are drawn in relation to the political feasibility of Basic Income.

Chapter 8 studies the notion of feasibility and suggests that there is a variety of feasibility tests that any policy proposal would need to pass if it were to be implemented. The different feasibilities are discussed in relation to Basic Income, and strategies to turn non-feasibility into feasibility are suggested.

There is no shortage of objections to Basic Income, and Chapter 9 combines three previously published short articles in order to tackle some of them. An argument against Basic Income's affordability is shown to be an argument for a particular Basic Income scheme's unaffordability, whereas to prove just one Basic Income scheme affordable is to prove Basic Income to be affordable. And arguments against something that is not a Basic Income are shown not to be arguments against Basic Income. The chapter shows the importance of employing the best available evidence and the best possible logic.

There would be many different routes to the implementation of a Basic Income, and Chapter 10 discusses some of them, particularly in relation to the contexts of the UK and Australia.

Chapter 11 relates to a particularly fraught perennial debate: whether the definition of Basic Income should include a statement of the amount that should be paid, and in particular whether only a Basic Income at subsistence level, somehow defined, should be termed a Basic Income. The chapter studies the concept of adequacy, defines subsistence levels in terms of Minimum Income Standards, shows that a Basic Income set at Minimum Income Standard levels would be infeasible to implement, and finds that a Basic Income scheme could bring households closer to those levels even if a Basic Income by itself could not.

Whether a Basic Income should be implemented for a single country, for a region, for one part of a federal country, or globally, has often been discussed, and the longest standing regional proposal is for a Eurodividend: a Basic Income for Europe, either for the European Union or for the Eurozone. Chapter 12 explores the advantages that a Eurodividend would offer, and suggests the research that that particular corner of the Basic Income debate now requires.

The upsurge in the Basic Income debate during the past ten years has often been driven by pilot projects and other experiments. Chapter 13 discusses the conditions that an experiment has to fulfil to be counted as a pilot project; reviews a number of past, current, and planned experiments to decide whether they are pilot projects; argues that microsimulation research provides much of the information that pilot projects can provide; and decides that pilot projects are still required to test those effects of Basic Income that microsimulation cannot test.

Part V of the book focuses on the United Kingdom. Although some of the other chapters in the book study the United Kingdom as a case study, their inclusion is mainly for the more general lessons that they offer. In this part of the book, the focus is firmly on the Basic Income debate in the United Kingdom.

Chapter 14 studies a number of UK policy changes and proposals in order to discover the factors that might determine whether a proposal is likely to be implemented. Two case studies are discussed: the Living

Wage campaign, which campaigns locally and nationally for a wage high enough to live on; and a shift in the direction of unconditional benefits.

Chapter 15 explores the history of the Basic Income debate in the UK and finds it to have been characterised throughout by research and by an educational approach. Three significant events are discussed to show how research evidence can be abused or ignored. The chapter concludes that essential to the health of the debate are careful definition, high-quality research, an educational approach accompanied by a diversity of approaches, and a wide variety of institutions involved in the debate.

Chapter 16 describes this author's fifteen year personal journey in microsimulation research: the employment of a computer programme with the UK's tax and benefits regulations coded into it and through which is passed financial data on a statistically significant sample of the population in order to discover the changes that implementing illustrative Basic Income schemes would bring about in relation to poverty, inequality, household net disposable income losses, numbers of households on means-tested benefits, and so on. The chapter describes methods developed and revised, results discovered, and conclusions drawn during the journey, and also the standard illustrative scheme that has evolved. Responses are given to a variety of questions, and avenues for future research are suggested.

This book contains no concluding chapter. This is for two reasons: first of all, most of the chapters offer their own conclusions, and as each chapter has already stood alone, and will continue to do so, it is those particular conclusions related to the particular issues under discussion in each chapter that will be important to the reader and to the wider Basic Income debate; and secondly, it is possible on the basis of the brief descriptions offered of the chapters here to draw some initial conclusions that the reader might wish to test out as they read those individual chapters in which they are particularly interested, or indeed while they read the rest of the book.

These are the tentative conclusions that we might draw:

- Clear and agreed definitions are essential to the integrity of the Basic Income debate, and particularly a clear and agreed definition of Basic Income;
- The debate must continue to be about the desirability of Basic Income, its feasibility, and its implementation;

- The debate should be as diverse as possible, in relation to the different disciplines employed, and in relation to the different perspectives and issues explored;
- High quality research, employing the best available methods, is essential to the health of the debate;
- The best logic available should be employed.

The chapters of this book represent a tiny proportion of the vast diversity of the now deep and widespread debate on Basic Income. There is so much more of it to study and understand, and there is much still to do.

Reference

Torry, M. (2021). *Basic income—A history*. Edward Elgar Publishing.

PART II

What is a Basic Income?

CHAPTER 2

Defining Basic Income

Introduction

There has been much discussion, in Basic Income Earth Network (BIEN, 2020, 2022a, 2022b) circles and elsewhere, as to how a Basic Income should be defined. The question is this: What does 'Basic Income' mean, and how can that meaning be expressed in a set of words? Related questions are these: What does 'Citizen's Income' mean? What does 'Universal Basic Income' mean? What does 'Citizen's Basic Income' mean? What does 'Basic Income Guarantee' mean? And what do 'unconditional' and 'universal' mean?

This chapter will first of all explore the meaning of 'definition': that is, what are we doing when we 'define' something? (How should we define 'define'? Take care, reader, that you do not disappear down an infinite vortex.) We shall discover a variety of ways of defining and will then apply those different methods to the task of defining a Basic Income, a Citizen's Income, and so on. Finally, we shall look at the policy implications of different definitions.

Why does any of this matter? It matters because mutual comprehension requires that different participants in a conversation should understand similar things by a particular word or group of words. If we mean different things by 'Basic Income' then people and organisations involved

M. Torry, *Basic Income—What, Why, and How?*,
Exploring the Basic Income Guarantee,
https://doi.org/10.1007/978-3-031-14248-2_2

in research and debate might think that they are understanding each other when in fact, they are not. While 'definition' and 'meaning' do not mean the same thing, and, as we shall see, two people can mean different things by the same words, for two people to agree on a definition of Basic Income can help each of them to have some idea about what the other one means by 'Basic Income' and can therefore enable useful dialogue to occur.

Different Ways of Defining

Usage

Ludwig Wittgenstein suggested that we discover the meaning of language by studying how language is used (Wittgenstein, 1967: 1), and, as the same word might be used in different ways in a multitude of different contexts, he offered the image of 'family resemblances' to describe the relationship between one use of a word and another (Wittgenstein 1967: 66–67).

By 'definition' we generally mean a set of words that indicates the 'meaning' of a word or group of words. This immediately poses a problem. If we study a particular use of a word and then construct a set of words to express the meaning of that use, then the use of the new set of words, and of each of its component words, will be specific to a particular context: so even if we employ the same definition (in the sense of the same set of words in the same order) in a different context, it will have a different meaning.

However, there really will be a family *resemblance*: and it is on this that dictionaries rely when they define a word or group of words. The Oxford English Dictionary not only offers a definition of each English word commonly in use, but it also lists the particular usages on which it has based its definition. There is no entry for 'Basic Income' or 'Citizen's Income' (which is interesting), but we do of course find both 'basic' and 'income'. 'Basic' used as an adjective is given a wide variety of definitions, the first two of which are as follows:

> a. Of, pertaining to, or forming a base; fundamental, essential: ... b. That is or constitutes a standard minimum amount in a scale of remuneration or the like. (Oxford University Press, 2022)

The dictionary also offers the following definition:

> Providing or having few or no amenities, accessories, functions, etc., beyond the ordinary or essential; of or designating the lowest standard acceptable or available; rudimentary: (Oxford University Press, 2022)

—of which it gives an example: 'Pastries and other sweets in the north can be pretty basic'.

English as spoken in the United States of America exhibits similar meanings:

> a. being the main or most important part of something … b. very simple, with nothing special added: 'The software is very basic.' (Cambridge University Press, 2022)

Whether the derogatory undertones are understood by a speaker using the word 'basic' in the context of 'Basic Income', or by someone hearing or reading the words, will depend on the speaker's, writer's, hearer's, or reader's previous experience of the word 'basic' and the context in which the word is being used; and whether these undertones will be encapsulated in definitions will again depend on the context. It is in relation to such undertones that meaning and definition can diverge. When we hear the term 'Basic Income' we might define it as 'an unconditional and nonwithdrawable income for every individual': but we might also understand the term to mean that in some respect the income will not be a very good one—an aspect of our understanding that might not appear in the stated definition.

The conclusion to draw from this discussion is that two people using the same words do not necessarily mean the same thing by them and that they might not mean the same thing by words that they use to explicate the meaning of those words. This means that to attempt to define 'Basic Income' by reference to current usage will deliver a variety of different definitions, and an even wider variety of understood meanings, with each definition and meaning being dependent on the particular uses of the words that the definer has experienced and the context in which the words are being used. There might or might not be a family resemblance between the different definitions and between the different meanings.

In relation to the global debate on Basic Income, a significant additional question has to be that of the transferability of definitions between different languages. The German '*Grundeinkommen*' offers a useful example. '*Grund*' in this context means 'foundation', so '*Grundeinkommen*' means a foundational income. There is no sense here that the income is not of good quality. '*Basiseinkommen*' has a similar meaning to '*Grundeinkommen*': it represents an income that provides a foundation on which people can build. So again, the question arises as to whether two people using a word will mean the same thing by it. An English speaker might translate '*Grundeinkommen*' as 'Basic Income' and understand some derogatory undertones that a German speaker would not understand when they heard the same word. The relationship between the various definitions of '*Grundeinkommen*' and the various definitions of 'Basic Income' will therefore be an interesting one.

Definition by Characteristics

What is sometimes called the 'classical' way of defining a definition is to envisage a category defined by a list of characteristics, with the category name being defined by names of characteristics. Thus the category 'table' is defined by the characteristics 'horizontal surface' and 'supported on legs'. Those entities that possess the characteristics are in the category, and those entities that do not are not: so a square is a rectangle because it has four sides, opposite sides are parallel, and the angles are right angles. But for anything other than simple cases of definition this strategy quickly breaks down because there are frequently cases where we cannot determine whether the entity concerned is in the category or not. Thus if to be a 'bird' something needs to fly, then an ostrich is not a bird and a bat is one. A folded drop-leaf table is not a table, whereas a stool is a table.

Eleanor Rosch (Rosch, 1999; Rosch & Lloyd, 1978) has suggested that categories are not the clear-cut things that we often think they are, and that it is often not the case that entities are either in the category or not in it; and neither is it the case that entities belong equally. Thus a robin is more a bird than an ostrich is, and a bat is on the boundary of the category. Rosch points out that in the real world we define categories in terms of prototypes and then decide whether something is in the category by asking how similar it is to the prototype. For the category 'bird' the prototype might be 'robin'. Mark Johnson (Johnson, 1993) has successfully used this means of definition to give a coherent account of how we categorise actions as moral or otherwise: we have in our minds a prototype lie and we then ask whether other actions are more or less like it.

So the question to ask is this: Is there a set of characteristics by which we can decide whether something belongs in the category labelled 'Basic Income'? There are a number of ways to approach this:

- Each user of the term 'Basic Income' could select their own preferred characteristics. The individual's autonomy would thus be honoured, but at the risk of losing mutual comprehension.
- We could study a wide variety of actual usages of the term 'Basic Income' and work out the lists of characteristics either stated or assumed by users of the term. If we could find characteristics employed in *all* actual usages, then we would have discovered the 'family likeness' and would be able to list a definitive set of characteristics. However, that does not mean that everyone would agree with the list. It would only take one user of the term 'Basic Income' to insist that they understood a characteristic not in the list to be essential to the definition of the category for the definition to become contentious and thus problematic in relation to attempts at mutual comprehension.
- An authority of some kind could decide on the list of characteristics that would qualify something as belonging to the category 'Basic Income'. This is our third definitional strategy.

ARecognised Authority

If a field of interest has related to it an organisation that those involved in that field believe to have some standing or authority, then participants might look to that organisation to supply definitions of terms. This will be by way of something like a social contract. In order to avoid the chaos of multiple definitions, participants might be willing to forego autonomy and to grant authority to the recognised organisation.

There are a number of ways in which the organisation might construct the expected definitions. It might construct a list of characteristics that something has to have in order to be included in the named category; or it might collect examples of the use of the term and on that basis decide on a definition; or it might employ a mixture of those methods: constructing a list of characteristics and testing the list against current usage. There might be various ways in which an organisation goes about the task. There might be an individual with the authority to make such decisions;

a small body of people might be elected or appointed to decide; or the entire membership might decide on a definition by a democratic process (although this method might in practice come down to an individual or small group making the decision because the wording of a resolution will always be words written by an individual or a small group).

Defining 'Basic Income'

'Basic Income' is frequently defined in relation to a list of characteristics. An income might belong in the category 'Basic Income' if it is 'unconditional', 'nonwithdrawable', and paid to 'each individual' rather than to households. However, as we have seen, meaning might be richer than definition. Usually unstated, but generally assumed, are some additional characteristics:

- That the income will be paid monthly, fortnightly, or weekly (or perhaps daily?). The Alaska Permanent Fund Dividend (Goldsmith, 2012: 49–50) is paid annually and is therefore not a Basic Income.
- That the income will not vary, although regular annual upratings will be expected. Again, the Alaska Permanent Fund dividend, which is the payment of a varying dividend, is not a Basic Income.
- That the income will vary with the recipient's age, with a 'standard' amount for working age adults, smaller amounts for children, and perhaps for young adults, and larger amounts for individuals over a defined state pension age. This assumption would appear to breach the 'unconditional' requirement, and strictly speaking it does: but because this conditionality is of a particular type, the breach is permitted. In relation to social security benefits, conditionalities exhibit two variables: ease of administration, and whether or not enquiry has to be made into an individual's situation or activity. Two of the expected advantages of a Basic Income are that it will be simple to administer, and that it will require no bureaucratic intrusion into the lives of recipients. Employment market status, household structure, and disability, are conditionalities about which enquiries have to be made, so none of them can be permitted to influence the level of someone's Basic Income. On the other hand, nobody would ever have to enquire into someone's age once the government's computer knew their date of birth. Their Basic

Income would begin at their birth, the computer would automatically increase their Basic Income as they ceased to be children, when they became working age adults, and when they passed state retirement age, and it would turn off their Basic Income when they died. There would be no bureaucratic intrusion, and, indeed, no active administration to be done.

These three assumptions are generally understood to belong to the definition of a Basic Income, but they are rarely stated. If 'definition' means a set of words that give some indication of the meaning of 'Basic Income', then the definition will rarely include these three assumptions. If by 'definition' we mean the understood meaning of 'Basic Income', then they do belong to the definition.

If we look for the words that generally accompany 'Basic Income' then we will often find the words 'unconditional', 'nonwithdrawable', and 'individual'. We might find 'regular', which can encapsulate the first assumption above; we might find a statement that the payment would be 'equal' or 'uniform', reflecting the second assumption; and we will generally find different levels of Basic Income for different age groups, reflecting the third assumption. So in the case of 'Basic Income', usage delivers a fairly consistent set of characteristics, and our first two definition methods converge.

We also find the third method in use. There are now multiple organisations involved in the Basic Income debate. In many countries we can find at least one organisation facilitating the debate, and in some countries there will be more than one. (In the UK, the Citizen's Basic Income Trust has been facilitating the debate for nearly forty years; Basic Income UK is a more recent campaigning organisation; and Citizen's Basic Income Network Scotland is now facilitating the debate in Scotland). The Basic Income Earth Network (BIEN, 2022b) is the debate's global umbrella organisation. Some of the national organisations affiliate with BIEN, but BIEN has no control over the activities of the national groups.

Each of these organisations has the authority to construct its own definition, but because each organisation's definition reflects common usage, and because the organisations are in network relationships with each other and with numerous writers on the subject, we might expect a certain amount of consistency. Quite often, 'unconditional', 'nonwithdrawable', and 'individual', or similar words, will be found, and the three assumptions (regular payment, nonvarying but upratable payments, and payments varying with age) will also be found.

Because BIEN is an umbrella organisation with affiliates, its own definition of Basic Income will need to reflect current usage, and in particular it will need to reflect current usage among its affiliates. This is not difficult to achieve. The wording on its website runs as follows:

> A basic income is a periodic cash payment unconditionally delivered to all on an individual basis, without means test or work requirement.
>
> That is, basic income has the following five characteristics:
>
> - Periodic: it is paid at regular intervals (for example every month), not as a one-off grant.
> - Cash payment: it is paid in an appropriate medium of exchange, allowing those who receive it to decide what they spend it on. It is not, therefore, paid either in kind (such as food or services) or in vouchers dedicated to a specific use.
> - Individual: it is paid on an individual basis—and not, for instance, to households.
> - Universal: it is paid to all, without means test.
> - Unconditional: it is paid without a requirement to work or to demonstrate willingness-to-work. (BIEN, 2022a)

As far as I can tell, nothing in this definition conflicts with any affiliate's definition, and it represents the consensus among affiliates and, most importantly, it reflects common usage of the term 'Basic Income'. BIEN can therefore confidently function as a 'recognised authority' in relation to the definition of Basic Income: and perhaps it should. A brief Ontario 'Basic Income' experiment described its 'Basic Income' like this:

> The payment will account for other income and ensure a minimum level of income is provided. Participants will receive:
>
> - Up to $16,989 per year for a single person, less 50% of any earned income
> - Up to $24,027 per year for a couple, less 50% of any earned income
> - Up to an additional $6000 per year for a person with a disability. (Ontario n.d.)

Such payments are neither 'individual' nor 'without means test'. They do not constitute a Basic Income, and perhaps BIEN should have said that.

The Amount of the Payment

A survey of BIEN's affiliated organisations in 2016 found that almost all of the definitions of Basic Income on their websites conformed to BIEN's definition, but that there was just one issue over which the national organisations disagreed: the amount of the payment.

All of the definitions of Basic Income employed by BIEN affiliates described it as unconditional, nonwithdrawable, and individual, although not necessarily in those precise words. They either said or assumed that the payment would be regular and of a consistent amount, that is, weekly or monthly, not annually; that payments would not vary (although they would be uprated); and the amount paid would differ with someone's age. Some stated that the Basic Income would be a right of citizenship, or of legal residence, and others might have been taken to assume this.

But there were differences when it came to the levels at which Basic Income would be paid. For some national organisations, only a working age adult unconditional, nonwithdrawable, regular and individual income at 'subsistence level' qualified as a Basic Income, whereas for other organisations an unconditional, nonwithdrawable, regular and individual income of any amount could count as one. The results of the survey can be found in the appendix [of the original congress paper. The situation today remains much the same as it was in 2016].

It might be thought that this leaves an umbrella organisation such as BIEN with a dilemma, but in fact it does not. BIEN is an authoritative organisation in the field, as are all of the national organisations. The difference is that BIEN has affiliates. If BIEN were to include 'at subsistence level' in its definition of Basic Income, then it would have to disaffiliate national organisations that did not require that (or they would disaffiliate themselves), whereas if it were not to include 'at subsistence level' in its definition of Basic Income then every national organisation would be able to remain affiliated. The fact that some of those organisations might choose to add an additional characteristic to their definition would only be relevant to affiliation if BIEN were to decide that it should be.

If BIEN did wish to say something about the level of Basic Income that would be agreeable to every affiliate, then there is just one possibility. The survey showed that.

- Some affiliates did not mention the issue, suggesting that the amount to be paid was not integral to the definition;
- Some said that a democratic process would be used to decide the amount;
- One mentioned a particular amount (Southern Africa);
- And some offered a description of the kind of life that the Basic Income would be expected to fund ('subsistence', 'dignity', 'participation', 'poverty line') in relation to the national context, but without specifying the relevant level of Basic Income.

BIEN could legitimately say that in each country the normal democratic process would determine the levels of Basic Income and their funding mechanisms. This would be entirely uncontentious.

'Universal', 'unconditional', 'citizen's', 'guarantee'

If we study the uses of the word 'universal' in the context of Basic Income, then we generally find that it means 'everyone within a national boundary', or perhaps 'everyone within a regional boundary'. For those campaigning for a global Basic Income, 'universal' means what it says: but generally 'universal' does not in fact mean universal. Does that matter? Not if everyone understands what is meant.

If within a particular jurisdiction a benefit is unconditional, then by definition it is universal within that jurisdiction. If it is universal then it is not necessarily unconditional. This means that 'unconditional' cannot be replaced by 'universal'. It might be thought that 'universal' in 'Universal Basic Income' is redundant. Strictly speaking, it is. Presumably 'Universal Basic Income' has become a common designation for a Basic Income because it emphasises an aspect of the income that its proponents wish to emphasise: the fact that it is for everyone.

'Basic Income' is sometimes described as 'Citizen's Income' (with the apostrophe before the s, because the income is for each individual citizen). It is partly because of the somewhat derogatory undertones of the word 'basic' in English that in 1992 the trustees of the Citizen's Basic Income Trust agreed to the suggestion made by the Joseph Rowntree Charitable Trust that we should speak of a 'Citizen's Income' rather than a 'Basic Income'; and the Green Party in the UK has often preferred 'Citizen's' to 'Basic'. However, the designation is not unproblematic, because the word 'citizen' does not necessarily include everyone who lives within a nation state's borders, so the word is not as all-encompassing as 'universal': but it does connect Basic Income with a discourse about citizens' rights; it avoids the negative connotations of 'basic'; and it encourages debate about the meaning of 'citizen'. The Scottish network, and the publisher of my *Citizen's Basic Income: A Christian social policy*, both independently asked that we should call the income a 'Citizen's Basic Income', and the trustees of what is now the Citizen's Basic Income Trust have now decided to do the same. The advantage of this designation is that it contains both 'Basic Income' and 'Citizen's'. The disadvantages are that it is longer than either 'Basic Income' or 'Citizen's Income', and that CBI can also mean the Confederation of British Industry.

Rather more problematic is the word 'guarantee'. During the early 1980s, at the beginning of the modern debate about Basic Income, Hermione Parker and Brandon Rhys Williams MP called a Basic Income a 'Basic Income Guarantee' (House of Commons Treasury & Civil Service Committee Sub-Committee, 1982, 1983; Parker, 1989). The word 'guarantee' was confusing because to guarantee an income is not necessarily to provide one. A means-tested benefit can guarantee someone an income by filling a gap between other income and a specified minimum income. When the British Government wanted a new name for its means-tested top-up for pensioners, it chose 'Minimum Income Guarantee': a rare example of accurate description. Because 'guarantee' can imply means-testing, the British Basic Income debate soon dropped the word, preferring 'Basic Income', then 'Citizen's Income', and now 'Citizen's Basic Income', with 'Basic Income' remaining a common description. The North American debate, however, retains the use of 'guarantee', causing occasional misunderstanding as to what is intended. Take, for instance, the wording on USBIG's website:

> The Basic Income Guarantee (BIG) is a government ensured guarantee that no one's income will fall below the level necessary to meet their most basic needs for any reason. ... The Basic Income gives every citizen a check for the full basic income every month, and taxes his or her earned income,

so that nearly everyone both pays taxes and receives a basic income. (USBIG, 2022)

Here 'Basic Income Guarantee' can mean a means-tested benefit, whereas 'Basic Income' does not. Because 'Basic Income' appears in both designations, this is potentially quite confusing, because someone could easily think that 'Basic Income' and 'Basic Income Guarantee' mean the same thing when in fact they do not. My recommendation would be that anyone using the term 'Basic Income Guarantee' should instead employ the term 'Minimum Income Guarantee', because that is more descriptive of what is intended, and it cannot be confused with 'Basic Income'.

Implications for the Basic Income Earth Network (BIEN, 2022b)

'Basic Income' has a clear definition—unconditional, nonwithdrawable, individual—and also carries with it three significant assumptions: regularity of payment, unvarying but upratable payments, and payments varying with age. Its meaning is clear, which is helpful to the debate about incomes paid unconditionally, nonwithdrawably, and to individuals. 'Citizen's Income' has the advantages that it does not suffer from the unfortunate undertones that 'Basic' can suffer from, and that it connects Basic Income with a citizen's rights discourse: but the downside is that in most jurisdictions the word 'citizen' is not entirely unproblematic. As long as we are clear that 'Citizen's Income' and 'Basic Income' mean the same thing, either or both of them can provide the clarity that the debate requires. Strictly speaking 'Universal Basic Income' means simply 'Basic Income': but the 'universal' is making a point. 'Basic Income', 'Citizen's Income', 'Citizen's Basic Income' and 'Universal Basic Income' will continue to provide the debate on unconditional, nonwithdrawable and individual incomes with the consistent definitional foundations that it needs.

It might be thought that it would helpful to reduce this variety to a single agreed term. First of all, there is no organisation with the authority to make the decision as to which that term should be; secondly, neither individuals nor organisations would be under any obligation to conform; and thirdly, the diversity is helpful in that it enables different aspects of a Basic Income to be emphasised: Basic Income its foundational nature; Citizen's Income its payment to each individual as a right; Citizen's

Basic Income both of those; and Universal Basic Income its payment to everyone.

'Guarantee' can cause confusion, and we should not be using it in association with 'Basic Income'.

Perhaps the most significant implication for BIEN relates to the question as to whether or not 'Basic Income' should imply an income at subsistence level. We have already recognised that any national organisation is at liberty to add this requirement to its definition of Basic Income, but that BIEN ought not to do so. We now need to recognise a number of problems that need to be faced by any individual or organisation that chooses to add the requirement to the definition:

- 'Subsistence level' is notoriously difficult to define. Every household behaves differently, and what one household counts as a subsistence income might be counted as utterly inadequate by another, and as overgenerous by yet another. Qualitative research can construct a list of expenditures regarded as necessary for participation in society (as in the Minimum Income Standards annual survey conducted for the Joseph Rowntree Foundation) (Davis et al., 2018): but such an approach can only obscure the wide variation in understandings of 'subsistence'. Government-specified subsistence levels are precisely that, and are driven largely or partly by political considerations.
- Governments tend to be cautious, and social policy is path dependent, so it is more likely that a Basic Income would start small, and would then grow, than that a large Basic Income would be implemented in the first instance. Organisations that insist that 'Basic Income' means an income at subsistence level will not help a government to ponder the possibility of making a start with a small Basic Income: and such an organisation will not be doing the kind of research required to enable a government to think rationally about whether a Basic Income might be feasible.
- Any organisation that decides that a payment is only a Basic Income if it is at a predetermined subsistence level is at risk of depriving itself of research results from organisations that research Basic Incomes at lower levels.

One solution to this problem would be to return to a set of terminology developed during the earlier period of the debate: a 'Full Basic Income' meant a Basic Income at subsistence level (somehow defined); a 'Partial Basic Income' meant one at a lower level; and a 'Transitional Basic Income' meant something in between. Some organisations might find this terminology helpful: and, because it assumes that a 'Basic Income' can be paid at any level, no organisation should find the terminology problematic.

Conclusion

Definition is a complex field, but it is one that anyone involved in the Basic Income debate needs to understand. Definitions matter. The more clarity we can achieve, the more useful will be our research results, and the more productive will be the debate.

The content of this chapter suggests that a recommendation should be made: That every individual and every organisation involved in the Basic Income debate should ask what they mean by the terms that they employ, and should seek the greatest possible clarity, including clarity over any unstated assumptions lying hidden behind the stated definitions; and also that BIEN should facilitate widespread debate about definitions in order to ensure that people working on Basic Income in different parts of the world can understand each other and can benefit most effectively from each other's research.

Acknowledgements This chapter publishes for the first time a paper presented at the Basic Income Earth Network (BIEN, 2022b) annual congress in 2017 in Lisbon, Portugal. Some of the material was first presented in another paper entitled '"Unconditional" and "Universal": Definitions and applications presented at the Federation for International Studies on Social Security conference at Sigtuna, Sweden, from the 5th to the 7th June 2017, the full version of which appears as Chapter 3 in this volume. The material contained in this chapter has frequently been quoted and referenced in the author's books, but this is the first time that it has been published in its entirety as originally presented at the 2017 BIEN congress.

Appendix

The appendix containing the definitions of Basic Income employed by BIEN's affiliated organisations can be found at the end of the original congress paper, which can be found at https://basicincome.org/wp-content/uploads/2015/01/Malcolm_Torry_Whats_a_definition_And_how_should_we_define_Basic_Income.pdf.

References

BIEN. (2020). The Basic Income Earth Network's Definition of Basic Income since the GA 2016. Retrieved March 26, 2022, from https://basicincome.org/wp-content/uploads/2020/07/Basic-Income-definition-longer-explanation-1.pdf.

BIEN. (2022a). About Basic Income. Retrieved March 26, 2022, from https://basicincome.org/about-basic-income.

BIEN. (2022b). About BIEN. Retrieved March 26, 2022, from https://basicincome.org/about-bien.

Cambridge University Press. (2022). Essential American English Dictionary. Retrieved March 26, 2022, from https://dictionary.cambridge.org/dictionary/essential-american-english/.

Davis, A., Hirsch, D., Padley, M., & Shepherd, C. (2018). *A Minimum Income Standard for the UK 2008–2018: Continuity and change*. Joseph Rowntree Foundation.

Goldsmith, S. (2012). The economic and social impacts of the Permanent Fund Dividend on Alaska. In K. Widerquist & M. W. Howard (Eds.), *Alaska's Permanent Fund Dividend: Examining its suitability as a model* (pp. 49–63). Palgrave Macmillan.

House of Commons Treasury and Civil Service Committee Sub-Committee. (1982). *The structure of personal income taxation and income support: Minutes of evidence*. HC 331–ix. Her Majesty's Stationery Office.

House of Commons Treasury and Civil Service Committee. (1983). *Enquiry into the structure of personal income taxation and income support* (Third special report, Session 1982–3). Her Majesty's Stationery Office.

Johnson, M. (1993). *Moral imagination: Implications of cognitive science for ethics*. Chicago University Press.

Ontario. (n.d.). Ontario's Basic Income Pilot: Studying the impact of a basic income. Retrieved March 26, 2022, from https://files.ontario.ca/170508_bi_brochure_eng_pg_by_pg_proof.pdf.

Oxford University Press. (2022). OED: Oxford English Dictionary. Retrieved March 26, 2022, from http://www.oed.com/.

Parker, H. (1989). *Instead of the dole: An enquiry into integration of the tax and benefit systems*. Routledge.
Rosch, E. (1999). Reclaiming concepts. In W. J. Freeman & R. Núñez (Eds.), Reclaiming cognition. *Journal of Consciousness Studies, 6*(11–12), 61–77.
Rosch, E., & Lloyd, B. B. (1978). *Cognition and categorization*. Lawrence Erlbaum.
USBIG. (2022). About the BIG. Retrieved March 26, 2022, from https://usbig.net/about-big/.
Wittgenstein, L. (1967). *Philosophical investigations* (G. E. M. Anscombe, Trans. 2nd ed.). Oxford University Press.

CHAPTER 3

'Unconditional' and 'universal': Definitions and Applications

Introduction

'Conditional cash transfers', 'Unconditional cash transfers', 'universal benefits', 'unconditional benefits', 'conditionalities' ... But what do these terms mean? How should they be defined? And are those two questions the same?

This chapter will explore a variety of different ways in which words are defined: according to current usage; by a legitimate authority on the basis of normative considerations; by a legitimate authority on the basis of current usage; or via a prototype. These methods will then be employed in order to define the terms 'unconditional' and 'universal', and, on the basis of the definitions constructed, relationships between the two terms will be discussed. How the terms are used in current social policy debate will be explored via case studies.

Whereas it might be difficult to envisage a variety of kinds of universality, it is possible to categorise different kinds of conditionality: those that we cannot affect; those that we have affected and that relate to events in the past (such as the payment of social insurance contributions); and those that we can affect and that relate to future or current events (such as paid employment). The different behavioural effects of the different kinds of conditionality will be discussed.

M. Torry, *Basic Income—What, Why, and How?*,
Exploring the Basic Income Guarantee,
https://doi.org/10.1007/978-3-031-14248-2_3

'Unconditional' and 'universal' will then be treated as ideal positions, and the question will be asked as to whether we might legitimately speak of degrees of unconditionality and degrees of universality: and, if so, whether levels of unconditionality and universality can be quantified. If so, levels of conditionality will need to be measured separately for each kind of conditionality.

Why does all of this matter? Only if different participants in a conversation understand similar things by a particular word or group of words will mutual comprehension be possible, will rational discussion be likely to occur, and will collaborative research be productive. If we mean different things by such terms as 'universal benefits' or 'unconditional cash transfers', then individuals and organisations involved in research and debate about such ideas might think that they are understanding each other when in fact they are not. While 'definition' and 'meaning' do not mean the same thing, and, as we shall see, two people can mean different things by the same words, for two people to agree on a definition of a term can help both of them to have some idea about what the other one means, which can enable useful dialogue to occur.

Definitions

What is the meaning of 'definition': that is, what are we doing when we 'define' something? ('How should we define "define"?' Take care, reader, that you do not disappear down an infinite regress.) We shall discover a variety of ways of defining, and we shall then apply those different methods to the task in hand.

There are a number of different ways of defining:

Usage

Ludwig Wittgenstein suggested that we discover the meaning of language by studying how language is used (Wittgenstein, 1967: 1), and, as the same word might be used in different ways in a multitude of different contexts, he offered the image of 'family resemblances' to describe the relationship between one use of a word and another (Wittgenstein, 1967: 66–67).

By 'definition' we generally mean a set of words that indicates the 'meaning' of a word or group of words. This immediately poses a problem. If we study a particular use of a word and then construct a set of words to express the meaning of that use, then the use of the new set of words, and of each of its component words, will be specific to a particular context: so even if we employ the same definition (in the sense of the same set of words in the same order), it will have different meanings in different contexts.

However, there really will be a family *resemblance*: and it is on this that dictionaries rely when they define a word or group of words. Thus the Oxford English Dictionary not only offers a definition of each English word commonly in use, but it also lists the particular usages on which it has based its definition.

Defining 'unconditional' in Relation to Its Use

The Oxford English Dictionary defines 'unconditional' as.

> Not limited by or subject to conditions or stipulations; absolute, unlimited, complete; (Oxford English Dictionary, 2022)

the entry on 'condition' contains the following:

> … Something demanded or required as a prerequisite to the granting or performance of something else; a provision, a stipulation. … In a legal instrument, e.g. a will, or contract, a provision on which its legal force or effect is made to depend. … Something that must exist or be present if something else is to be or take place; that on which anything else is contingent; a prerequisite. (Oxford English Dictionary, 2022)

and the entry on 'stipulation' includes.

> The action of specifying as one of the terms of a contract or agreement; a formulated term or condition of a contract or agreement. (Oxford English Dictionary, 2022)

The dictionary gives as one of its examples of the use of 'unconditional', 'The Kuwait authorities insisted that the [hijackers'] surrender was "unconditional"'; and as a use of 'condition' it offers a quotation from John Wesley: 'The word *condition* means neither more nor less than something *sine quâ non*, without which something else is not done'.

If usage is the key to a word's meaning, then we must seek examples of usage. Take these examples of uses of the words 'conditional', 'condition' and 'unconditional' drawn from an International Labour Office publication:

> Improvements in schooling are not restricted to conditional cash transfer programmes. Positive effects on schooling can also be observed for unconditional transfers or workfare programmes. ... Brazil's *Bolsa Familia* provides income transfers to poor households, on condition that they regularly send their children to school and that household members attend health clinics. ... In Chile, *Programa de Pensiones Asistenciales*, a non-contributory and unconditional social pension programme, is found to have reduced poverty amongst people in old age by about 9.2 per cent. (International Labour Office, 2010: viii, 2, 11)

This passage provides a useful case study in how the word 'unconditional' is used. In relation to its first use, 'unconditional' is employed in direct contrast to 'conditional', where the conditionality is clearly 'something demanded or required as a prerequisite': in this case, that parents send their children to school. The second use of 'unconditional' is interesting. The author appears to think it necessary to add 'non-contributory'. This suggests that in the author's mind 'unconditional' does not necessarily mean 'recipients do not have to have paid social insurance contributions of some kind'. Also, the pension is presumably paid only to individuals above a certain age, which suggests that it is conditional on the recipient's age: but this does not appear to compromise the payment's description as 'unconditional'.

There is clearly a wide variety of meanings of the word 'unconditional' in circulation. A categorisation might be helpful. There will be conditions that we cannot affect; there will be conditions that we have affected and that relate to events in the past (such as the payment of social insurance contributions); and there will be conditions that we can affect and that relate to future or current events (such as paid employment). The use of 'unconditional transfers' in the passage might suggest that none of these kinds of conditions apply, or it might imply that one or two of them do, with 'unconditional' applying to a type of condition that does not apply. The second usage of 'unconditional' is more explicit. Here a particular condition that we cannot affect, age, does apply. The author is clear that a conditionality related to past events (paying contributions) does not apply. We can reasonably assume that the author does not intend that conditions that we can affect and that relate to present or future events should apply.

It is clear that the word 'unconditional' can imply a variety of meanings and associated definitions broader than those represented in the Oxford English Dictionary.

Defining 'universal' in Relation to Its Use

The Oxford English Dictionary defines 'universal' as follows:

> Extending over or including the whole of something specified or implied, esp. the whole of a particular group or the whole world; comprehensive, complete; widely occurring or existing, prevalent over all. … Affecting or involving the whole of something specified or implied. … Modifying an agent noun, personal designation, or title, indicating that the role of the person concerned extends over or to all people, nations, etc. … Originating from the whole body or number of people specified or implied; done, given, made, etc., by all without exception. … *Of a service or facility: extended to, provided for, or accessible to all members of a community, regardless of wealth, social status, etc.* … (Oxford English Dictionary, 2022)

I have italicised this last entry because of its particular relevance to social security. The most recent example given is from the *South China Morning Post*: 'By last year, 94% of the mainland's populated areas had provided nine years of universal compulsory education' (Oxford English Dictionary, 2022). Here it is clear, as with other parts of the definition given above, that any use of the word 'universal' requires the specification of the community within which something applies, from which it comes, or to which it is supplied. By 'all without exception' is meant 'all without exception within the specified community'.

We shall employ the same International Labour Office publication as a case study:

> But despite the progress made in the materialization of the universal right to social security, very important gaps remain. … Non-contributory schemes include a broad range of schemes including universal schemes for all residents, some categorical schemes or means-tested schemes. … Categorical schemes could also be grouped as universal, if they cover all

> residents belonging to a certain category, or include resource conditions (social assistance schemes). They may include other types of conditions such as performing or accomplishing certain tasks. (International Labour Office, 2010: 1, 39)

Here we find three different uses of 'universal'. The first use applies to everyone, globally; and the second and third to everyone within a particular country. However, the second and third uses have different meanings, and we can only deduce these from the context. The second use implies that a 'universal' scheme is neither means-tested nor categorical, and therefore that it pays the same income to everyone, whereas the third use implies that universal schemes can be categorical or means-tested. While 'universal' always means 'extending over or including the whole of something specified or implied', the different uses here warn us to be clear about what precisely is universal: Is it the provision of an income? Or is it the provision of an income on certain conditions? The UK's 'Universal Credit' is the provision of a means-tested and work-tested income to everyone who fulfils the conditions (and would probably be better designated 'Unified Benefit'), whereas in the context of 'Universal Basic Income' 'universal' means that 'every individual unconditionally receives an income as a right of citizenship, independent of labour-market status' (Painter & Thoung, 2015: 18). ('Independent of labour-market status' is strictly redundant but is presumably added to emphasise the point.)

As with 'unconditional', the meaning of 'universal' is determined by its particular use, and care must be taken not to make untested assumptions about the word's meaning in a particular context.

Definition by Characteristics

What is sometimes called the 'classical' way of defining a definition is to envisage a category defined by a list of characteristics, with the category name being defined by the names of the characteristics. Thus a rectangle is a four-sided figure with opposite sides parallel and all four of its angles right angles: so a square is a rectangle because it has four sides, opposite sides are parallel, and the angles are right angles, whereas neither a triangle nor a circle is a rectangle. Those entities that possess the characteristics are in the category, and those entities that do not are not. But for anything other than simple cases of definition this strategy quickly breaks down because there are frequently cases where we cannot determine whether the entity concerned is in the category or not. Thus if to be a 'bird' something needs to fly, then an ostrich is not a bird and a bat is one. The category 'table' is defined by the characteristics 'horizontal surface' and 'supported on legs'. A folded drop-leaf table is not a table, whereas a stool is a table.

Eleanor Rosch (Rosch, 1999; Rosch & Lloyd, 1978) has suggested that categories are not the clear-cut things that we often think they are, and that it is often not the case that entities are either in the category or not in it; and neither is it the case that entities belong equally. Thus a robin is more a bird than an ostrich is, and a bat is on the boundary of the category. Rosch points out that in the real world we define categories in terms of prototypes and then decide whether something is in the category by asking how similar it is to the prototype. For the category 'bird' the prototype might be 'robin'. Mark Johnson (1993) has successfully used this means of definition to give a coherent account of how we categorise actions as moral or otherwise: we have in our minds a prototype lie and we then ask whether other actions are more or less like it.

So the question to ask is this: Is there a set of characteristics by which we can decide whether something belongs in the category labelled 'unconditional'? And similarly with the category labelled 'universal'? There are a number of ways to approach this:

- Each user of the terms 'universal' or 'unconditional' could select their own preferred characteristics. The individual's autonomy would thus be honoured, but at the risk of losing mutual comprehension.
- We could study a wide variety of actual usages of the terms and work out the lists of characteristics either stated or assumed by users of the terms. If we could find characteristics employed in *all* actual usages, then we would have discovered the 'family likeness' and would be able to list a definitive set of characteristics. However, that does not mean that everyone would agree with the list. It would only take one user of the terms 'universal' or 'unconditional' to insist that they understood a characteristic not in the list to be essential to the definition of the category for the definition to become problematic in relation to attempts at mutual comprehension.
- An authority of some kind could decide on the list of characteristics that would qualify something as belonging to the categories 'universal' or 'unconditional'.

A Recognised Authority

If a field of interest has related to it an organisation that those involved in that field believe to have some standing or authority, then participants might look to that organisation to supply definitions of terms. This will be by way of something like a social contract. In order to avoid the chaos of multiple definitions, participants might be willing to forego their autonomy and to grant authority to the recognised organisation.

There are a number of ways in which the organisation might construct the expected definitions. It might construct a list of characteristics that something has to have in order to be included in the named category; or it might collect examples of the use of the term and on that basis decide on a definition; or it might employ a mixture of those methods, constructing a list of characteristics and testing the list against current usage. There might be various ways in which an organisation might go about the task. There might be an individual within the authority to make such decisions about lists of characteristics; a small body of people might be elected or appointed to decide; or the entire membership might decide on definitions by a democratic process (although this method might in practice come down to an individual or a small group making the decision because the wording of a resolution will always be made up of words written by an individual or a small group).

Take the Foundation for International Studies on Social Security (2022) as an example of an authoritative organisation: One of the themes of its 2013 conference was 'The nature and impact of recent trends in universalism versus selectivity in social security (including targeting, conditionality, and the balance between rights and responsibilities)'. This assumes that 'universal' implies nonselective social security benefits rather than selective ones open to everyone who fulfils the conditions. This in turn suggests that 'universal' is being used to mean something close to 'unconditional'. One of the 2015 conference themes was 'The nature and impact of recent social security reforms (including targeting, coverage, conditionality, and the balance between rights and responsibilities)' (Foundation for International Studies on Social Security). In both of these quotations, 'conditionality' is in a list alongside 'coverage' and 'targeting'. In the social security context 'targeting' means either means-testing or some other method for directing resources at the worst off (although it might legitimately be suggested that reducing Income Tax rates and increasing the UK's Income Tax Personal Allowance tend to target wealthier members of society). 'Targeting' therefore implies conditionality, suggesting that means-testing is not included in the meaning of 'conditionality' as it is used here. Similarly, 'coverage' is universal if unconditional or in the context of conditions that can potentially be met by anyone, or it might be conditional. In the wording of these conference themes we find a certain lack of clarity in relation to the terms 'universal' and 'conditional'.

Given the ubiquity of the words 'universal' and 'unconditional' in social security discourse, and given the diversity of meanings of both of them that we have discovered, there would be a case for FISS researching and disseminating definitions of the two terms. It could do this by studying usage and drawing up definitions on that basis; or it could construct draft lists of characteristics that would need to be satisfied by social security benefits if they were to be included in the 'unconditional' or 'universal' categories and then test those lists against usage, or it could draw up lists of characteristics and put them to a vote of FISS members.

One approach that it could take would be to treat 'unconditional' and 'universal' as ideal positions and then promote the idea of degrees of unconditionality and degrees of universality. Clearly, quantification of such degrees would not be possible, but qualitative evaluation might be useful, particularly in relation to the different kinds of conditionality that we have discussed, and in relation to the two kinds of universality that we might call 'universality of provision' for incomes or other services offered equally to everyone within a jurisdiction, and 'universality of entitlement' for a universal right to a benefit or other service if certain conditions are met.

If such an evaluation is to be considered, then it will need to be undertaken separately for the three different kinds of conditionality and for the two different kinds of universality. An income or some other service provision would need to be evaluated separately in relation to whether it was conditional on factors that we cannot affect, factors relating to past events that we can affect (such as paying social insurance contributions), and factors relating to current and future events that we can affect (such as labour market status and household structure), and also in relation to whether it was universality of provision, universality of entitlement, or neither.

Policy Implications

Different Conditionalities Imply Different Behaviours

The existence of different kinds of conditionality might appear to be somewhat theoretical, but it is a theory with significant behavioural implications and therefore with policy implications.

Conditionalities relating to factors that we might be able to influence, such as household structure and labour market status, can result in moral hazard and in disincentives. Someone whose means-tested benefits depend on them not being employed might be hesitant to seek employment if their employment income and any remaining means-tested benefits would offer them little additional net income, or even a lower net income if they have to pay fares to work. Moral hazard will be a risk; and there will certainly be a level of disincentive that would not otherwise be experienced.

Factors relating to events in the past, such as paying social insurance contributions, do not act as a direct disincentive, and exhibit no moral hazard; and a disability, however originated, does not either. However, both the payment of contributions, and the existence of a disability, require bureaucratic enquiry, which can create stigma, and certainly creates complexity and administrative cost. So while it might look as if conditionalities relating to events in the past should not be a problem, they can be.

Conditionalities relating to factors over which we have no control, such as age, cause no problems at all. No enquiry is required, except when a child is born, or perhaps when a Basic Income is implemented if the state holds no birth date information: so the operative factor would appear to be not so much the nature of the conditionality but whether or not enquiry has to be made into an individual's situation. The same can be said of conditionalities related to events in the present or future. Enquiry has to be made into labour market status, household structure, and so on, so 'making enquiry' here acts as a proxy for conditionalities to be avoided.

This all suggests that when social policy is made, conditionalities about which enquiry has to be made should be avoided, whereas conditionalities that require no enquiry to be made are not a problem.

The Basic Income Debate

An increasingly significant factor in research and discussion of social security benefits is the now widespread global debate about the desirability and feasibility of a Basic Income: an unconditional and nonwithdrawable income paid to each individual.

In this context, it will be particularly important to be clear about the meanings of 'universal' and 'unconditional'. 'Universal' here generally means universal provision, in the sense that an income would actually be paid to everyone within a particular national or regional jurisdiction: although the restriction to those legally resident, or to citizens (somehow defined), might be necessary, and might compromise the proposed universality. In the context of the Basic Income debate, 'unconditional' generally means unconditional in relation to past, present or future events that we can affect, but not in relation to age, which is a condition that we cannot affect. Most illustrative Basic Income schemes assume that the Basic Income would vary in relation to the recipient's age (Torry, 2019, 2020, 2021).

The Basic Income debate raises the question of the relationship between 'universal' and 'unconditional'. If within a particular jurisdiction a benefit is unconditional, then by definition it is universal within that jurisdiction. If it is universal, then it is not necessarily unconditional. This means that 'unconditional' cannot necessarily be replaced by 'universal'. It might be thought that 'universal' in 'Universal Basic Income' is redundant. Strictly speaking, it is: so presumably 'Universal Basic Income' has become a common designation for a Basic Income because it emphasises an aspect of the income that its proponents might wish to emphasise: that the income is for everyone. What adding 'Universal' does not do is state Basic Income's unconditionality: so it might be more to the point to add 'unconditional' because an 'Unconditional Basic Income' would be both unconditional and universal.

As household structures and employment market behaviour become more diverse and complex, the unconditionality and therefore universality of Basic Income will look increasingly attractive: provided we recognise that 'unconditionality' does not preclude an age conditionality, and that 'universal' means universality of provision and not just universality of entitlement.

Acknowledgements This chapter publishes for the first time a paper entitled '"Unconditional" and "Universal": Definitions and applications' presented at the Federation for International Studies on Social Security conference at Sigtuna, Sweden, from the 5th to the 7th June 2017. The material contained in this chapter has frequently been quoted and referenced in the author's books, but this is the first time that the paper has been published in its entirety as originally presented at the Sigtuna conference. The original paper can be found at https://www.researchgate.net/publication/317648013_'Unconditional'_and_'universal'_definitions_and_applications.

References

Foundation for International Studies on Social Security. (2022). Welcome to the FISS website. Retrieved March 26, 2022, from http://fiss-socialsecurity.org/.

International Labour Office. (2010). *Effects of non-contributory social transfers in developing countries: A compendium*. International Labour Office. Retrieved March 26, 2022, from https://www.research.manchester.ac.uk/portal/files/32800126/FULL_TEXT.PDF.

Johnson, M. (1993). *Moral imagination: Implications of cognitive science for ethics*. Chicago University Press.

Oxford University Press. (2022). OED: Oxford English Dictionary. Retrieved March 26, 2022, from http://www.oed.com/.

Painter, A., & Thoung, C. (2015). *Creative citizen, creative state: The principled and pragmatic case for a Universal Basic Income*. Royal Society of Arts.

Rosch, E. (1999). 'Reclaiming concepts'. In W. J. Freeman & R. Núñez (Eds.). Reclaiming cognition. *Journal of Consciousness Studies, 6*(11–12), 61–77.

Rosch, E., & Lloyd, B. B. (1978). *Cognition and categorization*. Lawrence Erlbaum.

Torry, M. (2019). *Static microsimulation research on Citizen's Basic Income for the UK: A personal summary and further reflections* (Institute for Social and Economic Research Working Paper EM13/19). Institute for Social and Economic Research, University of Essex. Retrieved March 26, 2022, from https://www.iser.essex.ac.uk/research/publications/working-papers/euromod/em13-19.pdf.

Torry, M. (2020). *Evaluation of a Recovery Basic Income, and of a sustainable revenue neutral Citizen's Basic Income, with an appendix relating to different Universal Credit roll-out scenarios* (Institute for Social and Economic Research Working Paper EM7/20). Institute for Social and Economic Research, University of Essex. Retrieved March 26, 2022, from https://www.iser.essex.ac.uk/research/publications/working-papers/euromod/em7-20.pdf.

Torry, M. (2021). *Three income maintenance options for 2021* (Centre for Microsimulation and Policy Analysis report). Institute for Social and Economic Research, University of Essex. Retrieved March 26, 2022, from https://www.microsimulation.ac.uk/publications/publication-526555/.

Wittgenstein, L. (1967). *Philosophical investigations* (G. E. M. Anscombe, Trans. 2nd edn.). Oxford University Press.

CHAPTER 4

Basic Income and Basic Income Schemes: Definitions and Details

Introduction

A Basic Income is an unconditional, nonwithdrawable income paid to every individual as a right of citizenship. It is as simple as that. Basic Income has a number of different names: Citizen's Income, Basic Income, Citizen's Basic Income, Universal Basic Income. They all mean exactly the same: an unconditional income paid to every individual.

The amount paid to an individual would not depend on their income, it would not depend on their wealth, it would not depend on their household structure, it would not depend on their employment status, and it would not depend on anything else. Every individual of the same age would receive exactly the same: the same amount, every week or every month, automatically.

Older people might receive more than working age adults, younger adults less, and less for children. Does adjusting the amount with someone's age compromise Basic Income's unconditionality? No, it does not. What is unique about Basic Income, what matters, and what makes it work, is that it can be turned on at someone's birth, and turned off at their death, that no active administration is required in between, and that nothing that anyone can influence, or that requires enquiry of any kind, can affect it. Once the computer knows someone's date of birth, it never

M. Torry, *Basic Income—What, Why, and How?*,
Exploring the Basic Income Guarantee,
https://doi.org/10.1007/978-3-031-14248-2_4

needs to ask about their age: it can seamlessly adjust the amount that an individual is paid as their age changes. Everyone of the same age would receive exactly the same income, unconditionally.

Sometimes words are added, but they are not necessary. Basic Income is unconditional, so within the jurisdiction in which it is paid everybody gets it, so it is universal. There is no need to say that it is. Basic Income is unconditional, which means that it would not fall if other income rose, so it is nonwithdrawable. There is no need to say that it is. It is universal, and it is nonwithdrawable. But all we need to say is this: Every individual of the same age would receive exactly the same income, unconditionally.

The definition published by the Citizen's Basic Income Trust reads as follows:

> A Citizen's Basic Income is an unconditional, automatic and nonwithdrawable income for each individual as a right of citizenship. (A Citizen's Basic Income (CBI) is sometimes called a Basic Income (BI) or a Citizen's Income (CI))
>
> - 'Unconditional': A CBI would vary with age, but there would be no other conditions: so everyone of the same age would receive the same CBI, whatever their gender, employment status, family structure, contribution to society, housing costs, or anything else.
> - 'Automatic': Someone's CBI would be paid weekly or monthly, automatically.
> - 'Nonwithdrawable': CBIs would not be means-tested. Whether someone's earnings or wealth increased, decreased, or stayed the same, their Citizen's Basic Income would not change.
> - 'Individual': CBIs would be paid on an individual basis, and not on the basis of a couple or household.
> - 'As a right': Everybody legally resident in the UK would receive a CBI, subject to a minimum period of legal residency in the UK, and continuing residency for most of the year (Citizen's Basic Income Trust, 2018).

According to the definition published on the Basic Income Earth Network (BIEN) website:

> A basic income is a periodic cash payment unconditionally delivered to all on an individual basis, without means test or work requirement.

That is, basic income has the following five characteristics:

(1) Periodic: it is paid at regular intervals (for example every month), not as a one-off grant.
(2) Cash payment: it is paid in an appropriate medium of exchange, allowing those who receive it to decide what they spend it on. It is not, therefore, paid either in kind (such as food or services) or in vouchers dedicated to a specific use.
(3) Individual: it is paid on an individual basis—and not, for instance, to households.
(4) Universal: it is paid to all, without means test.
(5) Unconditional: it is paid without a requirement to work or to demonstrate willingness-to-work. (BIEN, 2022)

The different definitions exhibit different emphases, but they are perfectly consistent with each other, and they represent a consensus—and, after all, consensus is what definitions are about.

Basic Income, and Basic Income Schemes

A Basic Income is always as defined above, and anything that conforms to those definitions is a Basic Income. A Basic Income *scheme* is different: It specifies the levels of Basic Income to be paid to each age group, the frequency of the payments, and also the funding mechanism, which might be changes to the existing tax and benefits system, or maybe some other method. Consider two different Basic Income schemes: both would pay working age adult Basic Incomes somewhere around £70 per week, and different amounts for older and younger people; both would be largely funded by abolishing the Income Tax Personal Allowance and the National Insurance Contributions Primary Earnings Threshold; but one would abolish means-tested benefits, while the other would leave them in place and recalculate them on the basis that every individual in a household would now be receiving a Basic Income and that net earnings will have been changed by the abolition of the Income Tax Personal Allowance and the National Insurance Contributions Primary Earnings Threshold. The schemes would exhibit some very different effects. In particular, the scheme that abolished means-tested benefits would impose significant losses on low-income households at the point of implementation, whereas the scheme that retained means-tested benefits would not. The former would be politically infeasible, whereas the latter would not be (Torry, 2014, 2015).

[We might summarise the situation like this: A Basic Income would always have the same effects:

- A secure layer of income;
- Increased social cohesion;
- An absence of stigma;
- Administrative simplicity;
- Does not contribute to marginal withdrawal rates;
- Does not interfere with employment market decisions;
- Does not interfere with relationship decisions.

However, different Basic Income schemes could have very different effects:

- One scheme might increase inequality, whereas another might reduce it;
- One scheme might increase poverty, whereas another might reduce it;
- One scheme might impose losses on low-income households at the point of implementation, whereas another might not;
- One scheme might require very high-income tax rates, whereas another might not;
- One scheme might require additional funding from elsewhere, whereas another might not;
- One scheme might increase employment, whereas another might not;
- One scheme might be politically feasible, whereas another might not be].

Rothstein v. Torry

In November 2017, *Social Europe* published an article by Bo Rothstein entitled 'UBI: A bad idea for the welfare state' (Rothstein, 2017). The article sets out a definition of 'Unconditional Universal Basic Income'

(UUBI) as 'every citizen will be entitled to a basic income that frees them from the necessity of having a paid job'; and it adds the details that the level of UBI would be £800 per month and that 'all means-tested programs for those who cannot support themselves through paid work can be abolished'. Rothstein correctly identifies as an advantage of such a reform that it 'would force employers to create more acceptable and less demeaning types of work because people would not take jobs that they considered unsatisfactory. Releasing people from the compulsion to have a paid job would, according to the proponents, also mean strengthening the voluntary/civil society sector and cultural life'. Rothstein equally correctly identifies as disadvantages that his Basic Income scheme 'would be unsustainably expensive and would thereby jeopardize the state's ability to maintain quality in public services such as healthcare, education and care of the elderly'; that Basic Income would lose political legitimacy; and that 'people who can work [would] choose not to work'. Rothstein's verdict is that 'the basic error with the idea of unconditional basic income is its unconditionality', because that threatens 'the principle of reciprocity ... Breaking with this principle is most likely to lead to the dismantling of the type of broad-based social solidarity that built [the] welfare state.'

Not so. The main problem with the Basic Income that Rothstein discusses in his article is not its unconditionality: it is the flawed definition. As we have seen, the definition of Basic Income implies neither a particular amount, nor that means-tested benefits would be abolished, and it does not imply that the Basic Income would necessarily free people from paid employment. Rothstein has confused his particular Basic Income scheme with Basic Income.

Instead of a Basic Income scheme that pays £800 per month to every individual, and that abolishes means-tested benefits, we could pay £260 per month to every working age adult (with different amounts for children, young adults, and elderly people), and leave means-tested benefits in place and recalculate them on the basis that household members would be receiving Basic Incomes. Instead of leaving undefined the funding method for Basic Income, as Rothstein does, we could choose to fund it by reducing the Income Tax Personal Allowance and the National Insurance Contributions (NIC) Primary Earnings Threshold (so that Income Tax and NICs would be paid on more of someone's earned income), we could apply a flat rate of National Insurance Contribution of 12% to all earned income (rather than the current two-tier 12% and 2% structure), and we could increase Income Tax rates by just 3 percentage points. As research conducted at the Institute for Social and Economic Research shows (Torry, 2021), far from being 'unsustainably expensive', this scheme would require no additional public expenditure, and it would not affect expenditure on public services. Rothstein cannot show that his scheme would not impose significant losses on low-income households. This alternative scheme would not impose significant losses on low-income households, it would impose few losses on households in general, and it would still take a lot of households off means-tested benefits. Rothstein cannot tell us how his scheme would redistribute disposable income, or how it would affect poverty or inequality indices. This alternative scheme would redistribute from rich to poor, it would reduce every poverty index, and it would significantly reduce inequality. Rothstein tells us that his scheme would reduce the incentive to seek employment. For anyone taken off means-tested benefits by their Basic Income, this alternative scheme would reduce marginal deduction rates (the rate at which additional earned income is reduced by taxation and the withdrawal of means-tested benefits) (Torry, 2018b), and would therefore be likely to incentivise employment, self-employment, and new small businesses. It certainly would not disincentivise them. Far from compromising the reciprocity on which our society is built, it would enhance it. And this alternative scheme would not lose the advantages that Rothstein mentions. Because everyone would have a secure financial platform on which to build, this Basic Income scheme, like Rothstein's, would give to workers a greater ability to seek the employment or self-employment that they wanted, and would therefore encourage employers to supply better jobs in order to attract workers; and because this Basic Income scheme would give to each household more choice over its employment pattern, it would still encourage both caring and community activity. [See the note at the end of this chapter about the appendix].

Distinctions matter. A Basic Income is always an unconditional income paid to every individual, without means test and without work test. A Basic Income *scheme* specifies the rate at which the Basic Income would be paid for each age group, the funding mechanism, and changes to existing tax and benefits systems. There are many possible Basic Income schemes. As Rothstein correctly suggests, his chosen scheme would have many disadvantages. As I have shown, an alternative scheme might exhibit none of those disadvantages, and might offer many additional advantages.

Both of the schemes contain genuine Basic Incomes, but only one of them would be desirable and feasible.

Basic Income and Minimum Income Guarantee

A Basic Income is an unconditional, automatic and nonwithdrawable income for each individual as a right of citizenship. A Minimum Income Guarantee is very different: it is a level of disposable income below which a household is not allowed to fall. The amount of money that a government will need to pay to the household will therefore depend on the household's income from other sources (earnings, pensions, interest on savings, other benefits, and so on) and the composition of the household.

The 1970s Canadian and US experiments were Minimum Income Guarantee experiments rather than Basic Income experiments. The fact that those experiments exhibited clear health benefits and very little employment market withdrawal suggests that a Basic Income might have similar effects, but because a Minimum Income Guarantee and a Basic Income are not the same, that cannot be assumed.

Pitts et al. v. Torry

In the final edition of the journal *Renewal* for 2017, Frederick Pitts, Lorena Lombardozzi and Neil Warner suggest that the experience of the Speenhamland reforms of 1795 were 'an experiment in a kind of basic income' (Pitts et al., 2017: 150). They were not. They were an extension of means-tested poor relief to the working poor. The supplements paid out of the rates were designed to fill the gap between the worker's earnings and a specified minimum income that was related to the size of the family and the price of bread (Speizman, 1966: 45). The scheme was a Minimum Income Guarantee, and the supplements paid were a means-tested benefit. They were definitely not a Basic Income. The modern equivalents of the Speenhamland project are Working Tax Credits and so-called Universal Credit, and not Basic Income.

Not only is a Minimum Income Guarantee different from a Basic Income: the effects would be different. The Speenhamland payments fell if earnings rose, and rose if earnings fell. The Speenhamland supplement therefore functioned as a dynamic subsidy. Because it rose if wages fell, employers who cut wages knew that the supplement would make up for the wage cut. A Basic Income would remain the same whatever the individual's earnings, so it would be a static subsidy: that is, it would not rise if wages fell, so both employers and employees would know that if wages fell then employees' families would be worse off. In the context of a Basic Income, both collective bargaining and the National Minimum/Living Wage would be even more important than they are now, and the effort to maintain them would intensify.

Another difference relates to employment incentives. Within the communities that were paying the Speenhamland supplement, for breadwinners with large families there was no financial advantage to seeking increased wages, a better-paying job, or additional skills. Increased wages would mean a lower supplement. But because a Basic Income would never change, anyone currently on means-tested benefits whose Basic Income enabled them to come off them would immediately experience increased incentives to seek higher wages, or to seek additional skills in order to obtain a better-paying job. No longer would an increase in wages result in a loss of benefits, so an increase in earned income would result in a far greater increase in net income. (See the appendix for research results on the number of households that would be taken off means-tested benefits by a fairly modest Basic Income scheme).

Pitts, Lombardozzi and Warner are quite right to make a variety of criticisms of the Speenhamland approach. Means-tested in-work benefits such as the Speenhamland supplements, Working Tax Credits, and Universal Credit, do 'keep the cost of labour competitive with machines so that employers keep workers hanging on for longer than otherwise would be the case'; they do restrict 'the freedom of workers to sell their capacity to labour to employers as equal parties to a contract'; and they do 'render impossible the commodification of labour in a world still organised on the basis of the commodification of everything else' (Pitts et al., 2017: 149–150). A Basic Income, on the other hand, would never compromise 'the bargaining power of labour', and so would not contribute to 'falling or stagnating wages and deteriorating employment prospects' (Pitts et al., 2017: 151). Indeed, by providing a secure financial platform on which individuals and households could build, a Basic Income would increase workers' ability to start their own businesses, to turn down badly paid jobs, and to argue for wage increases.

The Basic Income enthusiasts that Pitts, Lomardozzi, and Warner have in their sights are those who suggest that a Basic Income would be a useful response to an automated economy in which fewer human workers would be required. It needs to be said that we cannot know the future of the employment market. Previous periods of technological change have seen new jobs created at the same time as existing jobs have been destroyed, and whether current and future technological change will have similar or different effects we cannot know. It is the fact that we cannot know the future shape of the employment market that is the argument for Basic Income. The benefits system that we are running in the UK is still a combination of the Poor Law and Speenhamland—that is, means-tested benefits both in and out of work. It is a system designed for a 1940s employment market characterised by long-term full-time jobs. This is even more true of Universal Credit. But the world has changed, and it will continue to change in ways that we cannot now predict. What we shall need is an income maintenance strategy that makes no assumptions about the future structure of the employment market, that incentivises employment, that provides as much freedom as possible for workers to choose how to deploy their labour, and that does not depress wages. Today's benefits system is precisely what is not required. A Basic Income might be the best option.

Conclusion

The Basic Income debate is important, it is increasingly lively, and the number of organisations and individuals engaged with it is increasing rapidly. If the debate is to be rational then it is essential that all of the players should agree on definitions, and that they should use them consistently.

Rothstein tells us that he is discussing Basic Income, whereas in fact he is discussing a particular Basic Income *scheme*. Pitts, Lomardozzi, and Warner tell us that the Speenhamland payments were a kind of Basic Income, whereas in fact they constituted a Minimum Income Guarantee: something entirely different. Such confusions are not helpful. What the Basic Income debate requires is not erroneous comparisons but high-quality research, careful logic, clear distinctions, and agreed definitions that everybody adheres to.

Acknowledgements This chapter is the first publication of a paper presented at the Basic Income Earth Network (BIEN, 2022) annual congress held in 2018 in Tampere, Finland. The original conference paper can be found here: https://basicincome.org/wp-content/uploads/2018/09/Basic-Income-and-Basic-Income-schemes-definitions-and-details.pdf. The articles referenced in the sections of the article titled 'Rothstein v. Torry' and 'Pitts et al. v. Torry' (Torry, 2018a, 2018c) appeared, respectively, in *Social Europe* and *Renewal*, and are republished in Chapter 9 of this volume. The additional section in square brackets, not in the original congress paper, is taken from a presentation on Basic Income prepared for a training course for Chinese interns working with BIEN in 2021.

Appendix

The appendix of the original conference paper consisted of microsimulation research results on an illustrative Basic Income scheme for the United Kingdom. The appendix can be found here: https://basicincome.org/wp-content/uploads/2018/09/Basic-Income-and-Basic-Income-schemes-definitions-and-details.pdf. A discussion of microsimulation research, and more up to date examples, can be found in Chapter 16 of this volume.

References

BIEN. (2022). About Basic Income. Retrieved March 26, 2022, from https://basicincome.org/about-basic-income.

Citizen's Basic Income Trust. (2022). Citizen's Basic Income. Retrieved March 26, 2022, from http://citizensincome.org/.

Citizen's Basic Income Trust. (2018). *Citizen's Basic Income: A brief introduction*. Citizen's Basic Income Trust.

Pitts, F. H., Lomardozzi, L., & Warner, N. (2017). Speenhamland, automation and the basic income: A warning from history? *Renewal, 25*(3–4), 145–155.

Rothstein, B. (2017, November 23). UBI: A bad idea for the welfare state. *Social Europe*. Retrieved March 26, 2022, from https://www.socialeurope.eu/ubi-bad-idea-welfare-state.

Speizman, M. D. (1966). Speenhamland: An experiment in guaranteed income. *Social Service Review, 40*(1), 44–55.

Torry, M. (2014). *Research note: A feasible way to implement a Citizen's Income* (EUROMOD Working Paper EM17/14). Institute for Social and Economic Research, University of Essex. Retrieved March 26, 2022, from www.iser.essex.ac.uk/research/publications/working-papers/euromod/em17-14.

Torry, M. (2015). *Two feasible ways to implement a revenue neutral Citizen's Income scheme* (EUROMOD Working Paper EM6/15). Institute for

Social and Economic Research, University of Essex. Retrieved March 26, 2022, from https://www.iser.essex.ac.uk/research/publications/working-papers/euromod/em6-15.

Torry, M. (2018a). Speenhamland, automation, and Basic Income: A response. *Renewal, 26*(1), 32–35.

Torry, M. (2018b). *An update, a correction, and an extension, of an evaluation of an illustrative Citizen's Basic Income scheme – addendum to EUROMOD working paper EM12/17* (Euromod Working Paper EM 12/17). Institute for Social and Economic Research, University of Essex. Retrieved March 26, 2022, from www.iser.essex.ac.uk/research/publications/working-papers/euromod/em12-17a.

Torry, M. (2018c). What is an Unconditional Basic Income? A response to Rothstein. In P. Van Parijs (Ed.), *Basic Income and the Left: A European debate* (pp. 110–115). Social Europe Ltd.

Torry, M. (2021). *Three income maintenance options for 2021* (Centre for Microsimulation and Policy Analysis report). Institute for Social and Economic Research, University of Essex. Retrieved March 26, 2022, from https://www.microsimulation.ac.uk/publications/publication-526555/.

PART III

Why Does Basic Income Matter?

CHAPTER 5

Basic Income the Preserver and Transformation of Capitalism

Introduction

Capitalism is:

> The possession of capital or wealth; an economic system in which private capital or wealth is used in the production or distribution of goods, and prices are determined mainly in a free market; the dominance of private owners of capital and of production for profit. (Oxford University Press, 2022)

A Basic Income is:

> an unconditional, automatic and nonwithdrawable income for each individual as a right of citizenship. (A Basic Income (BI) is sometimes called a Citizen's Basic Income (CBI), a Universal Basic Income (UBI), or a Citizen's Income (CI)).
>
> - 'Unconditional': A Basic Income would vary with age, but there would be no other conditions: so everyone of the same age would receive the same Basic Income, whatever their gender, employment status, family structure, contribution to society, housing costs, or anything else.

M. Torry, *Basic Income—What, Why, and How?*,
Exploring the Basic Income Guarantee,
https://doi.org/10.1007/978-3-031-14248-2_5

- 'Automatic': Someone's Basic Income would be paid weekly or monthly, automatically.
- 'Nonwithdrawable': Basic Incomes would not be means-tested. Whether someone's earnings or wealth increased, decreased, or stayed the same, their Basic Income would not change.
- 'Individual': Basic Incomes would be paid on an individual basis, and not on the basis of a couple or household.
- 'As a right': Everybody legally resident in the UK would receive a Basic Income, subject to a minimum period of legal residency in the UK, and continuing residency for most of the year (Citizen's Basic Income Trust, 2022).

This chapter will explore the nature and effects of capitalism, as defined above, and some of the ways in which a Basic Income would change those effects; and in particular it will study the characteristics of contemporary capitalism, the effects that contemporary capitalism is having on social and economic life, and the effects that a Basic Income might have on life in contemporary capitalism.

Different Meanings of 'capitalism'

Capitalism Understood as 'the possession of capital or wealth'

This definition of capitalism requires us to ask about the effects of an individual or organisation owning capital and/or wealth, and then, with capitalism understood in this way, about the effects of contemporary capitalism on social and economic life. We shall then ask about the effects that a Basic Income would be likely to have.

Capital is:

> Real or financial assets possessing a monetary value; the stock with which a company, corporation, or individual enters into business; the total sum of shareholders' contributions in a joint-stock company; accumulated wealth or goods, esp. as used in further production. (Oxford University Press, 2022)

Wealth is:

> Prosperity consisting in abundance of possessions; 'worldly goods', valuable possessions, esp. in great abundance: riches, affluence. ... Abundance of

> possessions or of valuable products, as characteristic of a people, country, or region; the collective riches of a people or country. ... A collective term for those things the abundant possession of which (by a person or a community) constitutes riches, or 'wealth' in the popular sense (Oxford University Press, 2022).

If 'capitalism' is understood as the possession of capital and/or wealth by certain individuals, and by implication not by others, or by certain organisations, and by implication not by others, then wealth inequality is inevitable; and because capital and wealth can generate income, and can provide access to other goods, such as higher education and good quality housing, then wealth inequality can result in income inequality, and potentially poverty for people with little or no wealth, little education, few skills, and poor housing. There will always be some people or organisations with more capital and/or wealth than others, and with more income than others. The differences in wealth and capital levels might be slight or they might be extreme, and differences in income levels likewise.

Contemporary capitalism is global in extent, and it exhibits increasing levels of inequality in relation to both income and wealth (Alvaredo et al., 2018). This matters, because a recent United Nations report has found that inequality stifles economic growth and poverty reduction, undermines social cohesion and stability, and negatively impacts the environment (Choo, 2019).

The question as to whether a Basic Income would reduce inequality does not have a simple answer. If a Basic Income were to be implemented on its own, then of course it would reduce income inequality, as it would make a larger proportional difference to the disposable incomes of low-income households than it would to the disposable incomes of higher-income households. However, a Basic Income never would be implemented on its own, because it would have to be funded, and different funding mechanisms would have different effects on inequality.

Here we must distinguish between Basic Income and a Basic Income *scheme*. A Basic Income is always an unconditional income for every individual. A Basic Income *scheme* is the Basic Income with its levels specified for each age group, the funding method specified in detail, and any changes to existing tax and benefits systems specified in detail. It would be the Basic Income scheme *as a whole* that would either decrease or increase income equality, not the Basic Income on its own. For instance, if in the United Kingdom (UK) a Basic Income were to be funded by abolishing existing means-tested benefits and by charging an additional flat income tax, then lots of low-income households would suffer significant losses (Torry, 2019: 4, 7, 11), and inequality could increase. If, on the other hand, existing means-tested benefits were to be retained, and recalculated on the basis that household members were receiving Basic Incomes, then, even with an additional flat tax rate, inequality would decrease (Torry, 2019: 26). Each country has a different tax and benefits system, so research would be required to ensure that any proposed Basic Income scheme would not accidentally increase inequality and poverty. The only method that can deliver the necessary research results is microsimulation (Torry, 2019, 2020, 2021).

It is often suggested that a carbon tax could be used to fund a Basic Income. Here again care would have to be taken. A carbon tax would increase the costs of transport and of heating homes, and the additional costs would constitute larger proportions of low-income households' disposable incomes than of the disposable incomes of higher-income households. A carbon tax could therefore increase both poverty and inequality. However, if carbon tax revenues were to be used to fund a Basic Income, then the Basic Income would constitute larger proportions of low-income households' disposable incomes than of the disposable incomes of higher-income households. What would be important would be to ensure that the positive effect of the Basic Income on low-income household disposable incomes would be greater than the negative effect of the carbon tax. There is an additional reason for combining a carbon tax with a Basic Income: If an inequality-reducing Basic Income scheme were to be implemented, then because the propensity to consume goods and services is higher among low-income households than among higher-income households, and because the secure layer of income constituted by the Basic Income might increase households' willingness to spend current income, the scheme could end up generating additional carbon dioxide emissions (Sager, 2017). Only a mechanism such as a carbon tax would be able to reduce them.

If a wealth tax were to be employed to fund a Basic Income, then we could be certain that inequality and poverty would decrease. Low-income households tend to have little or no wealth, so would not suffer the tax, and their Basic Incomes would increase their disposable incomes and potentially their wealth. Higher wealth households would receive Basic Incomes, but they would be paying wealth taxes of an amount greater than their Basic Incomes. We can therefore be sure that income poverty and income inequality would be reduced, and that wealth inequality would either be reduced as well or it would rise less steeply.

We can conclude that with capitalism understood as 'possession of capital or wealth', capitalism inevitably results in inequality, and potentially in poverty; that contemporary capitalism has experienced growing wealth and income inequality; and that a Basic Income could reduce income inequality and poverty, and could either reduce or slow the increase in wealth inequality, if care is taken over the details of the Basic Income scheme as a whole.

Capitalism Understood as 'an economic system in which private capital or wealth is used in the production or distribution of goods, and prices are determined mainly in a free market'

Ever since a spear was used to kill an animal, a rudimentary basket was used to collect fruit, and fruit was exchanged for a share of the kill, capitalism understood as 'an economic system in which private capital or wealth is used in the production or distribution of goods, and prices are determined mainly in a free market' has existed. But it has never been the only method for accessing goods and services. The kill would generally have been shared with the whole community, as the fruit would have been, regardless of who had worked to obtain those goods. And ever since then, alongside capitalism, collectively provided services have been an essential element in satisfying society's needs. The pendulum has often swung, either towards the distribution of goods in a free market and away from collective provision, or away from distribution in a free market and towards collective provision: but always there has been an element of both. For instance, defence of the community, whether local or national, has always been by collective provision; and food and clothing have generally been distributed through relatively free markets, although not always.

Contemporary capitalism has seen a significant swing of the pendulum towards the provision of goods and services by the market, and away from collective provision: in two senses, and not just one.

First of all, in relation to the individual or household: Here we have seen a trend away from free public provision and towards provision in a market. To take an example: In the UK, Legal Aid—government assistance with legal costs—used to be available in relation to family law:

and so, for instance, low-income families could apply for financial assistance with the costs of divorce proceedings. This could be particularly important where one party to the divorce was wealthy, and the other not. However, since 2012 Legal Aid has no longer been available for most family law cases, which means that legal assistance can usually only be obtained by the individuals concerned paying solicitors, to the disadvantage of the poorer partner (Marshall et al., 2018).

Secondly, in relation to the state, whether central or local government: here the swing of the pendulum has been constituted by services that were previously provided by state agencies now being contracted out to organisations in the private or voluntary sectors. If government contracts are awarded to non-profit voluntary organisations, then the organisations tend to become more like state agencies, any profits are not distributed, but are recycled into the service, and in practical terms people's experience of the service might be very like the experience of provision by the state. However, where services are contracted out to private organisations, profits are distributed to shareholders, short-term financial interests can dominate, and relative outcomes for service users can vary with the context, depending on the effectiveness of the state agencies that had previously managed the services (Lethbridge, 2019; Odendaal et al., 2018). A compounding factor is that governments can find it politically easier to reduce costs by privatising a service than to reduce the costs of existing state provision. This means that when we want to compare the relative effectivenesses of public services provided by private organisations and those provided by government agencies, it is important to compare the privately provided service with a publicly provided service with the same budget. Again to take the UK as an example: Some state services have been successfully contracted out for many decades, and sometimes for centuries. For instance, private provision of hospital laundry services can reap economies of scale unavailable to individual hospitals, and for a public service to create the management structure and physical plant that would be needed to reap similar economies of scale might be difficult and expensive to achieve. But some privatisations have been a disaster, both in terms of private providers being unable to provide an adequate service within the budget allocated, and in relation to the quality of the service. Some privatisations have had to be reversed. Healthcare and the probation service offer instructive examples (BBC, 2019; Ministry of Justice, 2019).

It is in relation to the first of these two kinds of privatisation—away from public provision for individuals and households, and towards the purchase of services in a market at the market price—that the Basic Income debate is relevant. This is because there are scholars, particularly in the United States, who argue that a Basic Income would enable the state to abolish a variety of means-tested benefits, and also a range of publicly provided services. As they see it, means-tested benefits create poverty traps, which makes it difficult for someone to get off them by earning additional income, which in turn, they claim, results in a dependency culture; and publicly provided services are, they claim, inefficient, and it would be better for people to be able to pay for education, healthcare, and so on, in a free market, because free markets are efficient by definition (Mead, 1992: ix; Murray, 1984: 204, 218, 227, 230; 1996: 50, 125; Pateman, 2005: 56).

It is of course true that means-tested benefits create poverty traps: but before any attempt is made simply to abolish them and replace them with a Basic Income, consideration would have to be given to whether low-income households would be made worse off, which could easily happen: in which case means-tested benefits would need to be retained and recalculated to take into account household members' Basic Incomes (Torry, 2019: 4, 7, 11, 26). As for the provision of services such as education and healthcare: There are two possibilities: public provision, and provision by a market. We shall take the UK's universal and unconditional National Health Service (NHS) as an example of public provision. It offers free visits to a General Practitioner (GP), and free inpatient and outpatient treatment in hospital, to every legal resident of the UK (National Health Service, 2020); it is paid for out of tax revenue; and general practitioners function as a rationing mechanism (House of Commons, 2014). An alternative would be a market in healthcare in which individuals would pay for the healthcare services that they received, either paying per item of healthcare, or paying insurance premiums to a company that would then pay for the healthcare that might be required.

The question to be addressed is this: Would it be possible to replace a system such as the NHS with a Basic Income and a market-based healthcare system? Superficially this might appear to be possible, because both the NHS and Basic Income can be described by the word 'unconditional'. However, the NHS exhibits an unconditionality very different from that of a Basic Income: it is an unconditionality of provision free at the point of use, rather than a constant free provision (Clarke, 2017). And so, for instance, one individual might make no use of NHS unconditional provision at any time during their life, whereas another might absorb healthcare that would have cost hundreds of thousands of pounds if purchased in a healthcare market. If the NHS were to be replaced by a Basic Income and a free market in healthcare, then the first of these two individuals would be in profit, and the second would be destitute and without the healthcare that they needed.

A further important factor to consider is that it would appear to be impossible to replace a publicly funded system such as the NHS with a market-based system that would be equally efficient and effective. Research has shown that the NHS has achieved better effectiveness and efficiency than any other OECD healthcare system, and that it is streets ahead of the United States' market-based system (Davis et al., 2014: 7). The main reason for the fact that a market-based healthcare system, which rations by price, is less effective and less efficient than a publicly provided system that rations by expert assessment of medical need, is that the apparently market-based system does not, in fact, operate in a classical free market, because the healthcare market suffers from multiple examples of asymmetric information and therefore multiple inefficiencies (Torry, 2017).

Capitalism understood as 'an economic system in which private capital or wealth is used in the production or distribution of goods, and prices are determined mainly in a free market' is an alluring prospect. Company managements and shareholders can believe public services to be opportunities for profit (although, as we have seen, they are often mistaken), and public servants can see privatisation as a means to save money and to achieve efficiency (again, they are often mistaken). Advocates of Basic Income from a certain end of the pollical spectrum can see a Basic Income as a means of replacing public services with services provided in a supposedly free market. As we have seen, this is an illusion. If anyone ever suggests the replacement of public services with a free market in services and a Basic Income, then the response has to be that unconditionality of constant provision and unconditionality of provision free at the point of need are totally different kinds of unconditionality, and that in any case it is far more efficient to provide healthcare and other services by public provision funded by taxation than by a market that simply cannot be efficient.

We have discovered that there is a sense in which Basic Income must not be allowed anywhere near capitalism understood as 'an economic system in which private capital or wealth is used in the production or distribution of goods, and prices are determined mainly in a free market': but that does not mean that there are no ways in which Basic Income and capitalism, understood in this sense, can be useful to each other. An important example is the employment market.

Although the relationship between a human being and their labour cannot be reduced to a market transaction in the same way as selling a car can be, there is a sense in which employment is a market transaction. If I agree to an employment contract, then I have sold my labour in a market, and the employer has bought it. This is the essence of capitalism understood as 'an economic system in which ... prices are determined mainly in a free market'. The market is not entirely free, because employment markets are highly regulated, mainly by employment rights and minimum wage legislation; and if the range of jobs available in an area is severely limited, then the person who needs an income and therefore a job might have only one employment option available to them, at a price decided by the employer, and they will not experience the employment market as a market within which choices can be made on the basis of price. However, if there is a range of jobs on offer, then the worker will experience a certain amount of freedom in relation to the prices that employers are willing to pay and that they are willing to accept. Self-employed workers might experience a little more freedom when they sell their skilled, semi-skilled or unskilled labour, because multiple individual contracts will be agreed upon, and the market might look rather more like the free market envisaged by the definition of capitalism. The question that we must therefore consider is this: How does Basic Income affect the employment market? (Here we shall mean both the employment and the self-employment markets).

First of all, a clarification: The price at which someone sells their labour is not the wage that is paid, because the worker will rarely receive the whole of the wage stated in the employment contract. Tax will be deducted, and then, if means-tested benefits are in payment, receipt of a wage will reduce the level of benefits received. The price that the worker receives for their labour will be the wage, minus tax, and minus the change in the benefits payment. (The price that the employer pays will be the wage, plus any statutory or contracted additions, such as social insurance and pension contributions: but that is not our concern here.) Of most relevance will be the price at the margin: that is, the amount of money received for one additional unit of labour; for it is that price that will determine whether the worker will work that hour, and therefore all of the hours up to that hour as well. This means that it will be the ***marginal*** deduction rate that matters: that is, the tax and loss of benefits related to that last hour of employment. For instance, Universal Credit regulations mean that one million families with children experience marginal deduction rates of between 70 and 80%, and that 900,000 families with children and receiving 'Tax Credits' will also be experiencing those rates (Finch et al., 2014: 19).

So what happens if the worker receives a Basic Income? A lot will depend on the detail of the scheme. For instance: if someone previously on means-tested benefits was taken off them by their Basic Income, then the marginal deduction rate would go down because they would no longer be suffering benefits withdrawal. This means that they would be more likely to seek additional income, either by working additional hours in their existing occupation, or by retraining and seeking a job at a higher wage. While motivation is a complex matter (Burchardt & Le Grand, 2002: 24), there is good evidence from natural and planned experiments that a reduced marginal deduction rate really does increase employment motivation, as the economic theory suggests that it should (Crossley & Jeon, 2007; Micheau & van Soest, 2008; O'Brien, 2007: 124; Parker & Sutherland 1988; Torry, 2018: 153–155), and the OECD (Organisation for Economic Co-operation and Development) has found that

> a reduction of marginal effective tax rates [marginal deduction rates] by 20% ... implies a rise in the probability of moving from unemployment to employment by nearly 10% ... . The strongest effects are found for the unemployed with a working partner, whose reemployment probability would increase by seven percentage points, from 51% to nearly 58%. (Organisation for Economic Cooperation & Development, 2005: 127)

A further effect of the implementation of a Basic Income scheme might be changes in wage levels: that is, in the prices that employers would be willing to pay for labour. If a wage is providing the whole of someone's subsistence income, and if the alternative to a wage is a means-tested benefit, with all of its complexity, sanctions, demotivation, and stigma (Dean & Mitchell, 2011; Welfare Reform Team, Oxford City Council, 2016), then the worker will accept the low wage, especially if he or she knows that a means-tested benefit and such other services as free school meals will be provided as well. However, a Basic Income might provide the worker with more options: for instance, the ability to start their own business, in the knowledge that if there is no income from it for a while then at least there will be a small secure income coming in; or the ability to be employed part-time and to allocate more time to voluntary community work. The wages of undesirable jobs would have to rise to attract workers (Liebermann, 2012: 93–95; Offe, 2008); and because the Basic Income would enable some workers to accept lower wages for more desirable jobs, and there would be more people looking for those jobs, wages for more desirable jobs could fall (Davis & Henrekson, 2005; Torry, 2018: 152).

A further consequence of a Basic Income scheme being implemented would be that low-paid employees would find themselves less likely to accept falling wage levels. At the moment, they might be on means-tested in-work benefits, which act as a dynamic subsidy—that is, the benefits rise in value as earned income falls, thus reducing workers' incentive to resist falling wages, and giving employers permission to reduce wages. A Basic Income would function as a static subsidy: that is, it would not change if wages fell. Workers whom the Basic Income had taken off means-tested benefits would find that their Basic Incomes would not rise as earned incomes fell, thus providing them with an incentive to resist wage reductions, and employers with a reduced ability to lower wages.

The changes that a Basic Income would bring about in the employment market would combine to improve workers' ability to choose the jobs that they would be willing to take, and to reject undesirable jobs; they would enable governments to reduce their reliance on means-tested benefits and on the accompanying sanctions regimes (Handler & Babcock, 2006); and they would take the employment market closer to being the kind of free market envisaged by a definition of capitalism as 'an economic system in which private capital or wealth is used in the production or distribution of goods, and prices are determined mainly in a free market'. A more equal balance of power between the employer and the worker would be good both for society and for the economy, because every firm would then have to provide the jobs that people already receiving totally secure small incomes would want. Research has shown that a combination of a Basic Income and progressive taxation could have a substantial effect on employment market activity: and that is before Basic Income's security of income and simplicity of administration have been taken into account (Colombino et al., 2010; Lo Vuolo, 2015: 35).

All manner of additional effects might also be felt. To take just one example: internships, which are currently the preserve of individuals whose parents can support them financially, would become financially feasible for individuals in part-time employment, to the benefit of social mobility and therefore of social cohesion (Werner & Goehler, 2010: 139–151).

The conclusion that we can draw is that a Basic Income would enable an individual worker, and therefore their household, to experience an employment market much closer to a free market than the employment market burdened with means-tested benefits that they might be experiencing today.

But it is not just the individual worker who would experience an employment market closer to a free market in which price regulates supply and demand. This would be good for industry as well (Van Parijs, 1990), even if it meant that some wages would have to rise in order to attract workers (Pech, 2010). The reason that rising wages can be good for industry is that they can result in greater efficiency because more rational decisions might be made about what can and what cannot be automated, and also about skills training. The result could be better job quality (Mayhew, 1991) along with increased efficiency for firms and public services. A further factor that would improve job quality is that during a strike a worker would retain their Basic Income, thus increasing their ability to seek improved pay and conditions (Gourevitch, 2016); and if someone's post was declared redundant, then the secure layer of income constituted by their Basic Income would provide them with more time to match their skills to the jobs on offer. Individuals and institutions would be more able to relate to each other as autonomous partners in constant negotiation, rather than being forced into the roles of supplicant and reluctant provider (Casassas, 2007; White, 2007).

We have seen that there are public services that could not be replaced by a Basic Income and a market in services, so in this respect Basic Income needs to be kept as far as possible from capitalism understood as 'an economic system in which private capital or wealth is used in the production or distribution of goods, and prices are determined mainly in a free market'. But we have also seen that in relation to the employment market, Basic Income could facilitate the better functioning of capitalism understood in this way, to the advantage of both workers and the owners of capital.

Capitalism as 'the dominance of private owners of capital and of production for profit'

This definition of capitalism reserves the word for an extreme example of the previous definition. This is somewhat problematic. If 'capitalism' means 'the *dominance* of private owners of capital and of production for profit', then the word is denied to those examples of private ownership of capital and of production for profit where dominance is not an issue. However, we shall accept for the time being that 'capitalism' can mean 'the dominance of private owners of capital and of production for profit', and ask how Basic Income might relate to capitalism so defined.

As we discovered in the previous section, with its broader definition of capitalism, a Basic Income could facilitate a market in labour that would better serve both workers and the owners of capital; and the fact that it would provide workers with a layer of income that would be completely secure, whatever their permanent or temporary employment market status, suggests that workers would have more employment and self-employment options available to them, and more options in relation to work more broadly defined: for instance, in relation to caring and voluntary community work. Private owners of capital, and production for profit, would therefore be able to dominate workers less easily.

There is legitimate debate as to how much of an 'exit' option a Basic Income might offer to workers: that is, whether a Basic Income really would provide workers with the ability to say 'no' to undesirable jobs (Birnbaum & De Wispelaere, 2016). For instance: if the only jobs in an area were both full-time and undesirable, then the 'exit' option would only be available to workers willing to move elsewhere. This means that the extent to which an exit option would be available could only be tested empirically, and would depend on local circumstances and on the details of the Basic Income scheme implemented: but in the context of a diverse employment market, and a Basic Income scheme that took a significant number of households off means-tested benefits, we could legitimately expect an increase in 'republican freedom': that is, the ability not to be dominated, at least in relation to the employment market (Casassas, 2007; Domènech & Raventós, 2007; White 2007). Although the guaranteed minimum income scheme tested nearly fifty years ago in Canada was not a Basic Income scheme, it did provide an increase in income security similar to the increase in security that a Basic Income scheme would provide, so we might be able to expect similar consequences. During the experiment, workers who became unemployed took longer to find the next job, suggesting that the income guarantee was enabling them to look for the right job rather than just any job (Forget, 2011). We would expect the income security provided by a Basic Income to have a similar effect. At the moment, in most countries, losing a job puts the whole of someone's income at risk, either because there is no safety net at all, or because the safety net is unpredictable. This makes finding a new job—any job—urgent. With a Basic Income scheme, the Basic Income would continue whatever happened to workers' employment market status; and because the Basic Income would be unconditional, there would be more of an option to fill any income gap with temporary employment, self-employment, and/or a search for an appropriate new job: options far less available in the context of means-tested and work-tested benefits.

Capitalism defined in terms of the dominance of capital is not a problem just for individual workers. It is a problem for governments and for whole societies. A clear example of the 'dominance of private owners of capital and of production for profit' is an increasingly global employment market that is driving down employment terms and conditions, and, even when they wish to, national governments are finding it difficult to insulate their societies from the effects of an increasingly insecure and often exploitative employment market. Countries working together are having some success, as in the European Union: but the slide into precarity for an increasing number of professions would appear to be inexorable (Standing 2011, 2014; University and College Union, 2016). Although no single policy instrument will be able to protect workers from an increasingly precarious employment experience, a Basic Income would help: by providing many individual workers with a greater ability to say 'no'; by providing a secure income on which a worker could build a mixture of self-employment and occasional employment if that might suit their circumstances, thus diversifying the employment market at the same time as enhancing workers' financial security; and by enabling households far more easily to choose employment patterns that suit their circumstances than they can in the context of rigid means-tested and work-tested benefits systems, thus strengthening families' resilience. Zero-hour contracts would not disappear, and neither should they, because they can be useful to some employers and to some employees: but a greater ability to say 'no' to exploitative contracts—the kind that forbids someone to work for other employers, and that requires them to accept shifts at short notice—would incentivise employers to offer non-exploitative contracts.

Conclusion

We have seen that in relation to capitalism understood as 'the possession of capital or wealth' and as 'an economic system in which private capital or wealth is used in the production or distribution of goods, and prices are determined mainly in a free market', a Basic Income could enable capitalism to function more efficiently for the economy, for society, for individuals, and for households. We have also seen that if capitalism is defined as 'the dominance of private owners of capital and of production for profit', then a Basic Income could help to protect individuals, households and societies from some of the effects of capitalism.

But there is one sense in which the principle at the heart of Basic Income is utterly opposed to capitalism, and we cannot end this so far entirely pragmatic chapter by failing to mention it. Every definition of capitalism that we have discussed assumes that everything has its price. There is nothing for free: and this goes as much for social policies ostensibly designed to protect societies from some of the unfortunate effects of capitalism as it does for the purchase of goods in a market. This is particularly clear in relation to social security benefits. Social insurance benefits, designed to protect workers during periods of illness and unemployment, have their price: the payment of contributions. Means-tested and work-tested benefits have their price: means tests, work tests, stigma, demeaning enquiry into personal circumstances, and so on. There are of course occasional social policies that are genuinely free of price ('priceless' in more senses than one). In many countries, education is offered without parents having to pay for it, although the principle is compromised if private education of better quality is available at a price. The UK's National Health Service and Child Benefit are two examples of public provision without a price. But the examples are rare. A Basic Income—an unconditional income for every individual—would be public provision without price, and so the very opposite of capitalism.

We can therefore conclude that Basic Income offers a tantalising possibility. It could work very happily alongside capitalism, and could facilitate the greater efficiency of the non-dominating varieties of it: for the owners of capital, for individual workers and their families, and for society as a whole; and, at the same time, it would offer a new paradigm: a wholly new way of organising the economy that would represent the polar opposite of capitalism. To implement a Basic Income scheme could therefore provide both our economies and our societies with the possibility of a non-disruptive transition into the kind of reform of capitalism that would reduce its ability to dominate and that would enable the price mechanism and the ownership of capital to act as servants of the economy, and therefore of a society founded on a different principle: the unconditionality principle, the principle of the gift. Whether we shall ever see such a society and such an economy I've no idea, but if we wish to see one, or if we should wish to see a society that has moved even slightly in that direction, then the argument of this chapter suggests that to implement a Basic Income scheme would provide an important element of the shift required.

Acknowledgements This chapter reproduces a paper prepared for the second Gyeonggi Province Basic Income International Conference that was planned to be held in the Republic of Korea in February 2020. The conference had to be cancelled because of rising coronavirus infections in Korea. A presentation based on the paper was given at an online conference held in September 2020.

References

Alvaredo, F., Chancel, L., Piketty, T., Saez, E., & Zucman, G. (2018). *World Inequality Report 2018*. World Inequality Lab. Retrieved March 26, 2022, from https://wir2018.wid.world/files/download/wir2018-full-report-english.pdf

BBC. (2019). *Virgin Care ends Staffordshire health contract over cost*. Retrieved March 26, 2022, from https://www.bbc.co.uk/news/uk-england-stoke-staffordshire-48121572

Birnbaum, S., & De Wispelaere, J. (2016). Basic Income in the capitalist economy: The mirage of 'exit' from employment. *Basic Income Studies, 11*(1), 61–74.

Burchardt, T., & Le Grand, J. (2002). *Constraint and opportunity: Identifying voluntary non-employment*. CASEpaper 55. Centre for Analysis of Social Exclusion, London School of Economics.

Casassas, D. (2007). Basic Income and the republican ideal: Rethinking material independence in contemporary societies. *Basic Income Studies, 2*(2), 1–7.

Choo, S. (2019). *A policymaker's guide on inequality*. United Nations Economic and Social Commission for Asia and the Pacific. Retrieved March 26,

2022, from https://www.unescap.org/sites/default/files/A%20policy%20maker%20guide%20on%20inequality%20191221.pdf

Citizen's Basic Income Trust. (2022). Citizen's Basic Income. Retrieved March 26, 2022, from https://citizensincome.org

Clarke, J. (2017). *Basic Income: Progressive dreams meet neoliberal realities*. Socialist Project. Retrieved March 26, 2022, from https://socialistproject.ca/2017/01/b1350/

Colombino, U., Locatelli, M., Narazani, E., & O'Donoghue, C. (2010). Alternative Basic Income mechanisms: An evaluation exercise with a microeconometric model. *Basic Income Studies, 5*(1), 1–31.

Crossley, T. F., & Jeon, S.-H. (2007). Joint taxation and the labour supply of married women: Evidence from the Canadian tax reform of 1988. *Fiscal Studies, 28*(3), 343–365.

Davis, S. J., & Henrekson, M. (2005). Tax effects on work activity, industry mix and shadow economy size: Evidence from rich-country comparisons. In R. Gomez-Salvador, A. Lamo, B. Petrongolo, M. Ward, & E. Wasmer (Eds.), *Labour supply and incentives to work in Europe* (pp. 44–104). Edward Elgar Publishing.

Davis, K., Stremikis, K., Squires, D., & Schoen, C. (2014). *Mirror, mirror on the wall: How the performance of the U.S. health care system compares internationally*. The Commonwealth Fund. Retrieved March 26, 2022, from www.commonwealthfund.org/~/media/files/publications/fund-report/2014/jun/1755_davis_mirror_mirror_2014.pdf

Dean, H., & Mitchell, G. (2011). *Wage top-ups and work incentives: The implications of the UK's Working Tax Credit scheme: A preliminary report*. London School of Economics.

Domènech, A., & Raventós, D. (2007). Property and republican freedom: An institutional approach to Basic Income. *Basic Income Studies, 2*(2), 1–8.

Finch, D., Corlett, A. & Alakeson, V. (2014). *Universal Credit: A policy under review*. Resolution Foundation. Retrieved March 26, 2022, from www.resolutionfoundation.org/app/uploads/2014/09/Universal-Credit-A-policy-under-review1.pdf

Forget, E. (2011). The town with no poverty: The health effects of a Canadian guaranteed annual income field experiment. *Canadian Public Policy, 37*(3), 283–305.

Gourevitch, A. (2016). The limits of a Basic Income: Means and ends of workplace democracy. *Basic Income Studies, 11*(1), 17–28.

Handler, J., & Babcock, A. (2006). The failure of workfare: Another reason for a Basic Income Guarantee. *Basic Income Studies, 1*(1), 1–22.

House of Commons. (2014, February 25 Tuesday). Oral answers to questions. Retrieved March 26, 2022, from www.publications.parliament.uk/pa/cm201314/cmhansrd/cm140225/debtext/140225-0001.htm

Lethbridge, J. (2019). *Empty promises: The impact of outsourcing on NHS services*. University of Greenwich. Retrieved March 26, 2022, from https://gala.gre.ac.uk/id/eprint/8084/

Liebermann, S. (2012). Germany: Far, though close – Problems and prospects of BI in Germany. In R. Caputo (Ed.), *Basic Income Guarantee and politics: International experiences and perspectives on the viability of Income Guarantee* (pp. 83–106). Palgrave Macmillan.

Lo Vuolo, R. M. (2015). Piketty's *Capital*, his critics and Basic Income. *Basic Income Studies, 10*(1), 29–43.

Marshall, E., Harper, S., & Stacey, H. (2018). *Family law and access to Legal Aid*. Public Law Project.

Mayhew, K. (1991). Basic Income as a lever for economic efficiency. *BIRG Bulletin*, (12), 10–12.

Mead, L. (1992). *The new politics of poverty: The non-working poor in America*. Harper Collins.

Micheau, P. C., & van Soest, A. (2008). How did the elimination of the US earnings test above the normal retirement age affect labour supply expectations. *Fiscal Studies, 29*(2), 197–231.

Ministry of Justice. (2019). *Government response to the Justice Committee's Ninth Report of Session 2017–19: Transforming rehabilitation*. Ministry of Justice. Retrieved March 26, 2022, from https://assets.publishing.service.gov.uk/government/uploads/system/uploads/attachment_data/file/809370/government-response-justice-committee_s-ninth-report-session-2017-19-transforming-rehabilitatio.pdf

Murray, C. (1984). *Losing ground: American social policy, 1950–1980*. Basic Books.

Murray, C. (1996). *Charles Murray and the underclass: The developing debate*. Institute of Economic Affairs.

National Health Service. (2020). *When you need to pay for NHS care*. Retrieved March 26, 2022, from https://www.nhs.uk/nhs-services/help-with-health-costs/when-you-need-to-pay-towards-nhs-care/

O'Brien, M. (2007). *Poverty, policy and the state*. Policy Press.

Odendaal W. A. Ward, K., Uneke, J., Uro-Chukwu, H., Chitama, D., Balakrishna, Y., & Kredo, T. (2018). *Contracting out to improve the use of clinical health services and health outcomes in low- and middle-income countries*. Cochrane. Retrieved March 26, 2022, from https://www.cochrane.org/CD008133/EPOC_contracting-out-improve-use-clinical-health-services-and-health-outcomes-low-and-middle-income

Offe, C. (2008). Basic Income and the labor contract. *Basic Income Studies, 3*(1), 1–30.

Organisation for Economic Cooperation and Development. (2005). *Employment outlook, 2005*. Organization for Economic Cooperation and Development.

Oxford University Press. (2022). Oxford English Dictionary. Retrieved March 26, 2022, from https://oed.com.

Parker, H., & Sutherland, H. (1988, February). How to get rid of the poverty trap: Basic Income plus national minimum wage. *Citizen's Income Bulletin*, (25), 11–14.

Pateman, C. (2005). Another way forward: Welfare, social reproduction, and a Basic Income. In L. Mead & C. Beem (Eds.), *Welfare reform and political theory* (pp. 34–64). Russell Sage Foundation.

Pech, W. (2010). Behavioral economics and the Basic Income Guarantee. *Basic Income Studies, 5*(2), 1–17.

Sager, L. (2017). *Income inequality and carbon consumption: Evidence from environmental Engel curves* (Working Paper 385). Grantham Research Institute on Climate Change and the Environment. Retrieved March 26, 2022, from http://www.lse.ac.uk/GranthamInstitute/publication/income-inequality-and-carbon-consumption-evidence-from-environmental-engel-curves/

Standing, G. (2011). *The Precariat: The new dangerous class*. Bloomsbury.

Standing, G. (2014). *A Precariat Charter: From denizens to citizens*. Bloomsbury.

Torry, M. (2017). Primary care, the basic necessity: Part I: Explorations in economics. In A. Papanikitas & J. Spicer (Eds.), *Handbook of primary care ethics* (pp. 369–375). CRC/Francis and Taylor.

Torry, M. (2018). *Why we need a Citizen's Basic Income: The desirability, feasibility and implementation of an unconditional income*. Policy Press.

Torry, M. (2019). *Static microsimulation research on Citizen's Basic Income for the UK: A personal summary and further reflections* (EUROMOD Working Paper EM13/19). Institute for Social and Economic Research. Retrieved March 26, 2022, from https://www.euromod.ac.uk/sites/default/files/working-papers/em13-19.pdf

Torry, M. (2020). *Evaluation of a Recovery Basic Income, and of a sustainable revenue neutral Citizen's Basic Income, with an appendix relating to different Universal Credit roll-out scenarios* (Institute for Social and Economic Research Working Paper EM7/20). Institute for Social and Economic Research, University of Essex. Retrieved March 26, 2022, from https://www.iser.essex.ac.uk/research/publications/working-papers/euromod/em7-20.pdf

Torry, M. (2021). *Three income maintenance options for 2021* (Centre for Microsimulation and Policy Analysis report). Institute for Social and Economic Research, University of Essex. Retrieved March 26, 2022, from https://www.microsimulation.ac.uk/publications/publication-526555/

University and College Union. (2016). *Precarious work in Higher Education: A snapshot of insecure contracts and institutional attitudes*. University and

College Union. Retrieved March 26, 2022, from www.ucu.org.uk/media/7995/Precarious-work-in-higher-education-a-snapshot-of-insecure-contracts-and-institutional-attitudes-Apr-16/pdf/ucu_precariouscontract_hereport_apr16.pdf

Van Parijs, P. (1990). The second marriage of justice and efficiency. *Journal of Social Policy, 19*(1), 1–25.

Welfare Reform Team, Oxford City Council. (2016). *Evaluation of European Social Fund Pilot Project 2014–2015.* Oxford City Council. Retrieved March 26, 2022, from www.oxford.gov.uk/downloads/file/2119/welfare_reform_european_social_fund_project_evaluation_report

Werner, G. W., & Goehler, A. (2010). *1.000 Euro für jeden.* Econ, Ullstein Buchverlage.

White, S. (2007). The Republican case for Basic Income: A plea for difficulty. *Basic Income Studies, 2*(2), 1–7.

CHAPTER 6

An Essential Dimension of the Social Minimum

Introduction

This chapter contributes to the discussion of a social minimum by conceptualising it in three dimensions: the different resources that need to be provided; the characteristics of the provision of those resources; and the ways in which delivery methods are structured.

The *Stanford Encyclopedia of Philosophy* defines a social minimum as 'that bundle of resources which suffices in the circumstances of a given society to enable someone to lead a minimally decent life', and a social minimum policy regime as 'a set of policies and institutions that serve to secure reasonable access to this social minimum for all members of the society' (White, 2015). For the purposes of this chapter, 'resources' means such different types of welfare provision as education, healthcare, income, and so on; 'characteristics' means such measurable characteristics of the resources as their quality, the level of equality of their provision, the ease with which the resources can be accessed, and the efficiency with which the resources are provided; and 'mode of delivery' means the way in which delivery is structured: for instance, whether healthcare is funded by individual insurance policies or by general taxation.

M. Torry, *Basic Income—What, Why, and How?*,
Exploring the Basic Income Guarantee,
https://doi.org/10.1007/978-3-031-14248-2_6

This chapter will construct a partial and provisional categorisation of the 'bundle of resources', and also a list of the characteristics of those resources that would be required if those resources are to promote a minimally decent life. Relationships between the various resources and the various characteristics will then be discussed, and then the characteristics' relationships with different modes of delivery.

Dimensions

In the academic literature, the welfare state is often discussed in terms of a number of dimensions of welfare, but the word 'dimension' can have a variety of meanings. Bo Rothstein defines the dimensions of the welfare state as (i) coverage; and (ii) allocation method (Rothstein, 1998: 20). Gilbert and Specht define four dimensions of social policy as (i) the bases of social allocation; (ii) the types of social provision; (iii) the strategies for delivery; and (iv) the ways to finance the provision made (Gilbert & Specht, 1974: 29). Gilbert and Terrell reiterate these dimensions, and add some more: equality, equity, and adequacy; and then still more: work incentives, childbearing, family stability, stigma/social integration; and such dimensions of allocation as attributed need, compensation, diagnostic differentiation, and means-tested need; and then more again (Gilbert & Terrell, 2013: 76–78, 102–106, 108–111). Rothstein's and Steinmo's institutional understanding of the welfare state suggests a spectrum along which we might locate 'client institution', 'user institution', and 'customer institution': a spectrum along which empowerment is at a minimum at the 'client institution' end, and at its maximum at the 'customer institution' end (Kumlin, 2002: 26; Rothstein & Steinmo, 2002: 15). Such a spectrum suggests a definition of 'dimension' with similarities to the word's core usage in relation to three-dimensional space. By the end of this chapter, we shall find ourselves with reasons for using the concept of a dimension in a similar way.

Resources Required for a 'minimally decent life'

For the purposes of this chapter I shall assume that 'a minimally decent life' and 'the avoidance of poverty' mean much the same. This does not mean that 'dimensions of poverty' and 'dimensions of the social minimum' are synonymous. Dimensions of poverty might be 'intensity', 'duration', or 'type' (poverty as the norm, poverty for the few, poverty as a constant risk, and so on) (Paugam, 2009: 8–9, 17). These would not apply to a social minimum. And we shall find ourselves formulating dimensions for the social minimum that do not apply to poverty. They would, of course, apply to the alleviation or abolition of poverty that the provision of a social minimum would imply.

I shall also leave to one side two somewhat extreme definitions of the social minimum: (i) an equal distribution of a society's wealth (Waldron, 1986: 21, 30; Widerquist, 2010: 474); and (ii) the 'minimum level of material wellbeing required before people are plunged into despair' (Waldron, 1986: 21). Instead, I shall ask what we might mean by 'a minimally decent life', and work out from that what resources might be required.

How should we decide what constitutes a minimally decent life? One approach to the avoidance of poverty, often called the 'Breadline Britain' tradition after the 1983 book of that title, is to ask a representative sample of a population what resources they think are required to enable someone to live a minimally decent life. (This is the process employed to set the Minimum Income Standards published annually by the Joseph Rowntree Foundation.) (Davis et al., 2016; Goedemé, 2020; Lansley & Mack, 1983, 2015). A second approach is the kind of social minimum that Barrientos suggests that Rawls has in mind: a 'justice-based social minimum' constructed via a society's democratic institutions (Barrientos, 2016: 154–156). Rawls proposes a social minimum that 'together with the whole family of social policies, maximises the life prospects of the least advantaged over time' (Rawls, 2001: 129–130). A third approach is to set out from the concept of 'human need', with 'need' defined in what might look like a normative fashion. This was the approach taken by Seebohm Rowntree in York a hundred years ago (Townsend, 1979: 32–34); and a similar approach stems from Abraham Maslow's hierarchy of human needs: first 'safety needs', then 'love needs', and finally 'esteem needs' (Maslow, 1943: 376–382), with 'safety needs' understood as biological (food, drink, and shelter) and as safety and security. A similar and fourth approach emerges from Amartya Sen's 'capabilities' approach to poverty. Here the question is this: What are the resources required to enable someone to exercise capabilities? Or, to state the obverse: what resources are required to avoid capabilities poverty? (Alkire, 2007: 91; Reader, 2006) This approach suggests that human need is in some way normative, whereas in fact it is to a large extent socially constructed (Dean, 2010: 46–47): but it remains true that someone for whom such lower level needs as food, drink and shelter have not been fulfilled will find their very existence threatened, their needs for affiliation, esteem, knowledge, the aesthetic, transcendence, and self-realisation (Maslow, 1943: 376–382) difficult to fulfil, and any potential capabilities difficult to exercise.

The 'Breadline Britain' approach to the social minimum automatically generates a list of resources required for a minimally decent life. The justice-based approach requires a similar method to be applied to the least advantaged individual. The third and fourth approaches can be understood either as similar one-stage processes (we need food, so food has to be provided), or as a two-stage process (we need health, so we need a healthcare system) (Reader, 2006: 337).

In a modern society, an income can substitute for some of these resources. This is clearly true of food and drink; it might or might not be true of shelter, although for most households it will be; and it might not be true of healthcare and education. The problems related to income are that the different approaches to the social minimum can deliver very different suggestions as to how much income is required for a social minimum, and that the income intended to provide for a social minimum might be chosen in relation to political and affordability constraints rather than in relation to any of the methods discussed above (Atkinson, 1990). The problem with healthcare is rather different. The problem here is that two different individuals might need radically different amounts of healthcare if they are both to live minimally decent lives: so in order to ensure that everyone in a society can lead a minimally decent life, healthcare itself has to be provided rather than an income with which to purchase it. It might be objected that an income can be used to purchase healthcare insurance. It can be for some, but not for everyone, as some individuals would be regarded as uninsurable; and, for society as a whole, an insurance-based healthcare system suffers from multiple market failures, and so is less efficient than government-provided universal and unconditional healthcare (Torry, 2017a). This means that income and healthcare are not substitutes, and it is no surprise that Stuart White defines a 'civic minimum' as constituted by both income and healthcare (White, 2003: 99, 131–32), and that Erik Thorbecke suggests that an income measure is not sufficient because 'it does not incorporate key dimensions of poverty such as life-expectancy (longevity), literacy, the provision of public goods, freedom and security': the attributes of social provision required to enable every individual to experience the 'capabilities and functioning' that Amartya Sen believed necessary for the avoidance of poverty (Thorbecke, 2007: 17). A further reason for separating healthcare and income is offered by Atkinson:

> Whereas a relative income standard has come to be used within country groupings, such as the EU [because the income required for participation in society will differ between different societies], there are good grounds for applying an absolute health deprivation standard [age at death, infant mortality rate, and so on], certainly when comparing across countries and, if adjustments are made over time, they are likely to be infrequent rather than annual. (Atkinson, 2009: 24)

Sufficient income to pay for food, drink and shelter (including clothing), and publicly provided healthcare, will be essential members of any list of necessary resources. Others might be education, public transport, policing, a courts system, legal representation, and perhaps social cohesion (De Boyser et al., 2009: 220). For the purposes of this chapter, I shall concentrate on income and healthcare.

Characteristics of the Resources

Each of these resources possesses a variety of characteristics—such as efficiency and equity—and, in different countries, different ways of delivering the resources will mean that the resources will be characterised by more or less equity, more or less efficiency, and so on.

Take healthcare as an example. The Commonwealth Fund, based in New York, has evaluated eleven OECD countries' healthcare systems in relation to a variety of characteristics and sub-characteristics:

- quality (effectiveness, safety, co-ordination, and person-centredness);
- ease of access (affordability and timeliness);
- efficiency (expenditures, administrative costs, administrative efficiency, appropriate use of resources, non-duplication);
- equity (understood as equality);
- 'healthy lives', in terms of 'mortality amenable to medical care, infant mortality, and healthy life expectancy at age 60' (Davis et al., 2014: 28–29) (a more general term is 'outcome').

The researchers find that the United Kingdom is ranked first overall and first in relation to most of the characteristics, and that the United States is ranked last overall and either last or a long way down the rankings in relation to most of the characteristics.

Each of the first four main indicators that the Commonwealth Fund measured relates to a characteristic of a healthcare system: its quality, its ease of access, its efficiency, and its equity. The fifth is somewhat different: healthy lives. A healthcare system is only partially responsible for the healthiness or otherwise of people's lives, and other factors can be more important. I shall translate this characteristic as 'outcome'.

The fact that the UK's healthcare system is doing so well in relation to most of the indicators, and that the US system is doing so badly, is an issue to which we shall return.

The first thing to say about the list above is that the division between characteristics and sub-characteristics (which the Commonwealth Fund calls 'indicators' and 'general characteristics') is somewhat arbitrary: both because any such categorisations are largely matters of subjective choice, and because each of the sub-characteristics could be regarded as characteristics. It is because the boundary between 'indicator' and 'general characteristic' is far from clear that I prefer the terminology 'characteristic' and 'sub-characteristic'.

The second and equally important question raised by this list is whether these characteristics are applicable to the other resources required for a minimally decent life in society. Take education as an example: all four characteristics are meaningful, as are their sub-characteristics. In relation to quality, all of effectiveness, safety, co-ordination, and person-centredness would apply; in relation to ease of access, affordability and timeliness are important; in relation to efficiency, expenditure, administrative costs, administrative efficiency, appropriate use of resources, and non-duplication, are relevant; equity matters; and the 'outcome' would be a well-educated population. The list feels as complete in relation to education as it does in relation to healthcare. The same might be true of emergency services and public transport, and might potentially be true of other resources that we might wish to add to the list.

However, the list of characteristics that might seem obvious in relation to healthcare and education might not be quite so appropriate in relation to income provision. So here we might require a different set of characteristics: or, if we employ the same list of characteristics, we shall find that the characteristics will mean different things in relation to the different resources, and that the lists of sub-characteristics will be different. None of this is a problem, as we can see if we study the method employed by the Commonwealth Fund. The Commonwealth Fund's researchers employed surveys and other empirical data to generate measurements of their chosen healthcare sub-characteristics in different countries, then combined those scores into scores for each characteristic, and then ranked countries in relation to those scores: and finally they employed a variety of methods to generate overall scores for each country's healthcare system (Davis et al., 2014: 28–29). We shall always be able to construct lists of characteristics and sub-characteristics, we shall always be able to conduct surveys to evaluate to what extent the characteristics are met in different contexts, and although it will never be possible to compare scores across different resources, we shall always be able to rank different contexts in relation to the characteristics of each individual resource, and we shall always be able to ascribe an overall ranking to each context for each resource. This is what matters: so it is not a problem that the lists of characteristics and sub-characteristics might be different for different resources.

Suppose that we wished to conduct a survey and collect other data to discover how people regard the income maintenance system in the UK. First of all, we would need to distinguish between earnings, other forms of income, the tax system, and the benefits system, and we would need to treat each of them separately. We would also need to treat different types of social security benefit differently: for instance, unconditional Child Benefit behaves very differently from such means-tested benefits as Jobseeker's Allowance, Child Tax Credits, Working Tax Credits, and Universal Credit. If we decided to set out from the list of characteristics employed by the Commonwealth Fund, we would quickly find ourselves dividing them. 'Effective' could mean 'prevents poverty' and 'incentivises employment'. 'Safety' could mean 'avoids bureaucratic intrusion' and 'ensures continuity of provision'. 'Co-ordinated' could mean 'fits with desired family and employment structure' and 'co-ordinates with other income streams'. 'Person-centred' could mean any or all of 'adapts to individual needs', 'avoids stigmatisation', and 'encourages personal choice'. 'Affordable' needs to apply to the claimant, so it could mean 'the claiming process is not costly in terms of money' and 'the claiming process is not costly in terms of time', and it might also mean 'does not result in overpayments that have to be paid back'. 'Timely' could mean 'payments are always made on time' and 'correct payments are made from the date of the claim'. 'Expenditure' refers to the total cost of each benefit, and 'administrative costs' and 'administrative efficiency' are what they say they are: but 'appropriate use of resources' could mean 'those who need more should receive more' and also 'the benefits system should provide everyone with the income that they need in order to live a minimally decent life in society'. 'Non-duplication' might or might not be a desirable feature of benefits systems. Non-duplication suggests administrative efficiency, but it might also be desirable for one income source, such as social security benefits, to incentivise the pursuit of other income sources, such as earnings.

Whether or not we choose to use the Commonwealth Fund's list of characteristics, once we have listed all of the possible sub-characteristics, we can employ the same method as the Commonwealth Fund (Davis et al., 2014: 28–29). We can use survey and other methods to construct scores for the different sub-characteristics, and then use a method similar to that used by the Commonwealth Fund researchers to construct overall scores for the characteristics, and from those we can construct rankings and overall rankings.

What the method does not require is that sub-characteristics should appear to be consistent. This is fortunate. 'Those who need more should receive more' and 'the benefits system should provide everyone with the income that they need to provide themselves with a minimally decent life in society' appear to be inconsistent because 'the benefits system should provide everyone with the income that they need to live a minimally decent life in society' might suggest universal and unconditional benefits, and 'those who need more should receive more' might suggest means-tested benefits. However, the inconsistency might be more linguistic than actual. The same amount of money to everyone will always increase the net incomes of low earners by a higher proportion than it increases the net incomes of higher earners (Rothstein, 2002: 210–211); and research on proposals to pay an unconditional income to every member of a population shows that such schemes can be designed to redistribute from rich to poor, to reduce poverty, to reduce inequality, to achieve zero net cost, to ensure almost zero losses for low-income households at the point of implementation, and to require minimal increases in rates of income tax (Torry, 2020a: 11–12; 2021: 9–12). But whether or not different characteristics are or are not consistent, and whether or not they appear to be consistent, the method is not compromised. Each sub-characteristic can always be separately scored for each resource in each context, the scores can be combined to create scores for characteristics (whether or not the same characteristics are listed for each resource), rankings can be calculated, and then overall rankings can be ascribed.

It therefore appears that the 'characteristics and sub-characteristics' method can be used in relation to income provision in much the same way as it can be used in other social policy fields. The kinds of surveys and other data-gathering exercises that have generated the international comparisons delivered by the Commonwealth Fund in relation to healthcare systems could easily be used to compare the benefits systems in different countries, and to compare different kinds of benefits within the same country. Equally interesting would be to spread the net further in order to take in other types of income provision, because the same method could just as easily be employed in relation to earned income and pensions income.

When we set out to construct a list of sub-characteristics to enable us to evaluate income maintenance, we set out from the list of characteristics appropriate for the evaluation of healthcare. The risk of doing this is that we might miss important characteristics and sub-characteristics that might relate to income provision but not to healthcare. One important characteristic that might be important in relation to income is revealed when we think of the social minimum in terms of its obverse: poverty. A 'poverty trap' occurs where institutional arrangements trap people in poverty. The more positive social minimum characteristic would be 'ease of progression'. Means-tested benefits can constitute traps, because, as earnings rise, benefits can be reduced at the same time as tax is paid, imposing a high marginal deduction rate, meaning that a household might benefit from only one-quarter of additional earned income: although this is an improvement on the 4% of additional earned income that could result from the withdrawal of previous means-tested benefits (Murphy & Reed, 2013: 25–27; Torry, 2020b: 29). Such universal and unconditional benefits as Child Benefit and the Winter Fuel Allowance do not cause such traps, and so offer ease of progression. Do such traps exist in the context of other social minimum resources? Arguably, yes. The question to be asked is whether the institutions involved prevent progress towards achieving a minimally decent life (Sindzingre, 2007: 63). So, for instance: in healthcare, do the budgetary and institutional boundaries between hospital care and local authority social care prevent progress towards independence following an accident or illness? What we are discussing here is the 'process freedom' that Amartya Sen discusses alongside the 'capabilities' freedom experienced in the situation to which process freedom will take us, and it suggests that there is a characteristic missing from all of our lists—effective pathways—and that this needs to be applied to all of the resources (Sen, 2009: 225–252, 370–371).

We have shown that the characteristics employed by the Commonwealth Fund to rank healthcare systems can also be employed for education provision, and might be useful in relation to income provision if different lists of sub-characteristics are employed. What we have not so far shown to be legitimate is to compare the scores generated by a characteristic of income provision across different countries with the scores generated by the same characteristic of healthcare. The indicators used would be different, which suggests that comparison would be impossible. What we *would* be able to compare would be the two *rankings* of the different countries in relation to that characteristic.

A similar question arises in relation to each country: In the Commonwealth Fund project each of the different scores given to characteristics is constructed from a wide variety of indicators for sub-characteristics: for instance, the 'quality' score is constructed from 44 different indicators (Davis et al., 2014: 28). A similar project for education provision would employ some indicators that might look similar, but there could also be substantial differences. The question to ask, therefore, is whether the fact that the quality scores across the different resources are constructed using different groups of indicators means that it is not possible to ask how a country's healthcare system compares with its education system. The answer is surely that it might not be possible to compare them in relation to their scores, but that it might be possible to compare them in relation to their rankings. So, in the same way that the Commonwealth Fund researchers were able to arrive at rankings for the healthcare systems of OECD countries, it might also be possible to arrive at rankings for the quality, access, efficiency, equity, and outcomes, of each country's other resources, and also to arrive at overall rankings for those resources. This is the kind of exercise that Thorbecke envisages when he asks for a welfare function that incorporates attributes of welfare provision, weights, thresholds of attributes, marginal benefits of attributes, and joint interactions (Thorbecke, 2007: 17), and that Atkinson is looking for when he explores the possibility of a welfare function with both income and health components. Atkinson of course recognises the difficulty of constructing overall scores, because methods for constructing scores will need to be agreed, and weights will need to be applied (Atkinson, 2009: 31–33; de Neuberg et al., 2009: 52). As we have suggested, it might be easier to create and compare rankings, and to create overall rankings out of rankings, than to create and compare scores, and create overall scores out of scores: but the question of how the different indicator scores are to be weighted in order to create the overall rankings at the national level and between countries does not go away. The Commonwealth Fund applied a variety of methods for creating rankings and overall rankings out of multiple indicators:

> We found that these alternative methods tended to consistently yield the same top-performing countries (the U.K. and Switzerland) and worst-performing countries (the U.S. and Canada). However, there was a fair amount of fluidity among the countries in the middle of the performance range, whose rankings were sensitive to relatively small changes in data or methodology. For this reason, overall rankings may overshadow important absolute differences in performance, warranting closer examination of the data when describing a particular country's performance. (Davis et al., 2014: 28–29)

I suspect that we would find the same combination of consistency and fluidity with the other social minimum resources.

A final question is this: Are the characteristics independent of each other? For instance: might there be a trade-off between equity and efficiency? Le Grand suggests that in relation to means-tested benefits there is such a trade-off between equity, understood as a reduction in poverty, and efficiency, understood as employment and savings incentives (Le Grand, 1990: 554). However, such a trade-off does not necessarily exist in relation to unconditional benefits, which, because they provide a higher proportion of net income for the poor than they do for the rich, can result in reductions in poverty and inequality; and because they are not withdrawn as earned and investment incomes rise, they do not compromise efficiency (Torry, 2021: 9–12). Trade-offs might or might not exist, but whether they do or not does not compromise the usefulness of generating rankings of characteristics.

The Construction of a Social Minimum Policy Regime

The Commonwealth Fund evaluates each country's healthcare system in relation to its characteristics, suggesting that there are two dimensions to healthcare provision: country, and characteristics. We have now extended the method to a variety of different resources, so we have added a third dimension: resources. However, in relation to the Commonwealth Fund's evaluation, the independent variable is better understood as a particular country's healthcare system's *mode of delivery*. It is the way that a healthcare system is structured that is being evaluated in relation to a variety of characteristics. It is the National Health Service's (NHS's) mode of delivery—that it is publicly funded, and free at the point of use—that makes the UK's NHS the highest ranked, and not the fact that it happens to be in the UK. It is not difficult to conclude that any country attempting to construct an ideal social minimum policy regime would choose to construct a healthcare system that shared characteristics with the UK's NHS: that is, a system publicly funded, and free at the point of use, with General Practitioners providing the essential rationing system (Torry, 2017a, 2017b). We can draw this conclusion in relation to healthcare in the UK because there is one dominant system, the NHS, and a subsidiary system, private healthcare, largely funded by insurance companies. It is therefore legitimate to say that the UK's healthcare system *is* the NHS.

With other resources it is less straightforward. For instance, in relation to income, different modes of delivery for the income required to provide food, drink, shelter, clothing, and the other necessities of a minimally decent life in society, could all be compared with each other. Where a country exhibits a variety of methods for providing one of the resources—for instance, in relation to income provision—each of the different modes of delivery (social insurance benefits, means-tested benefits, unconditional benefits, and so on) could be ranked separately. So if we were to construct a three-dimensional matrix, and the third dimension of our matrix were to be 'countries', then each country would need to be subdivided into its different systems. This offers the possibility of further refinement. If systems can be grouped—with, for instance, social insurance systems in different countries being grouped into 'social insurance' rather than into their separate countries, then, as in Fig. 6.1, the third dimension of the matrix becomes 'modes of delivery' rather than 'countries'. This is probably right: because, as we have recognised, it is systems that are being tested, and not countries. This third dimension could be understood as a generalisation of the empowerment spectrum developed by Kumlin (Kumlin, 2002: 26): a spectrum that enables him to conclude that means-testing and other forms of selectivity hamper citizen empowerment, whereas universal and unconditional provision does not. Along the same spectrum Atkinson concludes that in today's employment market social insurance needs to be complemented by an unconditional income rather than by a means-tested one because we no longer expect governments to ensure the full employment that would enable social insurance on its own to sustain a constant and stable income (Atkinson, 1993: 9, 19).

However, attempting to construct a three-dimensional matrix raises at least two questions. First of all, each dimension's constituents need to be consistent across the other two dimensions, so we are assuming that the same set of characteristics can apply to all of the resources and to all of the modes of delivery, and that all of the modes of delivery can apply to all of the resources. Is this legitimate? As a heuristic exercise, yes. However, we have already recognised that each different resource requires its own set of characteristics, and that categorisations of characteristics and sub-characteristics are always somewhat arbitrary. Similarly, we need to recognise that each mode of delivery will function differently in relation to the different resources. Unconditionality in relation to healthcare means

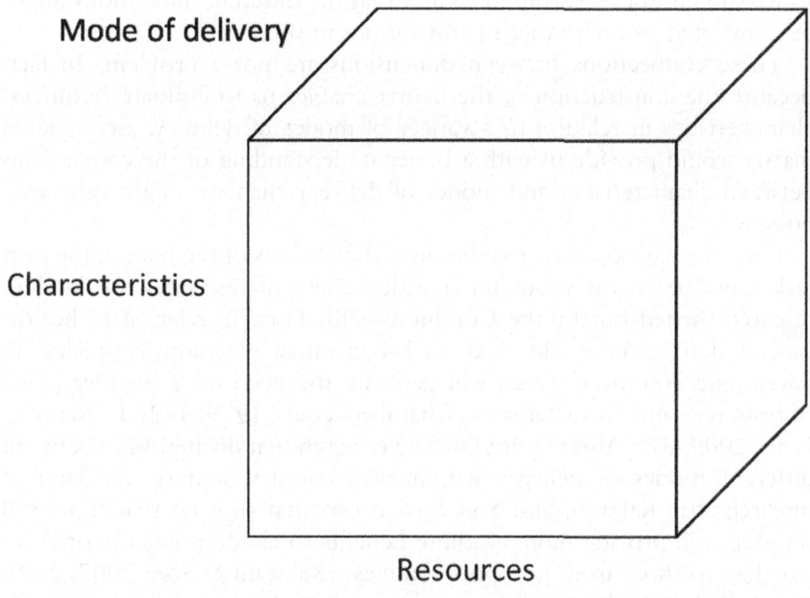

Fig. 6.1 A three-dimensional matrix: Dimensions of a social minimum (*Source* Torry [2019: 42])

unconditional access when healthcare is needed, whereas unconditionality in relation to income means a constant unconditional provision.

Secondly, attempting to construct a three-dimensional matrix raises the question: To what extent are the different dimensions independent of each other? For instance: In relation to the UK's healthcare system, a 'low administrative costs' sub-characteristic will be intimately related to a mode of delivery characterised by unconditionality. This raises a further question: Where characteristics and modes of delivery appear to be related to each other, what are the causal connections? As Rothstein and Steinmo suggest (Rothstein & Steinmo, 2002: 15–17), the ways in which welfare state institutions evolve through time determines the way that they function, and it is these institutions and their histories that to a large extent determine both the modes of delivery and the characteristics of welfare provision—so it is institutions that constitute the connection between the 'characteristics' and 'modes of delivery' dimensions of our matrix, and it is institutions that generate the mutual dependence of modes of delivery and characteristics. It is, after all, a *social* minimum that we are discussing, so we should not be surprised to find that the different dimensions might be connected to each other by institutions in society.

These connections between dimensions are not a problem. In fact, because the construction of the matrix enables us to evaluate resources' characteristics in relation to a variety of modes of delivery, a completed matrix would provide us with a better understanding of the connections between characteristics and modes of delivery than we might otherwise possess.

Once we have constructed the three dimensions of the matrix, the next task must be to carry out for a wide variety of resources the kind of research carried out by the Commonwealth Fund in relation to healthcare, and to carry it out across a broad range of countries, including developing countries, which will generate the need for a broader range of resources and characteristics (Chambers et al., 1979: 1–2; de Neuberg et al., 2009: 37). Also required will be research that distinguishes between different modes of delivery within each country, and so the kind of research that Kakwani and Son carried out that showed that 'universal transfers will provide more absolute benefits to children from poor families than to those from non-poor families' (Kakwani & Son, 2007: 269). We shall then be in a position to construct a three-dimensional matrix, with 'resources', 'characteristics', and 'modes of delivery' on the three axes; and from the completed matrix we shall be able to construct a social minimum policy regime. This is a considerable research agenda, but to pursue it could enable countries' populations to reach social minima, and the global population to reach a global social minimum.

Thorbecke suggests that 'there are too many unresolved questions left over to consider seriously using multidimensional measures in any truly operational sense' (Thorbecke, 2007: 18). Yes, there are unresolved questions, particularly in relation to the consistency of the same-named characteristics across the different resources, and in relation to the ways in which the different resources affect each other. However, as we have recognised, we are *ranking* modes of delivery rather than applying scores, so to list broad characteristics along an axis is not a problem.

In relation to the connections between different resources: if certain characteristics were not met in relation to income, such as timeliness, then health might be damaged; if the inequality of incomes were to increase, then again health might be damaged; with insufficient income, education might be compromised; and without sufficient education, there might be less income. Some of these relationships might be circular. Without sufficient income, health might be compromised; and ill health can compromise income. There might be unresolved questions here, but that does not compromise our ability to create a legitimate and comprehensible matrix, or our ability to employ the overall rankings for the modes of delivery of the different resources to construct the best available social minimum policy regime.

Conclusion

This chapter has defined the 'dimensions' of the social minimum to mean not the different resources that we need, or the different characteristics that resources might possess, but rather the 'resources', 'characteristics' and 'modes of delivery' dimensions of a matrix: a usage of 'dimension' closer to the word's core meaning in relation to three-dimensional space. An outstanding question is this: Which is the dimension to which we should pay most attention when constructing our social minimum policy regime? The first two dimensions of our matrix—resources and characteristics—are clearly essential to the provision of a social minimum. It now transpires that the third dimension—the 'mode of delivery' dimension—might be even more important in relation to the construction of the policy regime required, because it is this dimension that generates the different outcomes represented by the different rankings.

What is now required is further research to tackle the following questions:

- Is it possible to separate the different modes of delivery of a resource, such as healthcare, within a country?—that is, can the Commonwealth Fund's approach be employed in practice in relation to modes of delivery rather than to countries?
- Can the characteristics and sub-characteristics employed by the Commonwealth Fund in relation to healthcare be applied in practice to such other resources as education and income?
- Can the same ranking exercise that the Commonwealth Fund employed in relation to healthcare be transferred to income systems, education, public transport, and so on?
- When applied to different resources, how different would characteristics with the same name need to be for us to have to conclude that the three-dimensional matrix would need to be replaced by a series of 'mode of delivery/characteristics' grids, one for each resource?

What we have not attempted to state in this chapter is a set of levels that the characteristics of the different resources have to reach in order to constitute a social minimum. As we recognised when we studied a number of attempts to achieve that, there will always be a certain subjectivity related to the method chosen and to the way in which the method is constructed. What we have offered is a conceptualisation of the social minimum: it will consist of a number of different resources; there will be a variety of modes of delivery for each of those resources; and it will be possible to choose and evaluate characteristics for each resource, and to rank different modes of delivery in relation to the extent to which those characteristics are achieved. Whether or not any of the modes of delivery would deliver a somehow acceptable level of a social minimum is not here at issue. What the method would be able to offer would be a collection of modes of delivery for the different resources that together would achieve the maximum possible social minimum.

Acknowledgements This chapter was first published as Chapter 3, 'An Essential Dimension of the Social Minimum', in *Specifying and Securing a Social Minimum in the Battle Against Poverty*, edited by Toomas Kotkas, Ingrid Leijten, and Frans Pennings (Oxford: Hart Publishing, an imprint of Bloomsbury Publishing Plc, 2019), pp. 31–45. This was an amended version of a draft chapter presented at a meeting of authors at Jonsered, Sweden, on 13 and 14 September 2018, which was in turn a revision of a paper presented at a seminar at Oñati in Spain on 29 and 30 June 2017. I am most grateful to Jeff King for the commentary on the paper offered at the seminar, and for subsequent written comments; to Ben Warwick for commentary on the draft chapter at the authors' meeting; and to all of the participants at both the seminar and the authors' meeting. The publisher's permission to republish the chapter is gratefully acknowledged.

References

Alkire, S. (2007). Choosing dimensions: The capability approach and multidimensional poverty. In N. Kakwani & J. Silber (Eds.), *The many dimensions of poverty* (pp. 89–119). Palgrave Macmillan.

Atkinson, A. B. (1990). *A national minimum? A history of ambiguity in the determination of benefit scales in Britain*. London School of Economics.

Atkinson, A. B. (1993). *Beveridge, the national minimum, and its future in the European context*. London School of Economics.

Atkinson, A. B. (2009). Income, health and multi-dimensionality. In K. De Boyser, C. Dewilde, D. Dierickx, & J. Friedrichs (Eds.), *Between the social and the spatial: Exploring the multiple dimensions of poverty and social exclusion* (pp. 21–34). Ashgate.

Barrientos, A. (2016). Justice-based social assistance. *Global Social Policy, 16*(2), 151–165.

Chambers, R., Longhurst, R., Bradley, D., & Feacham, R. (1979). *Seasonal dimensions to rural poverty*. University of Sussex.

Davis, A., Hill, K., Hirsch, D., & Padley, M. (2016). *A minimum income standard for the UK in 2016*. Joseph Rowntree Foundation.

Davis, K., Stremikis, K., Squires, D., & Schoen, C. (2014). *Mirror, mirror, on the wall: How the performance of the US healthcare system compares internationally*. Commonwealth Fund.

Dean, H. (2010). *Understanding human need: Social issues, policy and practice*. Policy Press.

De Boyser, K., Dewilde, C., Dierickx, D., & Friedrichs, J. (Eds.). (2009). *Between the social and the spatial: Exploring the multiple dimensions of poverty and social exclusion*. Ashgate.

de Neuberg, C., Roelen, K., & Gassmann, F. (2009). Making policy analysis richer: Multi-dimensional poverty research and social policy design. In K. De Boyser, C. Dewilde, D. Dierickx, & J. Friedrichs (Eds.), *Between the social and the spatial: Exploring the multiple dimensions of poverty and social exclusion* (pp. 35–56). Ashgate.

Gilbert, N., & Specht, H. (1974). *Dimensions of social welfare policy*. Prentice Hall.

Gilbert, N., & Terrell, P. (2013). *Dimensions of social welfare policy*. Pearson Education.

Goedemé, T. (2020). The steep and winding road to comparable reference budgets in Europe. In C. Deeming (Ed.), *Minimum income standards and reference budgets: International and comparative policy perspectives* (pp. 255–270). Policy Press.

Kakwani, N., & Son, H.-H. (2007). On assessing pro-poorness of government programmes: International comparisons. In N. Kakwani & J. Silber (Eds.), *The many dimensions of poverty* (pp. 251–274). Palgrave Macmillan.

Kumlin, S. (2002). Institutions—experiences—preferences: How welfare state design affects political trust and ideology. In B. Rothstein & S. Steinmo (Eds.), *Restructuring the welfare state: Political institutions and policy change* (pp. 20–50). Palgrave Macmillan.

Lansley, S., & Mack, J. (1983). *Breadline Britain*. London Weekend Television.

Lansley, S., & Mack, J. (2015). *Breadline Britain*. Oneworld.

Le Grand, J. (1990). Equity versus efficiency: The elusive trade-off. *Ethics, 100*(3), 554–568.

Maslow, A. (1943). A theory of human motivation. *Psychological Review, 50*(4), 370–396.

Murphy, R., & Reed, H. (2013). *Financing the social state: Towards a full employment economy*. Centre for Labour and Social Studies.

Paugam, S. (2009). What forms does poverty take in European societies at the beginning of the twenty-first century? In K. De Boyser, C. Dewilde, D. Dierickx, & J. Friedrichs (Eds.), *Between the social and the spatial: Exploring the multiple dimensions of poverty and social exclusion* (pp. 3–20). Ashgate.

Rawls, J. (2001). *Justice as fairness: A restatement*. The Belknap Press of Harvard University Press.

Reader, S. (2006). Does a basic needs approach need capabilities? *The Journal of Political Philosophy, 14*(3), 337–350.

Rothstein, B. (1998). *Just institutions matter: The moral and political logic of the universal welfare state*. Cambridge University Press.

Rothstein, B. (2002). The universal welfare state as a social dilemma. In B. Rothstein & S. Steinmo (Eds.), *Restructuring the welfare state: Political institutions and policy change* (pp. 206–222). Palgrave Macmillan.

Rothstein, B., & Steinmo, S. (2002). Restructuring politics: Institutional analysis and the challenges of modern welfare states. In B. Rothstein & S. Steinmo (Eds.), *Restructuring the welfare state: Political institutions and policy change* (pp. 1–19). Palgrave Macmillan.

Sen, A. (2009). *The idea of justice*. Allen Lane.

Sindzingre, A. (2007). The multidimensionality of poverty: An institutionalist perspective. In N. Kakwani & J. Silber (Eds.), *The many dimensions of poverty* (pp. 52–74). Palgrave Macmillan.

Thorbecke, E. (2007). Multidimensional poverty: Conceptual and measurement issues. In N. Kakwani & J. Silber (Eds.), *The many dimensions of poverty* (pp. 3–19). Palgrave Macmillan.

Torry, M. (2017a). Primary care, the basic necessity: Part I: Explorations in economics. In A. Papanikitas & J. Spicer (Eds.), *Handbook of primary care ethics* (pp. 369–375). CRC/Francis and Taylor.

Torry, M. (2017b). Primary care, the basic necessity: Part II: Explorations in ethics. In A. Papanikitas & J. Spicer (Eds.), *Handbook of primary care ethics* (pp. 377–384). CRC/Francis and Taylor.

Torry, M. (2019). An essential dimension of the social minimum. In T. Kotkas, I. Leijten, & F. Pennings (Eds.), *Specifying and securing a social minimum in the battle against poverty* (pp. 31–45). Hart Publishing, an imprint of Bloomsbury Publishing Plc.

Torry, M. (2020a). *Evaluation of a recovery basic income, and of a sustainable revenue neutral Citizen's Basic Income, with an appendix relating to different Universal Credit roll-out scenarios.* Institute for Social and Economic Research Working Paper EM7/20. Colchester: Institute for Social and Economic Research, University of Essex. Retrieved March 26, 2022, from https://www.iser.essex.ac.uk/research/publications/working-papers/euromod/em7-20.pdf

Torry, M. (2020b). *A modern guide to citizen's basic income: A multidisciplinary approach.* Edward Elgar Publishing.

Torry, M. (2021). *Three income maintenance options for 2021.* Centre for Microsimulation and Policy Analysis report. Colchester: Institute for Social and Economic Research, University of Essex. Retrieved March 26, 2022, from https://www.microsimulation.ac.uk/publications/publication-526555/

Townsend, P. (1979). *Poverty in the United Kingdom.* Allen Lane.

Waldron, J. (1986). John Rawls and the social minimum. *The Journal of Applied Philosophy, 3*(1), 21–33.

White, S. (2003). *The civic minimum: On the rights and obligations of economic citizenship.* Oxford University Press.

White, S. (2015). Social minimum. In *The Stanford encyclopedia of philosophy.* Center for the Study of Language and Information, Stanford University. Retrieved March 26, 2022, from http://plato.stanford.edu/entries/social-minimum/

Widerquist, K. (2010). How the sufficiency minimum becomes a social maximum. *Utilitas, 22*(4), 474–480.

PART IV

How Might a Basic Income Happen?

CHAPTER 7

Only for Children?

Introduction

The United Kingdom (UK) already has an unconditional and nonwithdrawable income—for children. I shall therefore tell the story of how Family Allowance came about, how it became Child Benefit, and how it fares today; and at each stage of the story I shall seek reasons for why things happened as they did. Beyond hearings by parliamentary committees, there has been no legislative process relating to an unconditional and nonwithdrawable income for every adult citizen, but during the early 1970s there was an attempt to legislate a Tax Credits scheme that bore some resemblance to a Negative Income Tax. I shall draw lessons from that attempt. (The Tax Credits proposal of the early 1970s should not be confused with the last Labour Government's means-tested wages supplement, which it erroneously and confusingly called 'Tax Credits'.) I shall then study parliamentary committee discussions of universal benefits

Note: This chapter was originally published in 2012, and no attempt has been made to update the history recorded in it. An up-to-date and comprehensive history of Basic Income, including a detailed discussion of the history of the idea in the UK, is now available (Torry, 2021).

M. Torry, *Basic Income—What, Why, and How?*,
Exploring the Basic Income Guarantee,
https://doi.org/10.1007/978-3-031-14248-2_7

for adults, and the UK's implementation of something like a Citizen's Pension; and finally I shall discuss the factors that might determine whether the United Kingdom will ever legislate for a Basic Income.

Child Benefit is not the only universal aspect of the welfare state in the United Kingdom. In 1948, the previous patchwork of charitable, local authority, insurance-based and private healthcare provision was subsumed into the state-run National Health Service (NHS). The ways in which the NHS is organised have changed since then, and they are still changing, but the service still offers high-quality healthcare, is very good value for money, and is still free at the point of use. No government that wished to be re-elected would change that. Until the 1950s, prescriptions, dental care, false teeth, and spectacles, were free. That is now the case for selected groups only, but visits to a General Practitioner, stays in hospital, and all inpatient and outpatient treatment, remain free. The NHS is a rare and remarkable example of unconditionality.

Education in State-run schools is free; pensioners over seventy-five years old get free television licences; schoolchildren used to receive free milk at school; younger primary school children receive free school meals; and everyone on any kind of state pension receives the same winter fuel payment.

While important, none of these other unconditional and universal aspects of the UK's welfare state will be the subject of this chapter. What this chapter *will* be about is unconditional and universal cash benefits, whether paid to a demographic group, such as children, or to every citizen.

Terminology

Paul Spicker defines 'universal benefits' as 'given to whole categories of a population, like children or old people, without other tests' (Spicker, 2011: 117): but this leaves open the question as to whether contribution records that determine the level of payments count as a 'test'. In this chapter, I shall take 'universal benefits' to mean 'unconditional and nonwithdrawable cash payments made to every individual citizen as a right of citizenship'. Child Benefit is not universal in this sense because it is restricted to children, but otherwise it fits the definition because equal amounts are paid to every main carer of the same number of children regardless of that carer's income, employment status, household structure, or any other factor. There is another sense in which Child Benefit is not universal: a main carer only receives Child Benefit for a child up to nineteen years old if that child remains in full-time education: so strictly speaking the benefit is only universal for children below the statutory minimum school leaving age. Michael Hill prefers to call Child Benefit a 'contingent' benefit because only children receive it (Hill, 1990: 82–83), but I shall still call it 'universal' because every child who fulfils certain residence requirements gets it unconditionally and nonwithdrawably.

In the context of this book, a more important terminological point is that in the UK context we need to avoid 'guarantee' language. There are two reasons for this:

1. The previous government enacted a 'Minimum Income Guarantee', later called a 'Guarantee Credit' (Spicker, 2011: 80), for pensioners: a means-tested payment to bring their household income up to a prescribed level. This is as far from a universal benefit as it is possible to get.
2. The academic literature uses the term 'minimum income guarantee' for a prescribed level of net income to which a household is raised by a payment dependent on the level of earned income. For instance, James Meade formulated his Modified Social Dividend proposal in terms of a universal benefit (a 'Social Dividend') and an additional means-tested payment to bring an individual up to a 'minimum income guarantee' (Meade, 1978: 269–279).

In the UK, the normal term for an unconditional, nonwithdrawable income for every citizen is a Citizen's Income or a Basic Income. In English as used in the UK, the word 'basic' can have derogatory overtones, [so when originally published, this chapter employed] Citizen's Income terminology. (I shall leave to one side the important questions as to whether children are, can be, or should be, regarded as citizens. For the purposes of this chapter, they are citizens.)

'Allowance' is another word over which care needs to be taken. 'Child allowance', 'family allowance', or simply 'allowance', refer to payments made (in the case of child allowances, on behalf of the child to the main carer). 'Income Tax allowance' refers to an amount of earned income on which tax is not levied, tax only being levied on income above the 'tax threshold'.

The UK's Family Allowance and Child Benefit

Eleanor Rathbone's Family Endowment Society

The early history of social security benefits in the United Kingdom is one of the locally administered means test. The more recent history is mainly one of social insurance benefits topped up by means-tested benefits and increasingly replaced by them. The single universal benefit, Child Benefit, which evolved from Family Allowance, is therefore significant.

In 1796, the Prime Minister, William Pitt, wanted to make benefits 'where there are a large number of children a matter of right and honour, instead of a ground for opprobrium and contempt. This will make the large family a blessing, and not a curse' (Macnicol, 1980: 4). It did not happen, but in 1909 the Chancellor of the Exchequer, Lloyd George, established child tax allowances. During the First World War, the amount paid to a serviceman's family at home included an amount for each child. Those payments continued for six months on demobilisation. In 1918, Beatrice Webb, a significant social commentator, called for the payments to continue beyond that point (Macnicol, 1980: 5–10). During the 1890s, the Independent Labour Party had called for the 'endowment' of motherhood (Thane, 1996: 63–64), and Seebohm Rowntree, on the basis of his survey of poverty in York, had proposed a national minimum wage sufficient for a family with three children, and child allowances for the fourth and subsequent children. In this context, Eleanor Rathbone's 1911 pamphlet suggesting that children were society's responsibility, and her 1917 argument that a man's wage could not be expected to support a large family, contained nothing new. What *was* new was her establishment in 1917 of the Family Endowment Society, and then of the Children's Minimum Council, to pursue the cause of payments to mothers to enable them to care for their children (Macnicol, 1980: 10, 20–23; Thane, 1996: 202).

In 1924, Rathbone wrote *The Disinherited Family*, questioning the wisdom of expecting the same wage to be adequate for every family, whatever its size, especially as there was always a question over how much of a man's wage reached his wife. Rathbone discussed other countries' child allowances and the possibility of occupational schemes, and called for a universal state scheme in order to reduce class envy (Rathbone, 1986 [1924]: 139, 167, 353).

William Beveridge and his Report

William Beveridge wrote this in his epilogue to the 1949 edition of *The Disinherited Family*: 'I suffered instant and total conversion' (Beveridge in Rathbone, 1949: 270). He had read the book in 1924 when he was Director of the London School of Economics (LSE). In 1925 he chaired a Royal Commission on the mining industry and recommended child allowances, paid by employers, as a way of both providing for miners' families and not increasing the general level of wages. The General Strike intervened and the moment was lost, but not at the LSE, where child allowances were soon being paid.

In 1934, Beveridge was asked to sit on the Unemployment Insurance Statutory Committee, which reported on the state of the contributory unemployment benefit schemes fund. Child allowances were paid with Unemployment Benefit, which concerned Beveridge, as it meant that when someone returned to employment on low wages they could suffer a loss of income if they had a large family. Child allowances for every child was the only solution (Beveridge in Rathbone, 1949: 271), so when Beveridge was asked to chair an interdepartmental committee on the future of social insurance, he was already sure that child allowances should be in the report. The fact that universal benefits were not part of his brief did not perturb him: he simply made child allowances an assumption on which the rest of the report's findings were based (Beveridge, 1942: 154).

The reasons that Beveridge gave for assuming child allowances were that they would achieve a national minimum for families, that income out of work would not be higher than income in work, and that a decline in the birth rate would be arrested (Beveridge, 1942: 154). Rathbone would have wanted the emancipation of women from dependence on men in the list of reasons, but it was not, although another of her arguments had persuaded Beveridge: that a child allowance was 'an expression of the community's direct interest in children' (Beveridge, 1942: 155).

Beveridge based his report on *three* assumptions:

1. Full employment;
2. Everyone 'will be covered for comprehensive medical treatment and rehabilitation and for funeral expenses';
3. 'Children's allowances, which will be paid from the National Exchequer in respect of all children when the responsible parent is in

> receipt of insurance benefit or pension, and in respect of all children except one in other cases (Beveridge, 1942: 10: cf. 158, 163, 177).

It is surely significant that two of the three foundations that Beveridge thought essential to his social insurance edifice are universal benefits.

Beveridge argued that child allowances should be universal because 'little money can be saved by any reasonable income test' (Beveridge, 1942: 157), and that adjustments to child tax allowances could ensure that wealthier people would receive no net benefit from child allowances. The Chancellor of the Exchequer agreed that a flat rate and universal payment would be cheap to administer and was therefore desirable (Land, 1975: 193). Beveridge wanted the child allowances to be paid 'at rates averaging 8/- a week' (Beveridge, 1942: 177). (8/-, or 8s., means 'eight shillings': Until 1971 there were 20s. to the pound and 12d. ('twelve pence') to the shilling, so 8s. would have been equivalent to 40p if today's currency had been in use then). Beveridge had to compromise and agree not to pay an allowance for the first child in order to achieve this figure: but the Family Allowance Act of 1945 stipulated a payment of just 5s. [25p]. The Treasury achieved another victory: 'Family Allowance' rather than 'Child Allowance' prevailed. The Chancellor had argued that 'child allowance' would lead to the argument that sufficient should be paid to maintain a child, whereas 'family allowance' could be an allowance to assist in the support of a family, and no one would expect the Government to pay all of a family's subsistence costs (Macnicol, 1980: 193). What survived the debate was the universality of the payment, and in 1945 the Family Allowance Act was passed with all-party support.

The Family Allowance Act 1945: Why Did It Happen?

As Hilary Land suggests: 'In three years family allowances had gained the attention and the interest of the government that twenty years of campaigning by the Family Endowment Society had failed to achieve' (Land, 1975: 195). Here are just some of the reasons for that success:

1. *Poverty in large families*: The argument that the wage system did not and could not provide for the subsistence needs of large families had become widely accepted, and the 1930s had provided plenty

of surveys of poverty that Rathbone could publicise (Macnicol, 1980: 93). She and her Family Endowment Society had taken every opportunity, in and out of Parliament, to make the point that only child allowances could keep large families out of poverty, and the argument had finally been accepted by policymakers.

2. *Opposition from trades unions had melted away*: In 1928 and 1929 the Trade Union Congress (TUC) had discussed child allowances but had decided that it preferred child tax allowances: not surprisingly, given that most members of trades unions were men, that wage-earning men benefited from child tax allowances, and that their wives might benefit from child allowances. The 1930 TUC conference accepted from a working party the *minority* report, which advocated child tax allowances rather than child allowances (Land, 1975: 169).

   The next time the TUC discussed child allowances was during the Second World War. By then, more women were members of trades unions, and there were Labour ministers in the coalition government. The TUC therefore felt less isolated. The Labour Party had called both for child allowances and for a living wage, and had recognised that no realistic living wage would be able to keep large families out of poverty without child allowances being paid, particularly during the war. At its 1941 conference the TUC found itself more favourable toward the idea of family allowances (Thane, 1996: 226).
3. *Population decline*: In 1936, the Government's Population Investigation Committee had expressed concern about the falling birth rate, as it could foresee a growing elderly population with too few younger adults to do the necessary work. The need to maintain the birth rate in all social classes, and not just amongst the poor, argued for universal rather than means-tested child allowances (Land, 1975: 173).
4. *The state of young adults*: Army recruitment officers had expressed concern about the state of health of young adults, and child allowances were seen as a means of ensuring that the next generation would be better nourished (Land, 1975: 174)
5. *Disincentives in the labour market*: Beveridge was particularly keen to ensure that someone in work did not experience net income less than someone not in employment with the same size family. Only

child allowances for those in work could achieve that (Thane, 1996: 228). Larger tax allowances could *not* achieve it because the low paid often did not earn enough to benefit from their existing tax allowances (Land, 1975: 196).

6. *Fear of inflation*: Economist John Maynard Keynes was an unpaid advisor to the Cabinet during the Second World War. A major aim was controlling inflation, which was achieved through price controls and rationing. Wage control remained voluntary (Thane, 1996: 225–226), but there was concern that after the war wages might rise rapidly as price controls eased. Keynes argued for child allowances as a way of keeping large families out of poverty without wages having to rise (Macnicol, 1980: 176).
7. *A better Britain*: Members of the different political parties continued to offer the arguments that we might expect: the Conservatives that the Government should not interfere in a family's financial arrangements, and some Labour Members of Parliament that child allowances were a means of keeping wages low; but a general desire for a new start after the war meant that a comprehensible policy such as child allowances could gain considerable approval both across party lines in Parliament and amongst the general public. The fact that child tax allowances increased the incomes of the wealthy more than they increased those of the poor was beginning to be understood, and child allowances were beginning to look more in tune with the kind of country in which people wanted to live once the war was over (Land, 1975: 179).

The Parliamentary Debate

The 1943 parliamentary debate on Beveridge's report was rather fraught, and the Conservatives' opposition to its ideas might well have been one of the reasons for their defeat in the General Election of 1945; but the child allowances assumption underlying the report attracted widespread support (Land, 1975: 205). The Treasury then employed delaying tactics (Macnicol, 1980: 191), but in 1945 the Family Allowances Act was passed.

An important question raised during the debate was whether the allowance should be paid to the father or to the mother. Rathbone threatened to vote against the Act if the allowances were paid to the father, a free vote was offered, and the amendment to pay the allowance to the mother was passed (Land, 1975: 221; Macnicol, 1980: 193). The first Family Allowances were paid on August 6, 1946.

A significant aspect of the debate in Parliament was that there was little discussion of the *objectives* of child allowances (Land, 1975: 221). This might have been because each Member of Parliament (MP) could find something to like in child allowances (whether the relief of poverty, the suppression of wages, the reduction of labour market disincentives, or possibly for some Conservatives a hope that to increase working-class incomes might increase their share of the vote at the next General Election): but they all knew that other Members had very different reasons for wanting them and did not want to risk a fractious debate that might risk losing child allowances. The Government's aim was to keep wages down (Macnicol, 1980: 172, 202). It certainly was not to improve the status of women.

In her biography of Eleanor Rathbone, Mary Stokes writes:

> Family Allowances . . . could be approached from so many directions, with such an infinite variety of emphasis and application. It could be handled as a problem of vital statistics, housing administration, minimum wage legislation, child nutrition, national insurance, teachers' salary scales, coal-mining economics, feminism, social philosophy or pure finance. That is perhaps one reason why Eleanor's handling of it never became . . . tedious by repetition. (Stokes, 1949: quoted in Freeman, 1998: 2)

This insight offers us a clue to Rathbone's success in getting child allowances onto the statute book. She was able to persuade individuals and groups of the advantages of the idea in relation to their own interests. Child allowances were part of the solution to a wide variety of problems: hence a level of support could be built which was able to submerge objections from trades unions, and also the generally unspoken objection that child allowances paid to the mother would reduce her dependence on the father (Land, 1975: 227).

Crucial were two particular conversions, Beveridge's and Keynes'. Beveridge saw that child allowances would reduce disincentives in the labour market, and Keynes that they would help to keep inflation under control (Land, 1975: 227).

So why did Family Allowances happen? The reasons are as follows:

1. Persistent campaigning over a long period of time;
2. One good book;
3. Accidental convergence of different interests on a single policy change;
4. Two crucial conversions.

The only connection with reducing inequality and empowering women was that these were among *Rathbone's* aims. They were essential to the process because they motivated her.

The Rediscovery of Poverty During the 1960s, and the Birth of Child Benefit

Beveridge eventually got his National Insurance Acts in 1946, and in 1948 a National Assistance Act was passed to provide means-tested benefits for people with insufficient contributions records. However, National Insurance benefits were generally paid at levels below National Assistance levels, largely because National Assistance took into account housing costs and National Insurance benefits did not. The United Kingdom therefore found itself still mired in a largely means-tested system (Atkinson, 1969: 24). The situation was not helped by government neglect of Family Allowances, which by 1960 were paying only 8s. [40p] per week for the second child and 10s. [50p] per week for each subsequent child in a family (Townsend, 1979: 162–163). By the mid-1960s this was a serious problem because a family on means-tested benefits could claim benefits for *every* child, and the payments were age-related, with payments for older children being significantly higher than those for younger children. Fourteen per cent of families in work with six children or more were living below National Assistance levels, and half of all families below that level had three or fewer children (Atkinson, 1969: 24).

A serious problem was that child tax allowances were worth more to families on higher incomes. (The allowance reduced taxable pay, which for someone paying higher rate tax reduced the amount of earned income taxed in the higher rate tax rate band: whereas for someone who did not pay higher rate tax, the allowance reduced the amount of pay taxed in a lower rate tax rate band. A compounding factor was that some people's pay was only just over, or in some cases was below, the tax threshold. The child tax allowance therefore made little or no difference to their net income.) The problem had to some extent been ameliorated by a 'clawback' mechanism that reduced the tax allowance by an amount for each child for whom Family Allowance was in payment. The significance of this seemingly insignificant piece of history is that it marked the first direct relationship between the tax and benefits systems (Banting, 1979: 95).

An important context for the next stage in the development of universal benefits in the United Kingdom—the transition from Family Allowance to Child Benefit—was the flurry of social scientific study of poverty that occurred during the early 1960s. Significant books were Richard Titmuss's 1962 *Income Distribution and Social Change*, and Brian Abel-Smith and Peter Townsend's 1965 *The Poor and the Poorest: A new analysis of the Ministry of Labour's Family Expenditure Surveys of 1953–54 and 1960.* Their close study of official statistics, including family expenditure data, revealed substantial income inequality and almost one in five families on incomes below half the average. More important for the public understanding of the realities of poverty was the television play *Cathy Come Home*, broadcast in 1966, which tells the story of a family in which the male breadwinner is injured and loses his job, leading to unemployment, homelessness, and the removal of the family's children into the care of the Social Services.

This 'rediscovery of poverty' gave birth in 1965 to the Child Poverty Action Group (CPAG), which argued for a Family Allowance for the first child in a family and for the child tax allowance to be abolished in favour of higher Family Allowances (Hill, 1990: 41). In 1968, Family Allowance was raised to 15s. [75p] for each child, and then to 18 s. [90p] (Atkinson, 1969: 85). Families out of work had amounts equal to their Family Allowance deducted from their benefits, and instead received age-related child allowances. Family allowance of 90p per week was only 74% of the means-tested allowance for a child under five years of age, and 50% of the means-tested allowance for a child aged between 11 and 13 years (Atkinson, 1969: 86), meaning that if a parent with a large family returned to work then they could experience a considerable loss of income. A compounding factor was that Family Allowance was taxed, whereas means-tested benefits were not.

There was thus considerable logic in CPAG's campaign for the abolition of child tax allowances (which didn't benefit the lowest earning families) and payment of child allowances for every child in a family at a rate higher than that of the current Family Allowance. That such a change would improve labour market incentives was an important argument (Atkinson, 1969: 141). By 1968, child allowances for every child in the family had been termed 'Child Benefit' and had gained considerable support in government, but then the Labour administration was replaced by Edward Heath's Conservative Government.

By the time of Labour's return to power in 1974, there was a consensus that a universal child benefit (that is, payment for every child) would be useful, and that it should be accompanied by the phasing out of child tax allowances. A Bill received a second reading in May 1975, but no start date was given. The next year Cabinet minutes leaked to Frank Field, director of CPAG, and published in *New Society* on June 17, 1976, revealed government concern that to abolish tax allowances and to pay a Child Benefit higher than Family Allowance would reduce net incomes of men and thus cause wage inflation; and that the change from tax revenue foregone to an increased payment to the mother would look as if public expenditure had increased even though it had not (Spicker, 2011: 118).

CPAG convened a 'Child Benefit Now' campaign, trades unions gave their support (particularly those with high numbers of women members), Barbara Castle MP (from 1974 Secretary of State for Health and Social Services, but consigned to the back benches when James Callaghan replaced Harold Wilson as Prime Minister in 1976) gave parliamentary support, and, whilst both trades unions and the government remained divided, Child Benefit was eventually established (McCarthy, 1986: 274).

Why Did Child Benefit Happen?

Again, individuals were significant: Margaret Herbison MP (a former minister of social security) gathered support for Child Benefit amongst MPs and journalists; Barbara Castle was far from silent on the matter; Frank Field campaigned consistently; and the cabinet mole was crucial. As time went by, and ministers came and went, the balance within the cabinet shifted against those wanting a means-tested approach to poverty in working families, and the Labour Party's historic suspicion of means tests eventually defeated the critics of Child Benefit (Banting, 1979: 102–103). (Many Labour Party members could still remember the 1930s household means test, which took the assets and income of everyone living in the household fully into account when benefits were calculated.) Equally significant of course was 20-years' positive experience of Family

Allowance and a resultant growing understanding that universal benefits experience high take-up, that they are simple and therefore cheap to administer, that they don't attract stigma, that the mother is more likely to spend money on the children than is the father (so a universal benefit paid to the mother will on average be of more value to the children than a tax allowance or a means-tested benefit paid to the father), and that universal benefits ameliorate the poverty and unemployment traps (because they do not reduce the net effect of additional earnings in the way that taxation and means tests do) (Barr & Coulter, 1991: 279–280; Spicker, 2011: 119).

Child Benefit entered the statute book because enough MPs could find reasons to support it, because a successful public campaign and the leaked cabinet minutes had reduced opposition, and because the trades unions now contained more women members, and opinion amongst trade union members was therefore more divided. The pursuit of greater equality for women was a motivator for some of those involved (Barr & Coulter, 1991: 295), and was therefore significant, but more important was an understanding that poverty in working families mattered and that something had to be done about it.

Preserving Child Benefit

From 1979 to 1997 there was again a Conservative government, and from 1979 Child Benefit was uprated in line with prices rather than wages (Hill, 1990: 57). In 1985, the Secretary of State for Social Security, Norman Fowler, reviewed social security benefits. The Government replaced Family Income Supplement (a means-tested in-work benefit that the previous administration had established) with the more generous but still means-tested Family Credit, whereas Child Benefit was frozen. The result was a marked shift towards means-testing (Barr & Coulter, 1991: 282). 'Targeting' was the aim, but unfortunately means-tested benefits constitute a less efficient form of targeting than universal benefits accompanied by a progressive tax system.

CPAG joined in the debate by publishing research on mothers' experience of Child Benefit:

> [Child Benefit] is essential to a large majority of mothers in providing for the needs of their children ... [and] it is a reliable payment made reliably

> and directly to them ... A large majority of mothers supports the continuation of the universal payment of child benefit for each child. (Walsh & Lister, 1985: 42)

The late 1980s saw Conservative voices questioning the future of Child Benefit. CPAG was vigorous in its defence: 'The government should not be asking how much can be "saved" from Child Benefit, but how this valuable multi-purpose benefit can be maintained and improved as an investment in the future into the twenty-first century . . . The case for more emphasis on Child Benefit is, in part, the case against *over*-use of means-tested benefits, because of their defects' (Brown, 1988: xiii, 15)—especially their labour market disincentive effects. Child Benefit was much to be preferred to means-tested provision because it provides a secure floor to a family's income, and it recognises the whole community's responsibility for the care of the next generation (Brown, 1988: 20, 35, 43; 1990: 15). CPAG complained, as others had before, that Child Benefit was counted as public expenditure whereas child tax allowances were not, which skewed the argument towards regressive tax allowances and away from universal and thus progressive Child Benefit (Brown, 1988: 63), despite the fact that when Child Benefit was phased in there was cross-party agreement that it should be viewed as similar to a tax allowance, and that the 1979 Conservative government viewed it as similar to a tax credit (Brown, 1988: 25). Holly Sutherland and Hermione Parker, working at the London School of Economics, showed that from the point of view of claimants, administrators, and taxpayers, Child Benefit was preferable to child tax allowances, and also concluded that a Basic Income would be preferable to means-tested benefits (Parker and Sutherland, no date: 133). Child Benefit survived, and when John Major became Prime Minister his first act was to unfreeze it.

At the Conservative Party conference in 2010, the Chancellor of the Exchequer announced that Child Benefit would be withdrawn from every household containing at least one higher rate taxpayer. [In order to avoid having to find out which wealthier individuals lived in households in which Child Benefit was being claimed, Child Benefit was not withdrawn from households containing high earners, but instead anyone earning more than £50,000 per annum and living in a household in which Child Benefit was received had to pay a tax charge that increased as earned incomes rose above £50,000 per annum (Spicker, 2011: 120). What seems particularly unjust about the new tax charge is that a household containing two earners, both just under the threshold, would pay no tax charge, whereas an identical household with just one earner just over the threshold would do so. As we shall see, the fact that the proposal required the establishment of new investigative or administrative systems, and thus additional civil servants, might have been one of the causes of departmental enthusiasm that could have helped to propel the proposal onto the statute book.]

Tax Credits

We have studied Child Benefit: a legislated universal benefit that is still with us. We now turn to proposals that did not make it onto the statute book, and first of all to the Heath Government's 1972 Tax Credit proposals, not because they constitute a universal benefit (although they share some of their characteristics) but because the attempt to establish a Tax Credits scheme in the United Kingdom offers lessons to those who might wish to see a Basic Income established.

The reader is reminded that the Tax Credits scheme of the early 1970s was for genuine tax credits. Households (and not individuals) would have been awarded tax credits. These would have replaced tax allowances, would have been paid in full if earned income dropped to zero, and would have been withdrawn at a specified rate as earned income rose. As earned income continued to rise, the tax credits would have ceased to be paid out and the worker would have started to pay tax. (The Labour Government's recent 'Tax Credits' scheme, introduced in 2003, is a means-tested benefit, it is not tax credits, it should not have been called tax credits, and it should not be confused with the genuine article.)

As the Heath Government's consultation paper said:

> The tax credit system is a reform which embodies the socially valuable device of paying tax credits, to the extent that they are not used against tax due, positively as a benefit . . . [so as to] bring together what people pay and what they receive . . . Fewer people will be means-tested and others means-tested less often, and for the community there will be a large saving in administrative staff. (Her Majesty's Government, 1972: iii)

Not everyone would have benefited from the scheme. Anyone self-employed, or employed and earning less than £8 per week, would have been excluded. Also excluded would have been employed married women

(Her Majesty's Government, 1972: 5). In 1971, a married woman was given the right to have her income assessed separately for income tax, rather than her earnings being included on her husband's tax return along with her income from other sources. A married man received a tax allowance higher than that for a single person, and a married woman received a single person's allowance to set against her earnings. The result was a financial advantage for married men. The Tax Credits consultation paper maintained this position by granting a £4 per week tax credit to each single person, a £6 tax credit to a married man, and a continuing tax allowance to each married woman (Her Majesty's Government, 1972: 18).

The number of people in the scheme would have risen over time because someone already in the scheme who became unemployed would have had their tax credit paid through the Department of Health and Social Security or through the Department of Employment (Her Majesty's Government, 1972: 3), but otherwise all tax credits would have been calculated by the employer who would have deducted tax from all earned income at 30% and set the tax credit against the tax due. A major difference between tax credits and income tax allowances was that tax credits would have operated on a weekly basis, whereas tax allowances operate on an annual basis, so no longer would the employer have had to manage complex ongoing calculations to ensure that by the end of the year the right amount of tax had been deducted. A major advantage of the scheme was that poorer families would have benefited from it, whereas often they did not earn sufficient income to benefit fully from tax allowances (Her Majesty's Government, 1972: 28).

The parliamentary select committee that examined submissions to the consultation recommended that the withdrawal rate for Tax Credits should be 30 per cent (whereas the withdrawal rate for the means-tested Family Income Supplement was 50%), that additional Tax Credits should be allocated for such conditions as blindness, that married women should receive a single person's Tax Credit rather than a tax allowance, that a married woman should be able to transfer half of her Tax Credit to her husband if he did not qualify for one, and that Child Tax Credits should be paid to the mother (or to whoever had care of the children) as cash payments at the Post Office (Her Majesty's Government, 1972: 5, 20–24). Family Income Supplement would have been abolished, but not other means-tested benefits, which would still have been needed (House of Commons Select Committee on Tax-Credit, 1973: 7): though as the

Tax Credits scheme had matured fewer families would have had need of means-tested benefits.

A minority report suggested that as only Family Income Supplement would be replaced, it would be preferable to solve the problem of working poverty by establishing a National Minimum Wage and increasing tax allowances (House of Commons Select Committee on Tax-Credit, 1973: 74): but the majority of the committee members recommended acceptance of the Tax Credits scheme because it appeared

> to offer the possibility of improving the amount of income retained from increased earnings . . . The effect of the scheme [was] to give the same treatment to the very large majority of the population, with scope for differential treatment by giving selective help to those in greatest need and levying differential taxation on the highest paid. (House of Commons Select Committee on Tax Credit, 1973: 7)

The Conservative Government was defeated in the 1974 General Election, and a new Labour administration preferred Family Income Supplement to Tax Credits. Since then we have had Family Credit (minor revisions of Family Income Supplement) and Gordon Brown's 'Tax Credits' (further revisions of Family Income Supplement but now administered by Her Majesty's Revenue and Customs rather than by the Department of Social Security).

Why did Tax Credits not happen? There was an enthusiast, Sir Arthur Cockfield, and there were sufficient reasons for supporting the proposals to enable Members of Parliament with a variety of interests to support them. The Tax Credits scheme would have reduced working poverty, provided a greater incentive to increase earned income, and increased administrative efficiency. Even though the scheme was not entirely a tidy one, it would clearly have met these objectives. If the Heath Government had survived its difficulties with the trades unions in 1972 then we might now have had nearly 40 years' experience of genuine tax credits. Admittedly, the scheme was not a universal one, and it was not entirely individualised. Nonetheless, increasing numbers of people would have found themselves within it. The Tax Credits scheme would have provided an additional paradigm alongside Child Benefit, contributory benefits, and means-tested benefits, and it would have enabled a more informed debate to take place on the extent to which the tax and benefits systems should and could be integrated with each other, and on the relative advantages and disadvantages of the tax credit and universal benefit approaches to integration. In particular, the experience of tax credits might eventually have enabled the Government to ask about different options for recording in the national accounts revenue foregone and benefits paid out.

Genuine tax credits did not entirely disappear from the agenda. In 1979, Philip Vince developed for the Liberal Party a scheme of 'tax-free credits, some of them universal and some withdrawn as other income rises' (Vince, 1986: 5); and in 1983 Richard Wainwright MP presented an uprated version of the scheme to the Treasury and Civil Service Committee's enquiry into 'the Structure of Personal Income Taxation and Income Support' (Parker, 1989: 168–189; Vince, 2011). The tax credit scheme was party policy, but it was the policy of a party with few Members of Parliament and little influence. During the early 1990s, a Basic Income was Liberal Democrat Party policy, and the same reason meant that nothing happened.

Juliet Rhys Williams' Minority Report

Just as Tax Credits did not get onto the statute book, neither has a Basic Income scheme. A Basic Income has never been the subject of a government green paper (consultation document), but it has been discussed by parliamentary select committees, and there are lessons to be learnt from understanding those discussions.

The UK debate about a Basic Income arguably goes back to the eighteenth century and to Thomas Paine and others like him who recognised every citizen's natural right to a subsistence income: a right, because all citizens are 'born, and always continue, free and equal in respect of their Rights' (Claeys, 1989: 125; Paine, [1792] 2006: 62). On this basis, Paine developed a scheme for incomes for the poorest (Paine, [1792] 2006: 146, 148). It was left to others to draw the conclusion that equal natural rights meant equal incomes (Torry, 2021: 36–64). Amongst those were Mabel and Dennis Milner and Bertram Pickard, all Quakers, who established the State Bonus League to campaign for a 'state bonus' of 9s. [45p] for each citizen (Macnicol, 1980: 9; Torry, 2021: 67–75; Van Trier, 1995: 31–142). The Labour Party Executive Committee discussed the idea in 1921 and rejected it.

When William Beveridge presented his report on *Social Insurance and Allied Services* in 1942, Lady Juliet Rhys Williams, Secretary of the Women's Liberal Federation (Harris, 1981: 258), issued a minority report, subsequently published in a more developed form as *Something to look forward to* (Rhys Williams, 1943). Her concern was that a combination of social insurance and means-tested benefits would involve high marginal deduction rates as earned income rose, and would therefore provide little incentive to earn a living. Coercion would therefore be needed to get people to work, and 'once the power of the State is made use of as a means of making a man work against his will' (Rhys Williams, 1943: 13), other coercions could easily follow. 'The hope of gain is infinitely preferable to the fear of punishment and the fear of want as a motive for human labour... The real objection to the Beveridge scheme does not lie in its shortcomings in respect of the abolition of want, which could be made good, but in its serious attack upon the will to work' (Rhys Williams, 1943: 45, 141). In particular, part-time labour must be possible in industries that require less labour, but part-time employment did not provide a subsistence income and would have made a man unavailable for other work and so unable to receive national insurance unemployment benefit.

Rhys Williams proposed a new contract:

> The State owes precisely the same benefits to all of its citizens, and should in no circumstances pay more to one than to another of the same sex and age, except in return for services rendered ... Therefore the same benefits [should be paid] to the employed and healthy as to the idle and sick. ... The prevention of want must be regarded as being the duty of the State to all its citizens and not merely to a favoured few. (Rhys Williams, 1943: 139, 145)

In Rhys Williams' scheme there would have been 'no more adult dependents' (Rhys Williams, 1943: 151), and women would have received an income in their own right, though interestingly 19s. [95p] per week rather than the 21s. [£1.05] for men. The result would have been that workers would have received 'the whole benefit of wages (less taxation)' (Rhys Williams, 1943: 147). To cope with differential housing costs Lady Rhys Williams recommended different levels of payment in different regions.

This really was meant to be a *contract*, and the scheme required visits to the Labour Exchange for anyone not in employment, and any work offered would have had to be accepted. This provision reintroduced fear (of losing the state income) into employment incentives (Rhys Williams, 1943: 167), but Rhys Williams clearly expected the reduced marginal deduction rates to be sufficient incentive to people to look for and accept any employment on offer.

In 1953, Rhys Williams listed the advantages of her equal payment for all citizens: administrative simplicity, raised employment incentives, the avoidance of means-testing, increased possibilities for useful activity during periods of unemployment, and an improvement in married women's status (Rhys Williams, 1953: 138). As H. S. Booker suggested in relation to the scheme: 'Is there anything fundamentally wrong with a subsidy on wages if there are appropriate safeguards?' (Booker, 1946: 232): and what better safeguard than *not* losing the state's contribution to one's income when earned income rises? Under the National Insurance Act, a man, wife and child could earn £3 per week and be only 5s. [25p] better off. Under Rhys Williams' scheme they would have been £1 16s. [£1.80] better off.

Like Mother, Like Son

Juliet Rhys Williams' son Sir Brandon Rhys Williams was a Conservative Member of Parliament, and when in March 1973 a select committee evaluated the Tax Credits proposal he was a witness (House of Commons Select Committee on Tax-Credit, 1973). In 1982, a Treasury and Civil Service Committee Sub-Committee heard evidence on 'the Structure of Personal Income Taxation and Income Support', and, as well as considering the Liberal Party's tax credits scheme, it received from Sir Brandon Rhys Williams a memorandum recommending a 'Basic Income Guarantee': that is, a Basic Income. ('Guarantee' here means that the citizen is guaranteed to receive an unconditional income. This was before the use of 'guarantee' for a guaranteed net income level, so its use did not cause any confusion.) 'Every British Citizen should be awarded a personal allowance of a value related to personal status, not to resources' (House of Commons Treasury and Civil Service Committee Sub-Committee, 1982: 423; cf. Rhys Williams, 1989).

Rhys Williams also submitted a synopsis of the scheme from his colleague, Hermione Parker: 'Every citizen would be entitled to a personal basic income or PBI. These guaranteed basic incomes would replace virtually all existing benefits and allowances' (House of Commons Treasury and Civil Service Committee Sub-Committee, 1982: 425; cf. Parker, 1982, 1989, 1995). The committee examined Brandon Rhys Williams on the proposals. The final exchange is instructive:

> *Chairman*: There seem to me to be many benefits of this system.
> *BRW*: There are.
> *C*: Clearly you are expressing them very eloquently. Clearly they would go a long way toward easing the unemployment and poverty traps.
> *BRW*: There would not be any unemployment under these schemes. You would not need to register as unemployed. There would be people who were not in full-time work but they would not need to have themselves labelled as unemployed. If they got an opportunity of work or casual work they could take it and nobody would have to know.
> *C*: Are you saying that the unemployment benefit trap would be virtually eradicated by this?
> *BRW*: Certainly.
> *C*: Also it would be administratively much simpler.
> *BRW*: Yes, it would.
> *C*: I wonder what degree of redistribution of resources there would be or is that one of the matters that could be flexible within the system?
> *BRW*: This is optional. This is why I have not put figures in my paper because you could make the scheme do what you liked. If you want to help people on low wages or low incomes you can tilt the tax and benefit structure in such a way that it is redistributive in certain directions.
> *C*: May I say that you will observe that owing to pressure of other engagements we have lost our third member and are now therefore non quorate. Thank you very much. (House of Commons Treasury & Civil Service Committee Sub-Committee, 1982: 459).

The committee recommended that the Government should consider a Basic Income as an option for reform, but that more work needed to be done on the idea: 'We recommend that the Government should put such work in hand' (House of Commons Treasury & Civil Service Committee, 1983: para 13.35; as cited in Parker, 1989: 100).

There is no evidence of this happening.

Committees of Enquiry

In 1984, the Basic Income Research Group (BIRG) was convened by Peter Ashby, an employee of the National Council for Voluntary Organisations. BIRG subsequently helped to establish the Basic Income European Network (BIEN), became a charitable trust, in 1994 became the Citizen's Income Trust (CIT), [and then in 2017 the Citizen's Basic Income Trust (CBIT)]. For nearly forty years it has promoted debate on Basic Income, published a regular journal (originally the *BIRG Bulletin*, now the *Citizen's Income Newsletter*), organised meetings, maintained a library and website, and responded to requests for information. During the past few years perhaps its most significant activity has been to contribute evidence to parliamentary committees.

In 2007, the Trust submitted evidence to the House of Commons Work and Pensions Committee's enquiry into benefits simplification. Its submission, a fully costed and revenue-neutral Basic Income scheme, was printed as evidence in the committee's report (House of Commons Work and Pensions Committee, 2007: Ev 84–90), but no witnesses from the Trust were called. During the committee's discussion with witnesses, Donald Hirsch explained that the Joseph Rowntree Foundation had estimated that a Basic Income would require a basic tax rate of 46%. (He did not say whether this included National Insurance Contributions.) 'We did not think the country was quite ready for that particular form' (House of Commons Work and Pensions Committee, 2007: Ev 14). The Citizen's Income Trust's carefully calculated tax rate of 33% (22% Income Tax + 11% National Insurance Contribution) did not get a mention, suggesting that none of the committee members had read the submission.

In 1994, the Labour Party's Commission on Social Justice, chaired by Sir Gordon Borrie, issued its report: *Social Justice: Strategies for national renewal*. The Commission studied the difficulties experienced by the existing tax and benefits system, and explored options for change. The Commission's report gave a Basic Income an honourable mention: 'It would be unwise … to rule out a move towards Citizen's Income in future: if it turns out to be the case that earnings simply cannot provide a stable income for a growing proportion of people, then the notion of some guaranteed income, outside the labour market, could become increasingly attractive' (Commission on Social Justice, 1994: 263–4). It also commented favourably on a Participation Income: an income conditional on participating in some way in society (Commission on Social Justice, 1994: 264–265). Just as nothing happened following the 1982 Select Committee's hearing to which Brandon Rhys Williams gave evidence, so the Labour Party did nothing further on a Basic Income. What did happen when Labour came to power in 1997 was a National Minimum Wage. This was a good thing in itself, but it did little to sort out the complexities and disincentives of means-tested benefits.

In 2010, Iain Duncan Smith MP became Secretary of State for Social Security. While the Conservative Party had been in opposition he had established a Centre for Social Justice (CSJ) with which the Citizen's Income Trust exchanged a certain amount of correspondence, particularly in relation to the CSJ's publication *Dynamic Benefits* (Centre for Social Justice, 2009). That report's main recommendation was for 'Universal Credits', a means-tested benefit to replace several existing means-tested benefits in such a way as to reduce the overall marginal deduction rate. 'The Universal Credit system is one benefit, with a work-focused component and living costs component, withdrawn at a uniform rate above an earnings disregard, which is determined by household type' (Centre for Social Justice, 2009: 265). This idea found its way into the new coalition government's consultation paper, *21st Century Welfare* (Department for Work and Pensions, 2010a): 'The Universal Credit would gradually be reduced as post-tax household incomes rose. ... A single withdrawal rate would make it clearer and simpler to calculate the financial gains from work and for people to be confident of being better off by taking a job and progressing to more hours and higher pay once in work' (Department for Work and Pensions, 2010a: 21). Legislative proposals followed: *Universal Credit: welfare that works* (Department for Work and Pensions, 2010b): 'As earnings rise, we expect Universal Credit will be withdrawn at a constant rate of around 65 pence for each pound of net earnings' (Department for Work and Pensions, 2010b: 13). At each stage the Citizen's Income Trust participated in the debate: by corresponding with the Centre for Social Justice, by sending a submission in response to the consultation, and by commenting on the draft legislation; and it published its contributions in the *Citizen's Income Newsletter* (Citizen's Income Trust, 2010, 2011). The message was this: A Universal Credit is a useful few steps along the road to a Basic Income, and it would take only a few more steps to create a Basic Income and secure the benefits which that would offer in terms of income security, employment incentives, poverty reduction, and social cohesion. Another possibility, of course, is that the

Universal Credit would make means-tested benefits more acceptable by reducing marginal deduction rates, thus postponing debate on whether we need a new income maintenance structure.

(It is a pity that the unified benefit has been termed 'Universal Credit'. While the 'credit' usage is consistent with Gordon Brown's use of the term for *his* 'Tax Credits', it is not consistent with the use of 'credit' for the 1972 Heath Government's proposal for genuine tax credits. It would have been better to term the means-tested payment a 'benefit'. It is also a pity that it has been called 'universal'. It is not. 'Unified Benefit' would have been a far better description of the proposal.)

Citizen's Pension

At the end of 2010, Steven Webb, Minister for Pensions in the coalition government, proposed a single flat-rate state retirement pension; on March 8, 2011, Iain Duncan Smith expressed approval of the plan for a basic state pension of £140 per week; and in April 2011 one of the options contained in a Department for Work and Pensions consultation document, *A State Pension for the 21st Century*, was a single tier state pension of £140 per week for every individual with a thirty year National Insurance Contribution record (Department for Work and Pensions, 2011: 10, 29–35). This is not strictly a Citizen's Pension [(an unconditional and equal pension for every individual above retirement age)] but it would only take the substitution of a residence condition for the contribution record condition for it to become one.

The current pattern of state pension provision is composed of two contributory elements, one of which is earnings related, and an additional means-tested element for individuals whose income in retirement does not reach a stated minimum. This structure makes it difficult for people to know what level of state pension they will receive when they retire, and thus difficult for them to plan for the future, so there is little incentive for those on low incomes to take out private pensions; and because savings are taken into account in the calculation of means-tested pension supplements, in a somewhat complex way, there is little incentive for those on low incomes to save in other ways for their retirement. A genuine Citizen's Pension would take no account of savings, or of private or occupational pensions, and so would encourage people to take out private pensions and to save in other ways, and for everyone with a 30-year contribution record the proposed single-tier state pension would have the same effect because it would already be above the level of the current guaranteed retirement income.

Steven Webb was no newcomer to a Basic Income. In 1990 he published a book on the subject with Samuel Brittan, *Beyond the Welfare State: An Examination of Basic Incomes in a Market Economy*: 'A Basic Income is a payment received by every person or household adequate to provide a minimum income, based only on age and family status, but otherwise unconditional' (Brittan & Webb, 1990: 1). (Because the proposed payment was to be calculated on a household basis, and not on an individual basis, it was not strictly a Basic Income. If it had been individualised then it would have been one.) In 2004, the Pensions Policy Institute studied New Zealand's Citizen's Pension (James & Curry, 2010; O'Connell, 2004), so the idea had already received a certain amount of public debate: debate in which the Citizen's Income Trust participated (Citizen's Income Trust, 2004). So the new pension proposal had not come from nowhere—it had come from an interested individual and from existing debate: a pattern that we have seen before.

The Citizen's Income Trust made a submission to the consultation on *A state Pension for the 21st Century* and published its submission in an edition of the *Citizen's Income Newsletter*.

Discussion

So why did nothing follow Juliet Rhys Williams' minority report? Here we had a significant book, and a context of debate about the future of the tax and benefits system. And why did nothing happen following Brandon Rhys Williams' interventions? Here we had thorough research and a feasible scheme. In the case of the Universal Credit proposal, we had a ministerial champion and thorough research, and similarly with Steven Webb's pension proposal. In both cases, we had identifiable problems that needed to be fixed (high marginal deduction rates, and disincentives to save for retirement). In the case of Universal Credit, the parliamentary champion was a secretary of state who persuaded the Chancellor of the Exchequer that in the medium term his scheme would save money even though it might cost money to establish it. Universal Credit has happened. Steven Webb was a junior minister and a member of the junior party in the coalition, but his secretary of state understood and backed his plan. The first of two options listed in *A State Pension for the 21st Century* retained the current structure of first and second state pensions and increased the rate at which the second pension would become flat rate. The second option was for the single tier state pension. The consultation document was clear that the first option did not meet the Department's own reform criteria as well as the second option did. A flat rate single-tier state pension for everyone with a 30-year contribution record is what happened.

Contributions to parliamentary committee debate about a Basic Income have been only that, and have lacked parliamentary champions. Neither Juliet Rhys Williams nor Brandon Rhys Williams were ministers. This might suggest that major reform requires a ministerial champion. However, there is another distinction to be drawn: Both Juliet and Brandon Rhys Williams were attempting to change the entire benefits system, whereas Universal Credit and a single tier state pension are for particular demographic or contingency groups: for people on means-tested benefits, and for the elderly. Similarly, Family Allowance and Child Benefit were only for children. It is somewhat challenging to have to recognise that the last major overhaul of the United Kingdom's benefits structure occurred after a serious recession and during a major war. In such a context the apparent difficulties faced by major fiscal reform fade into insignificance beside other national difficulties. The question for us is this: Is that the only context in which we might expect reform of the system as a whole?

Clearly, no such change will ever occur without some previous discussion of the issues that the system faces, and of the options for change. That condition has been met to some extent in relation to Basic Income: although it has to be said that debate has taken place mainly amongst those professionally and academically interested, rather than among policymakers. Since the mid-1980s there has been exponential growth in the volume of academic debate on income maintenance reform proposals: Negative Income Tax, Tax Credits, and a Basic Income. Some of this interest has been generated from within academic departments because the originally rather thin field has offered plenty of opportunity for theses and dissertations and for the publication of books and articles. Some of the debate has been generated by think tanks. We have already mentioned the Centre for Social Justice, but some general purpose think tanks have also occasionally dabbled in the field; and the Citizen's Basic Income Trust has, of course, played its own part in promoting and publicising debate on Basic Income. One of the reasons for interest in academic departments is that universal benefits can be the subject matter for research and debate in a wide variety of disciplines: economics, social policy, sociology, moral philosophy, theology, and more. A rather narrower field of disciplines will be of interest to policymakers.

Here is not the place to rehearse the numerous arguments both for and against universal benefits, though more *systematic* work on those arguments, and on the ways in which arguments in different fields do or do not connect, would be welcome. Here our task is to ask whether there is any possibility that the United Kingdom's policymaking process will ever turn research and debate into additional legislated universal benefits, and perhaps to ask the rather more pressing question as to whether the universal aspects of the welfare state that we currently possess (Child Benefit and the National Health Service) will survive the current Government.

General political trends will be an important factor. The additional tax imposed on households receiving Child Benefit is part of a general trend towards conditionality. This trend is evidenced in both the Conservative and Labour Parties, particularly in relation to increasingly onerous conditions placed on Job Seeker's Allowance recipients, on recipients of Incapacity Benefit, and on households in receipt of Universal Credit.

Another factor which might determine whether further universal benefits reach the statute book lies in Harris's suggestion as to why Juliet Rhys Williams' scheme never happened: 'Like most schemes for abolishing bureaucrats, Lady Juliet's proposals met with an official wall of silence' (Harris, 1981: 258). Family Allowances did not abolish anything, and so added to the total number of civil servants. Child Tax Allowances disappeared when Child Benefit was established, but there were plenty of other tax allowances for Inland Revenue staff to administer. Whether this factor had any influence over the process which led to Family Allowance and Child Benefit is difficult to determine, but it is clearly possible. The two Rhys Williams' proposals would have shrunk the number of staff administering Income Tax, National Insurance Contributions, and means-tested benefits. This might have been a reason for the proposals being ignored. Civil servants' attitudes to proposed legislation clearly colour the ways in which those civil servants might formulate a reform proposal, recommend it to ministers or fail to recommend it, and calculate its costs and benefits: though how significant this factor might be in any particular case will of course be difficult to determine. It is not obvious that the 1970s Tax Credit scheme would have reduced the number of civil servants.

Civil servants were therefore content to facilitate the project. Universal Credit has rationalised to some extent the current patchwork of means-tested benefits, and has reduced marginal deduction rates. It might or might not have reduced civil service numbers. Because the proposal for a single tier state pension retains contribution records, any reduction in staff numbers resulting from the change will be small. The government's proposal to tax higher rate taxpayers if they live in households receiving Child Benefit is more likely to have increased the number of jobs in Her Majesty's Revenue and Customs than to decrease it.

A further significant factor, which we have already mentioned, is this: Our national accounts count benefits payments as public expenditure, but do not count as public expenditure the tax foregone by the government through the mechanism of tax allowances. This means that any proposal to shift income maintenance policy from tax allowances to cash payments will suffer from a disadvantage, and any proposal to shift policy in the opposite direction will experience a positive advantage. This is entirely irrational.

This accounting difficulty poses no problem to the new state pension, of course. Public expenditure will be affected very little, the second option in *A State Pension for the 21st Century* will tackle some recognised problems in the current system, there was existing debate and research on the proposal, and it had a ministerial champion. It has happened.

Things are rather different for a Basic Income, which is by definition payable to every citizen. The Basic Income itself would take little administration, whereas fewer people would be on means-tested benefits, and so fewer civil servants would be required. Personal tax allowances would be turned into cash payments, so Her Majesty's Revenue and Customs might require fewer staff. The national accounts would show higher public expenditure even though revenue foregone through tax allowances would decline by the same amount that benefits payments increased. It does not look good for Basic Income.

One hope for a Basic Income in the United Kingdom is for a significant parliamentary champion to emerge who understands the tax and benefits system and its disincentive effects, who is willing to put the arguments for universal benefits in and out of parliament, and who has sufficient influence to persuade colleagues that the tax and benefits system matters and that it is high time for radical change.

A rather different hope is that Child Benefit will survive as a universal benefit; that a Citizen's Pension will be enacted as a natural extension of the new single tier pension; that a 'universal grant' will be established for young adults to encourage education and training; that a universal 'mature worker's grant' will be established to encourage flexible labour market patterns amongst the over fifties; and that filling the 25 to 50-year old gap will then seem obvious.

A possibly impossible task is to persuade the British public that a Basic Income is a good idea. Research by DVL Smith Associates in 1991 showed that 'few respondents had a clear understanding of the UK system of pensions and benefits' (DVL Smith and Associates, 1991: 5), and many people could not comprehend reform options when they were explained (DVL Smith and Associates, 1991: 29). Debate amongst apparently intelligent members of the Conservative Party in 2010 about the government's initial proposals for depriving some families of Child Benefit ('They don't need it') showed a woeful ignorance of the efficiency and incentives advantages of universal benefits, of the context of a progressive tax system (which withdraws from wealthy families far more than they receive in Child Benefit), and of the disadvantages of means-testing.

What *is* required is rational debate among ministers in the Treasury and the Department for Work and Pensions about the way in which we keep our national accounts, about the administrative waste of means-testing, and about the increased employment incentive and social cohesion that a Basic Income would deliver. We also, of course, need a Chancellor of the Exchequer able to understand these things. The Citizen's Income Trust's research in 2006 suggests that there would be parliamentary support for a major review of income maintenance policy and for serious consideration being given to a Basic Income (Citizen's Income Trust, 2007), and Bochel and Defty have found a diversity of views on social policy issues among Conservative Members of Parliament, and an interesting willingness to question previous policy positions (Bochel, 2011: 13; Bochel & Defty, 2007). It is therefore possible that a minister who decided to consult on an extension of universal benefits might find more of a welcome in Parliament than they might expect.

Acknowledgements This chapter was first published as Chapter 14, 'The United Kingdom: Only for children?' in *Basic Income Guarantee and Politics: International experiences and perspectives on the viability of income guarantee*, edited by Richard Caputo, New York: Palgrave Macmillan, 2012, pp. 235–63 (Torry, 2012). The publisher's permission to republish the chapter in this volume is gratefully acknowledged. I remain grateful to all of those who read and commented on the first draft of the original chapter and particularly to Professor Hartley Dean, Dr. Tony Fitzpatrick, Professor Ruth Lister, Ms. Anne Miller, and Mr. Philip Vince.

Bibliography

Abel-Smith, B., & Townsend, P. (1965). *The poor and the poorest: A new analysis of the Ministry of Labour's Family Expenditure Surveys of 1953–54 and 1960.* Bell.

Atkinson, A. B. (1969). *Poverty in Britain and the reform of social security.* Cambridge University Press.

Banting, K. G. (1979). *Poverty, politics and policy: Britain in the 1960s.* Macmillan.

Barr, N., & Coulter, F. (1991). Social security: Solution or problem? In J. Hills (Ed.), *The state of welfare: The welfare state in Britain since 1974* (pp. 274–337). Clarendon Press.

Beveridge, Sir W. (1942). *Social insurance and allied services.* Cmd 6404. Her Majesty's Stationery Office.

Bochel, H. (2011). Conservative approaches to social policy since 1997. In H. Bochel (Ed.), *The Conservative Party and social policy* (pp. 1–22). Policy Press.

Bochel, H., & Defty, A. (2007). *Welfare policy under new labour.* Policy Press.

Booker, H. S. (1946). Lady Rhys Williams' proposals for the amalgamation of direct taxation with social insurance. *The Economic Journal, 56*(222), 230–243.

Brittan, S., & Webb, S. (1990). *Beyond the welfare state: An examination of basic Incomes in a market economy.* Aberdeen University Press.

Brown, J. (1988). *Child benefit: Investing in the future.* Child Poverty Action Group.

Brown, J. (1990). *Child benefit: Options for the 1990s.* Save Child Benefit / Child Poverty Action Group.

Centre for Social Justice. (2009). *Dynamic benefits: Towards welfare that works.* Centre for Social Justice.

Citizen's Income Trust. (2004). Further support for a citizen's pension. *Citizen's Income Newsletter*, 2004(2), 1–2. Citizen's Income Trust.

Citizen's Income Trust. (2007). Both the House of Commons and the House of Lords support a citizen's income approach to the reform of tax and benefits. *Citizen's Income Newsletter*, 2007(2), 1–2. Citizen's Income Trust.

Citizen's Income Trust. (2010). A response to *21st Century Welfare*. *Citizen's Income Newsletter*, 2010(3), 3–9. Citizen's Income Trust.

Citizen's Income Trust. (2011). With apologies to 'Yes, Minister'. *Citizen's Income Newsletter*, 2011(1), 16. Citizen's Income Trust.

Claeys, G. (1989). *Thomas Paine: Social and political thought*. Unwin Hyman.

Commission on Social Justice. (1994). *Social justice: Strategies for national renewal*. Vintage.

Creedy, J., & Disney, R. (1985). *Social insurance in transition*. Clarendon Press.

Department for Work and Pensions. (2010a). *21st century welfare*. Cm 7913. The Stationery Office.

Department for Work and Pensions. (2010b). *Universal Credit: Welfare that works*. Cm 7957. The Stationery Office.

Department for Work and Pensions. (2011). *A state pension for the 21st century*. Cm 8053. The Stationery Office.

DVL Smith & Associates. (1991). *Basic income: A research report*. Prepared for Age Concern England.

Freeman, C. (1998). *Family allowances, technical change, inequality, and social policy*. The Eleanor Rathbone Lecture, 1996. Liverpool University Press.

Harris, J. (1981). Some aspects of social policy in Britain during the Second World War. In W. J. Mommsen (Ed.), *The emergence of the welfare state in Britain and Germany, 1850–1950* (pp. 247–262). Croom Helm.

Her Majesty's Government. (1972). *Proposals for a tax-credit system*. Cmnd. 5116. Her Majesty's Stationery Office.

Hill, M. (1990). *Social security policy in Britain*. Edward Elgar.

House of Commons Select Committee on Tax-Credit. (1973). *Report and proceedings of the committee*. Session 1972–73, Volume I. 341–I. Her Majesty's Stationery Office.

House of Commons Treasury and Civil Service Committee Sub-Committee. (1982). *The structure of personal income taxation and income support: Minutes of evidence*. HC 331–ix. Her Majesty's Stationery Office.

House of Commons Treasury and Civil Service Committee. (1983). *Enquiry into the structure of personal income taxation and income support*, Third Special Report, Session 1982–3. Her Majesty's Stationery Office.

House of Commons Work and Pensions Committee. (2007). *Benefit simplification*. Seventh Report of Session 2006–7. HC 463. The Stationery Office.

James, S., & Curry, C. (2010). *A foundation pension: A PPI evaluation of NAPF* [National Association of Pension Funds] *proposals*. Pensions Policy Institute.

Land, H. (1975). The introduction of family allowances: An act of historic justice? In P. Hall, H. Land, R. Parker, & A. Webb (Eds.), *Change, choice and conflict in social policy* (pp. 157–230). Heinemann.

Macnicol, J. (1980). *The movement for family allowances, 1918–1945: A study in social policy development*. Heinemann.

McCarthy, M. (1986). *Campaigning for the poor: CPAG and the politics of welfare*. Croom Helm.

Meade, J. E. (1978). *The structure and reform of direct taxation*. Report of a committee chaired by Professor J. E. Meade. London: George Allen and Unwin, for the Institute for Fiscal Studies.
O'Connell, A. (2004). *Citizen's pension: An introduction*. Pensions Policy Institute.
Paine, T. (2006). *The rights of man*. The Echo Library. First published in 1791–1792.
Parker, H. (1982). *The moral hazard of social benefits: A study of the impact of social benefits and income tax on incentives to work*. Institute of Economic Affairs.
Parker, H. (1989). *Instead of the dole: An enquiry into integration of the tax and benefit systems*. Routledge.
Parker, H. (1995). *Taxes, benefits and family life: The seven deadly traps*. Institute of Economic Affairs.
Parker, H., & Sutherland, H. (No date). *Child tax allowances? A comparison of child benefit, child tax reliefs, and basic incomes as instruments of family policy*. Suntory-Toyota International Centre for Economics and Related Disciplines, London School of Economics and Political Science.
Rathbone, E. (1949). *Family allowances*. George Allen and Unwin (A new edition of *The disinherited family* with an epilogue by William Beveridge)
Rathbone, E. (1986). *The disinherited family*. Falling Wall Press. First published in 1924.
Rhys Williams, B. (1989). *Stepping stones to independence: National Insurance after 1990*. Aberdeen University Press.
Rhys Williams, J. (1943). *Something to look forward to*. MacDonald and Co.
Rhys Williams, J. (1953). *Taxation and incentives*. William Hodge and Co.
Spicker, P. (2011). *How social security works: An introduction to benefits in Britain*. Policy Press.
Stokes, M. (1949). *Eleanor Rathbone: A biography*. Gollancz.
Thane, P. (1996). *Foundations of the welfare state* (2nd ed.). Longman.
Titmuss, R. (1962). *Income distribution and social change*. Allen and Unwin.
Torry, M. (2012). The United Kingdom: Only for children? In R. Caputo (Ed.), *Basic income guarantee and politics: International experiences and perspectives on the viability of income guarantee* (pp. 235–263). Palgrave Macmillan.
Torry, M. (2021). *Basic Income: A history*. Edward Elgar Publishing.
Townsend, P. (1979). *Poverty in the United Kingdom*. Penguin.
Van Trier, W. (1995). *Every one a king*. Departement Sociologie Katholieke, Universiteit Leuven.
Vince, P. (1986). Basic incomes: Some practical considerations. *BIRG Bulletin* (Spring 1986): 5–8. Basic Income Research Group.
Vince, P. (2011). Correspondence with the author, dated 6th April 2011.
Walsh, A., & Lister, R. (1985). *Mother's life-line*. Child Poverty Action Group.

CHAPTER 8

A Basic Income is Feasible: But What Do We Mean by 'Feasible'?

Introduction

'Is a Basic Income feasible?' Here 'feasible' means 'capable of being done, effected, or accomplished' (dictionary.com). So the question that we are asking here is this: Is a Basic Income capable of being legislated and implemented? But in order to ask that question, we shall first of all need to provide a context, and secondly we shall need to break the question down into a series of related questions. The context in view here is the

This chapter, written as a conference paper in 2014, assumes that with the implementation of a Basic Income it would be feasible to abolish most means-tested benefits. This approach was subsequently shown to result in substantial disposable income losses for lots of low-income households, which means that although a significant number of households would be taken off means-tested benefits, and lots more households would be brought within striking distance of coming off them, means-tested benefits would have to be retained and recalculated to take into account households' Basic Incomes and their changed earned incomes as a result of the changes to the income tax system required to pay for the Basic Incomes (Torry, 2019; and see Chapter 16 in this volume).

M. Torry, *Basic Income—What, Why, and How?*,
Exploring the Basic Income Guarantee,
https://doi.org/10.1007/978-3-031-14248-2_8

UK. A Basic Income of particular specified levels for different age groups might be feasible in Canada but not in the UK, or vice versa. And in order to answer the general question 'Is a Basic Income feasible in the UK?' we shall have to ask such questions as 'Is a Basic Income financially feasible?' and 'Is a Basic Income politically feasible?'—and that latter question will itself need to be broken down into two separate questions: 'Does a Basic Income cohere with the ideological positions of the UK's major political parties?' and 'Given the way in which social policy achieves implementation in the UK, is it possible that a Basic Income might be implemented?'

Financial Feasibility

The obvious answer to the question 'Would a Basic Income be financially feasible?' is of course 'yes' if we mean by the question 'Could a Basic Income be funded by reducing tax allowances and means-tested and contributory benefits?' A revenue-neutral Basic Income scheme would be possible if constructed in that way (Torry, 2020, 2021).

The concept of financial feasibility might also relate to the number of individuals who would suffer significant losses if a revenue-neutral Basic Income scheme were to be implemented. We might somewhat arbitrarily decide that feasibility in this sense might be defined as: 'No more than 5% of individuals should suffer a loss of disposable income of more than 15%, and no more than 10% of individuals should suffer a loss of disposable income of more than 10%' (Torry, 2012); or we might decide on the criterion 'no more than 2% of low income households should experience household net disposable income losses of more than 5%' (Torry, 2021).

By using the EUROMOD computer programme and Family Resource Survey data, we can discover the gains and losses that would be experienced by a 0.1% sample of the UK population if a specified benefits reform were to be implemented. Research [in 2021] showed that it would be possible to implement a Basic Income scheme that would be paid for by reducing tax allowances and means-tested benefits and by adjusting Income Tax and National Insurance Contribution rates slightly, and that would fulfil the latter household losses criterion (Torry, 2021).

Basic Incomes of different levels, and paid for by different adjustments to tax thresholds, tax rates, and means-tested and contributory benefits, would deliver different patterns of gains and losses, and further research in this area will always be useful. But having said that, we should not be overly concerned about losses of say five per cent. A household that suffers a loss in means-tested benefits of that magnitude will generally find it very difficult to make up that loss. If we assume a household loss of £10 per week, a Universal Credit taper rate of 65%, and National Insurance Contributions of 11%, then additional earnings of about £40 per week will be required to deliver the necessary additional £10 of net income. With a Basic Income the situation is very different. The Basic Income would not be withdrawn, but Income Tax (at say 25%) would be payable on all or most earned income. A household loss of £10 per week could be made up by earning an additional £13.33 per week. It would therefore be far easier for a household to make up losses at the point of implementation of a Basic Income than it is in relation to losses imposed by changes in means-tested benefits regulations.

We can conclude that in relation to revenue neutrality, and in relation to households' ability to handle losses at the point of implementation, a Basic Income scheme could be designed that would be financially feasible.

Psychological Feasibility

There are some public policy fields in which public opinion plays only a small part in policymaking (Richardson, 1969): but in the benefits sphere public opinion matters, and in the UK it might be in relation to the public mindset that a Basic Income will be less feasible than in relation to any of the other feasibility types.

My experience of explaining a Basic Income to groups of intelligent people is that, at the beginning of the conversation, at the forefront of people's minds are such understandable presuppositions as 'to reduce poverty we need to give more money to the poor', 'to reduce inequality we need to give more money to the poor', 'if you give more money to the poor then they might not work', 'the rich don't need benefits'.

I might draw the group's attention to Child Benefit. This gives the same amount of money to every family with the same number of children, *and* it reduces poverty because it provides additional income for families with the lowest incomes, *and* it reduces inequality because it constitutes a higher proportion of total income for those with low incomes than it does for those with high incomes. Child Benefit provides additional income for those with the lowest incomes, but because it is not withdrawn as earned income rises, it does not act as an employment disincentive and so is more likely to encourage additional gainful employment than means-tested benefits do. The wealthy pay more in Income Tax than they receive in Child Benefit, so it hardly matters that they receive Child Benefit: and it is better that they do receive it because to give the benefit to every family with children is administratively efficient. I might also draw the group's attention to means-tested benefits. These give more to the poor than to the rich, but because the benefits are withdrawn as earnings rise, they prevent families from earning their way out of poverty, they make it less likely that people will seek gainful employment, and they therefore tend to increase inequality.

When I suggest that the intentions behind the group's presuppositions are better served by Child Benefit than by means-tested benefits, and that a Basic Income would also serve those intentions better than means-tested benefits currently do, I can see the penny drop for some of the group's members. They have understood. But by the end of the session, there will still be some members of the group who cannot see beyond the idea that if the poor need more money then means-testing is the obvious way to make sure that they get the money that they need.

The presuppositions are so difficult to shake off because we have lived with them for so long. Since Elizabethan times we have operated means tests, with the State giving more to the poor than to the rich and then withdrawing benefits as other income rises. Four centuries ago this might have been the only option, but in the context of a progressive tax system unconditional and nonwithdrawable benefits are the administratively efficient way to provide those with low incomes with additional income, and at the same time to ensure that they experience no employment disincentives.

The question for us here is this: Is it possible to shift the public mindset? Is it possible that sufficient numbers of people will understand that in the context of a progressive tax system a universal benefit is a more constructive way of targeting money on the poor than means-testing will ever be?—that universal benefits make people more likely to work, and not less?—that the tax system takes far more from the wealthy than they receive in universal benefits, so it's no problem that they receive benefits along with everybody else?

Since William James wrote *The Varieties of Religious Experience*, we have known quite a lot about individual conversion experiences, both religious and otherwise (James, 2012; Sargant, 1976) and, more relevantly,

Serge Moscovici has shown how a minority within a group can convert the majority to their viewpoint:

> A minority, which by definition expresses a deviant judgment, a judgment contrary to the norms respected by the social group, convinces some members of the group, who may accept its judgment in private. They will be reluctant to do so publicly, however, either for fear of losing face or to avoid the risk of speaking or acting in a deviant fashion in the presence of others. (Moscovici, 1980: 211)

If individual but unexpressed conversions then occur, public compliance with the view expressed by the majority can for a long time coexist with an increasing minority thinking differently. Then one act of courage can reveal how opinion is shifting, and a snowball effect can then occur because

> a consistent minority can exert an influence to the same extent as a consistent majority, and ... the former will generally have a greater effect on a deeper level, while the latter often has less, or none, at that level. (Moscovici, 1980: 214–216)

Moscovici's research related to groups and institutions, and we ought not to assume that a whole society will function in the same way: but the UK's recent experience of a rapid shift of public opinion towards same sex marriage suggests that the same process might also occur on a societal level. That particular transition might be informative, particularly in relation to the incremental practical steps by which it occurred. Within just sixty years the UK has seen the decriminalisation of homosexual activity, anti-discrimination legislation, equalities legislation, civil partnerships, and now same-sex marriage. The same process occurred with equalities legislation generally. Starting with the Race Discrimination Act in 1965 and the Equal Pay Act in 1970, the UK Government has legislated for various equalities when doing so has been somewhat ahead of public opinion. Each legislative step changed public behaviour and propelled an already changing public opinion more quickly along its trajectory and thus prepared the ground for the next legislative step that was slightly ahead of public opinion. The public opinion trajectory was always clear, so although it might have looked as if the Government was taking a risk, in fact it was not.

There are loud voices opposed to universal benefits, including the press. This is why party leaders feel a need to express opposition to universal benefits, and why during a speech made on the 6 June 2013 Ed Miliband MP said that 'it doesn't make sense to continue sending a cheque every year for Winter Fuel Allowance to the richest pensioners in the country'. However, the silent majority know both how efficient Child Benefit is and how well it serves those on the lowest incomes. Households containing children, and with at least one adult paying higher rate tax, would now appreciate not having the value of Child Benefit withdrawn through the tax system. There might therefore be a silent majority in favour of universal benefits, but perhaps not knowing that they are a majority. The only way to test this would be for the Government to argue for turning means-tested benefits into a new universal benefit and then to make the change: preferably for a group within society that the majority could regard as deserving in some way, so that the experiment becomes a test of public appreciation of universal benefits rather than a test of public attitudes towards groups within society.

There is a precedent. It was a slow and somewhat fraught process, but during the 1970s Family Allowance for every child except the first in each family became Child Benefit: an unconditional benefit for every child. The mechanism by which the change occurred is that Child Tax Allowances were abolished, and Family Allowance was extended to the first child in each family. Effectively, a tax allowance became a new universal benefit. The change was achieved with almost no public opposition (Torry, 2013: 22–25). There is therefore no reason for not making similar attempts, and every reason for doing so.

Groups regarded by the public as deserving, and for whom the Government might therefore attempt transitions from tax allowances and means-tested benefits to unconditional and nonwithdrawable benefits, might be young adults and pre-retirement working age adults (perhaps with National Insurance contribution records functioning as a gateway for the latter group, as they do for the new Single-Tier State Pension).

My hunch is that we would see the same process as we have seen for same-sex marriage, and that the popularity of the changes for young adults and for pre-retirement adults would reveal and embed a public opinion shifting towards understanding the advantages of universal, unconditional and nonwithdrawable benefits. The silent majority will have become conscious of their approval, and might have become vocal about it; and the minority willing and able to express the advantages of unconditional and nonwithdrawable benefits will have converted the rest of society.

Institutional Feasibility

This section of the chapter will be much shorter because this feasibility is easier to demonstrate than financial feasibility, and far easier to demonstrate than the possibility of psychological feasibility.

The UK has been paying Family Allowance to every family with more than one child since 1946; and it has been paying Child Benefit for every child since the 1970s. The administration is simple and efficient, almost no fraud occurs, and error rates are negligible (Torry, 2013: 22–25). To pay a Basic Income to every adult would be even easier because every child who leaves school is allocated a unique National Insurance Number. Just as importantly, it would be easy to administer an unconditional and nonwithdrawable benefit for any particular age cohort; and whether for the entire population, or for a particular age cohort, the unconditional and nonwithdrawable nature of the benefit would make computerisation simple in the extreme.

A Basic Income would be institutionally feasible; and equally institutionally feasible would be an unconditional and nonwithdrawable benefit for any particular age cohort.

Behavioural Feasibility

We might think that in order to demonstrate behavioural feasibility we would need to show that a Basic Income would work for households in the sense of providing them with an ideal income maintenance system, somehow defined. Such a demonstration would not be possible. Take the case of housing costs. In London in particular, but also across much of the South-east and elsewhere, housing is becoming unaffordable for large sections of the population, forcing households into living at some distance from their workplaces, or in accommodation too small for their needs, or with too insecure a tenure. An unconditional benefit high enough to enable every household to pay for the accommodation that it needs, as well as other living expenses, would be unaffordable without politically unsustainable increases in Income Tax rates. For the time being, Housing Benefit, calculated in relation to both housing costs and ability to pay, will be required; and because it is households that live in houses and flats, Housing Benefit will need to continue to be paid on the basis of the household as the claimant unit, unlike the Basic Income, which will be paid equally to every individual of the same age (Torry, 2013: 268–270).

Similarly with Council Tax Benefit. The assistance that the Government gives to those with too low an income to pay Council Tax (a local tax that pays for local services) has now been localised, and although Council Tax is always based on the value of the household's accommodation, Council Tax Benefit is differently calculated by every Local Authority. There is no reason in principle why a Basic Income could not be paid at a sufficiently high level to enable Council Tax Benefit to be abolished; but the fact that Council Tax is paid by households and not by individuals, and the fact that Council Tax can be of very different amounts for different households, means that for the time being we must view it in the same way as Housing Benefit: as an unfortunate part of the current system which for the time being a Basic Income will be able to do nothing about.

However, the replacement of other means-tested benefits with a Basic Income would make a considerable difference to many households, because it would provide them with new options in relation to employment patterns. Take the example of a household in which the male adult has been unemployed for more than a year and the female adult is in low-paying employment. Currently, most of the value of the woman's earnings is deducted from the household's means-tested Jobseeker's Allowance; if the man finds a job then much of the value of the woman's earnings will be deducted from the household's Working Tax Credits [and now from its Universal Credit]. If Jobseeker's Allowance and Tax Credits were to be replaced by a Basic Income then whether he was in employment or not she could earn as much as she wished and the household's Basic Incomes would not change. The household would be in a radically different position. If their Basic Incomes were not enough to live on, and Housing Benefit was still in payment, then both partners would have a substantial incentive to earn sufficient income to enable the household to escape from means-testing altogether: and creating additional net income would be much more possible with a Basic Income because the Basic Income would provide a solid income floor that would never be withdrawn.

All we need to show is that all households would either experience no change if a Basic Income were to be implemented, or would find themselves in a better position: not necessarily in terms of net income on the day of implementation (because for some households net income might go down slightly), but in terms of employment options and the net income possibilities attached to those options. If attempted new behaviours produced advantageous outcomes—whether that be in terms of work-life balance, or increasing net income, or both—then the Basic Income will have been behaviourally feasible.

A potential problem with behavioural feasibility is that, while we might be able to predict behavioural feasibility, it will not be possible to demonstrate it in advance. This is not necessarily a problem, particularly if implementation of a Basic Income is phased in, either by providing every citizen with a very small Basic Income and then increasing it, or by establishing a Basic Income for one demographic group at a time. If an unconditional and nonwithdrawable Pre-Retirement Income were to be paid to adults between the age of 55 and retirement age, paid for by reducing personal tax allowances and means-tested and other benefits, then that group would experience behavioural changes, and policymakers would be able to evaluate both the changes and their acceptability. This would provide valuable evidence about the behavioural feasibility that might follow the implementation of Basic Incomes for other demographic groups.

Behavioural feasibility matters, but not initially. Implementation of a Basic Income can begin without the behavioural feasibility of a Basic Income for every citizen having been demonstrated. This means that behavioural feasibility functions rather like psychological feasibility. They are both requirements for successful implementation of a Basic Income, but neither is required prior to the commencement of Basic Income implementation.

Political Feasibility

There are two related meanings of 'political feasibility' that we might express by the following two questions: (1) Does a Basic Income cohere with the ideological positions of the UK's major political parties? (parties in the plural because a Basic Income's implementation would require all-party support); and (2) Given the way in which social policy achieves implementation in the UK, is it possible that a Basic Income might be implemented?

Political Ideologies

Research has shown that the main recent and current political ideologies in the UK—the New Right, Socialism, One Nation Conservatism, Liberalism, Social Democracy, and New Labour's 'Third Way', and also for a Green perspective—the ideology itself generates arguments for a Basic Income, arguments for a Basic Income have in fact been developed by proponents of the different ideologies, and any arguments against a Basic Income developed by proponents of the ideologies are generic: that is, whatever the ideology espoused by the objector, the objections are of the form 'A Basic Income would be too expensive', 'We should not pay people to do nothing', 'Rich people do not need it', or 'A Basic Income would discourage people from seeking employment' (Torry, 2013: 228). One of the appendices to *Money for Everyone* (Torry, 2013: website appendix 13) also examines the ideologies attached to Old Labour (and the Co-operative Movement) and to the Post-War Consensus, and finds the same to be true: the ideologies themselves, and their proponents, offer arguments for a Basic Income, whereas arguments against a Basic Income are the generic ones listed above.

This all suggests that a Basic Income would be politically feasible in the sense that every mainstream UK political ideology, and every proponent of these ideologies, can find reasons to support the implementation of a Basic Income, and any arguments against implementation are not related to those ideologies, and can be answered.

The Policy Process

It might be important to be able to show that no mainstream UK political ideology would necessarily be a barrier to the implementation of a Basic Income, but if the ways in which policy is made in the UK would preclude the implementation of a Basic Income, then ideological acceptability would be irrelevant. I shall therefore give most of the rest of this chapter to the question: Given the way in which social policy achieves implementation in the UK, is it possible for a Basic Income to be implemented?

Here I shall take as my guide Michael Hill's *The Public Policy Process* (Hill, 2009):

> The policy process is a complex and multi-layered one. It is … a complex political process in which there are many actors: politicians, pressure groups, civil servants, publicly employed professionals, and even sometimes those who see themselves as the passive recipients of policy. (Hill, 2009: 4)

A first step in understanding the policy process in relation to a particular proposal is to ask about the geographical location of relevant factors (Hill, 2009: 47). For instance: are global factors significant, or do we only need to take account of factors relating to the social and economic environment of the UK (which are, of course, influenced by global factors)? To take a different policy proposal: A 'Tobin' tax on currency transactions (Adam et al., 2011: 151–153, 195–215) might be feasible at a very low level in an individual country, but the fact that banking is a global industry, and that currency exchange can occur in numerous financial centres around the world, means that a Tobin tax at a level that might discourage banks from undertaking currency exchanges in the UK is not feasible. In the case of a Basic Income, it might be thought that a relevant geographical factor would be the free movement of labour in Europe. Would a Basic Income in the UK encourage higher levels of inward migration? The answer to this question is probably 'no' unless the Basic Income were to be set at a level higher than current means-tested and universal benefits. The UK already has an unconditional and nonwithdrawable Child Benefit, payable to anyone with the care of children if they ordinarily reside in the UK, they have a right to be there, and they are physically present in the country (Her Majesty's Revenue and Customs, 2022). Child Benefit is rarely accused of fuelling inward migration. More generally, a Basic Income at a level not above that of existing benefits would provide no additional incentive to migrate to the UK. This means that while it might have looked as if the social and economic environments in other countries might be relevant factors, they might not be, and we can concentrate on institutions and processes within the UK.

Crucial to the policy process are the institutions for which ideas and evidence are inputs, and legislation and implementation are outputs. In the case of the UK, in the field of social security benefits, this means ministers, government departments, and Parliament. Any one part of this tripartite system can block or delay policy change, and all three parts have to cooperate to enable change to occur (Hill, 2009: 68, 73). Also essential to the policy process will be a policy community or policy network concerned about a particular issue, or perhaps about a variety of issues. Such networks (around which information passes) and communities (groups of organisations more intimately engaged in the policy process) (Smith, 1993: 56–65) will often be complex, with some members more concerned about one aspect of an issue, and some more concerned about another; and they will overlap with other networks and communities (Hill, 2009: 58–66). In relation to a Basic Income, networks concerned with poverty alleviation, poverty abolition, employment incentives, individual freedom, and the voluntary sector, will all be relevant, as will be the already quite well-developed network gathered around the idea of a Basic Income.

But however effective interest groups might appear to be, however well-organised policy networks and policy communities might appear, and however adequate the general public's understanding and approval of a policy proposal might be, only if the policy community, including the government, the civil service, and parliamentary institutions, can line up to create the necessary change will the policy change occur (Hill, 2009: 87). If they do all line up behind the proposal then members of the policy community will exchange research and other resources with each other in order to achieve policy implementation. If they do not all line up then the community will revert to being a powerless network (Smith, 1993: 82–83).

As Hill suggests, institutions relate to institutions, which means that as well as individual proponents of a policy change relating to individuals within the tripartite system, it is important that institutions within the policy networks, and communities attached to a policy proposal, should relate to other institutions (Hill, 2009: 88). Think tanks are important because they are institutions that can relate to institutions. Important to both individual and institutional relationships with the Government, the civil service, and Parliament, will be a recognition that every actor in the system is to some extent self-interested. Each member of parliament, each minister, and each civil servant, will to some extent be influenced by their own interests; and if supporting a proposal would be clearly against their own interests then they would be unlikely to support it. So, for instance, civil servants would be unlikely to support proposals that might reduce the size of their departments (Hill, 2009: 90, 102). They might also be somewhat unenthusiastic about a policy change that appears to be impossible to implement. Successful implementation of a policy can enhance a civil service career. Impending implementation failure will lead to capable civil servants seeking transfer from the department or section involved, for obvious reasons.

What we have said so far about the policy process makes it look as if it might be orderly and rational, but that is generally far from the truth. Hill describes the policy environment as like a soup within which problems [which are socially constructed (Anglund, 1999: 151)], policy options (again socially constructed), and political factors (constantly influenced by societal pressures), swirl in unpredictable ways. Policy change is generally incremental because that is the only kind that looks feasible within such a complex environment (Hill, 2009: 157, 164); because incremental change enables learning and useful adaptation to occur (Richardson, 1999: 67); and because political pressures in a variety of directions will often only allow minor policy changes, and will frequently result in a pendulum effect: for instance, between means-testing and universality (Barkai, 1998). Another reason for change generally being incremental is that because we have a permanent civil service in the UK, civil servants have to serve consecutive ministers with often very different ideological positions, and seeking consensus is the most likely way to avoid turbulence as governments change (Hill, 2009: 186). (Civil servants achieve the control that they do because ministers have little time available and must therefore rely on civil servants to give regulatory and legislative effect to their ideas.) Yet more reasons for incremental change are that evidence can only be collected from existing systems; that it is often easier to implement changes to existing systems than to build entirely new systems (Hill, 2009: 188); and that small incremental changes are generally easier for the different parties within a policy network to understand than major system changes would be. The media, which are an important and influential component of any policy network, will often not be capable of expressing simply and accurately the smallest policy changes, or public opinion related to them (Hill, 2009: 167; Jacobs & Shapiro, 1999: 136), and are therefore highly unlikely to be capable of expressing accurately the reasons for major systems changes: so again, consensus and incremental change will be the safest option.

The policy process is often described as a series of steps, for instance:

1. Precise definition of policy objectives;
2. Instruments chosen;
3. Implementation arrangements formulated; and
4. Rules for implementation: (Hill, 2009: 174):

whereas in practice ‘policy formulation is a piecemeal activity’ (Hill, 2009: 173) within which the different theoretical steps merge into each other (Hill, 2009: 191). Take the example of changes to the benefits system. Theoretically, the minister will take to Parliament a Bill prepared by civil servants according to instructions given by the minister; Parliament will turn the Bill into an Act; and the new policy will then be implemented by civil servants. Things are rarely as simple as that. For instance: if new computer software is required to implement the benefits changes, then the computer company writing the software will be an interested party, will attempt to influence both the policy and its regulations, and will often succeed in doing so because their statement that computerisation would be cheaper or easier if changes were made, or that computerisation would be impossible if changes were not made, would be difficult to contradict. The computer company possesses ‘expert power’ in the situation (French & Raven, 1959; Hill, 2009: 191), even if it is not very expert.

When it comes to implementation of a new policy, the situation is equally complex, and precisely how the policy is implemented will depend on the characteristics of the policy, on any accompanying regulations, and on the organisations involved in implementation: the relationships between them; their feedback to ministers, Parliament, and the civil service; and the ways in which their staff (functioning as ‘street-level bureaucrats’ [Hill, 2009: 299]) implement the policy and exercise discretion in relation to regulations. A further factor will be public response to implementation (Hill, 2009: 212).

We can draw some initial conclusions in relation to the feasibility of a Basic Income:

- Institutional representation of the policy idea is essential: that is, broadly based think tanks and academic departments actively involved in research, dissemination, and education, and perhaps a better resourced Citizen’s Income Trust [, and, internationally, Basic Income Earth Network (BIEN)];
- A policy network or community is required in which institutions and individuals representing the media, community groups, academia, political parties, trades unions, employers’ organisations, and generally as wide a range of interests as possible, will relate well to each other, will relate consistently to the issues of poverty, the poverty

trap, and a Basic Income, and will together relate to Parliament, the Government, and the civil service;

- An important task will be to prepare draft legislation [This happened in 2018 (Citizen's Basic Income Trust, 2018)], regulations, and implementation strategies [A report on this was published in 2016 (Torry, 2016b)], because these will make it clear that some of the complexities related to other policy options would not apply to a Basic Income—and, in particular, that computerisation would be simple, institutional arrangements for implementation would be radically simple, and there would be no street-level bureaucrats to worry about;
- Implementation of a Basic Income would need to be incremental: that is, implementation one demographic group at a time rather than as a single project for the entire age range (Torry, 2013: 49–52); and
- Careful study of current government priorities will be required throughout. Current themes are the disaggregation of the public sector (which suggests that the Basic Incomes should be managed by a separate agency); explicit standards; output controls; and discipline and parsimony in relation to resources (all easy to achieve with a Basic Income) (Hill, 2009: 291).

Our discussion and its conclusions suggest a range of criteria by which we might judge whether or not a Basic Income is likely to be politically feasible in the sense of a positive response to the question: Given the way in which social policy achieves implementation in the UK, is it possible that a Basic Income might be implemented?

- It will need to address two problems both recognised as serious problems needing solutions: poverty, and the poverty trap;
- It will need to garner government, parliamentary, and civil service support, and this will require public understanding and support (a point made by John McDonnell MP at a meeting at the House of Commons on 4 March 2014);
- An active policy community will need to include trades unions and other social institutions;
- Policy change will need to be, and be seen to be, an incremental change or a series of incremental changes (and the existence of pilot

projects of some kind will be useful to represent the incremental and proven nature of the change envisaged);

- Implementation will need to be, and be seen to be, feasible, both in relation to the transition and in relation to ongoing administration; and
- The media will need to be actively involved in the policy network, and both this and public understanding will depend on clearly deserving social groups benefiting from the proposed change or changes—which is again an argument for incremental implementation.

Any compromise over the characteristics of unconditional and nonwithdrawable benefits—for instance, by applying conditions of any kind to their receipt—would destroy the policy proposal, would not deliver the benefits that an unconditional and nonwithdrawable benefit would offer, and would make it more difficult to establish an unconditional and nonwithdrawable benefit for the next demographic group. Here commitment to unconditionality and nonwithdrawability by individual and institutional members of relevant policy networks and communities, and their carefully and consistently expressed arguments for these characteristics, will be essential.

Relationships Between Feasibilities

Ivan Steiner has identified three types of group tasks:

- Additive: all group members do the same thing. The outcome is the sum of contributions (as in a tug of war);
- Conjunctive: the performance depends on the performance of the least talented. All members' contributions are needed for success, and the links between the elements are often crucial (as in a relay race); and
- Disjunctive: here accomplishment depends on the performance of the most talented member. The group remains better than that individual because even the best at something does not necessarily know all of the right answers (as in a pub quiz). Here the major requirement is that less talented members of the group should not be able to hold back the most talented member (Steiner, 1972).

We might employ this categorisation of group tasks analogically to discuss the relationships between the different kinds of feasibility that we have discussed.

If we term the pre-implementation feasibilities required for the establishment of an unconditional and nonwithdrawable benefit for a demographic group financial, institutional, psychological, ideological, and policy process feasibilities, then the argument of this chapter suggests that if one of the feasibilities is absent or weak then it is difficult to see how implementation is likely to be possible. This means that the relationships are not disjunctive. Some of the feasibilities relate to each other (for instance, psychological and policy process feasibilities form a circular, or possibly a spiral, process), so here an element of additivity might be present: but generally the feasibilities are independent of each other (Pasquali, 2012: 60, 188), and because they are all required it would appear that we are looking at conjunctive feasibilities. The order in which the feasibilities are established is important—for instance, financial and institutional feasibilities and a certain amount of psychological feasibility will need to be in place before ideological and policy process feasibilities can be built; and behavioural feasibility then needs to generate the next tranche of psychological feasibility so that the next demographic group can be tackled. This makes the relay race analogy even more relevant.

The conjunctive nature of the feasibilities that we have been studying has practical importance because it means that for implementation of a Basic Income to be feasible, even for an individual demographic group, sufficient work needs to be done on all of the feasibilities, and none can be neglected.

Conclusion

At the BIEN Congress held in Münich in 2012, De Wispelaere's and Noguera's categorisation of feasibilities was discussed (De Wispelaere & Noguera, 2012): strategic feasibility (that is, the feasibility of persuading policymaking institutions to enact a new policy); institutional feasibility; psychological feasibility; and behavioural feasibility. De Wispelaere and Nogeura had hypothesised that before implementation of a Basic Income could take place, both strategic and psychological feasibilities would have to have been established, and that after implementation both behavioural and institutional feasibility would have had to be evidenced in order for the policy change to be sustainable (De Wispelaere & Noguera, 2012:

21). The suggestion was made then that the only pre-implementation requirements were psychological feasibility and strategic feasibility (their term for a combination of administrative and policy process feasibilities)—that is, that both the general public and policymaking institutions would need to be persuaded. The argument of this chapter suggests that that suggestion is of only limited applicability.

Our discussions of psychological feasibility, behavioural feasibility, and the policy process, suggest that the establishment of a Basic Income for the whole population is unlikely to be feasible. What might be feasible would be an unconditional and nonwithdrawable benefit payable to a demographic group perceived as somehow deserving. Such a benefit would need to be shown to be both institutionally feasible and financially feasible. These tasks would not be difficult to achieve. A public understanding of the deservingness of the social group would then provide sufficient psychological feasibility to enable the policy process to embrace the possibility of implementation, and would enable ideological positions to develop and the necessary political commitments to be expressed. Behavioural feasibility would follow implementation, as would the psychological feasibility necessary for an unconditional and nonwithdrawable benefit to be implemented for the next demographic group. Basic Income established for successive demographic groups (a Citizen's Pension, a Pre-Retirement Income, an Education and Training Income, and an enhanced Child Benefit) would narrow the age range without a Basic Income sufficiently to enable it to become psychologically feasible for a Basic Income to be considered for working age adults, and for the policy process to embrace the idea as a necessary completion of a task already nearly completed.

It would appear that the only way forwards for the UK would be the implementation of a Basic Income for one demographic group at a time. What this chapter has shown is that the implementation of a Basic Income by that route would be entirely feasible, provided that at every stage we have put the necessary work into all of the different feasibilities required.

Acknowledgements This chapter publishes for the first time a conference paper, 'A Basic Income is feasible. But what do we mean by "feasible"?', presented at the Basic Income Earth Network (BIEN) congress in Montreal in June 2014. The paper has been quoted and referenced in a variety of chapters, articles, and books, and in particular in Malcolm Torry, *The Feasibility of Citizen's Income*

(Torry, 2016a), of which it formed the basis: but this is the first time that the paper has been published as originally presented at the congress.

Readers might wish to note that when the list of feasibilities developed in the conference paper was used to construct the book *The Feasibility of Citizen's Income*, 'institutional feasibility' was relabelled 'administrative feasibility'; 'financial feasibility' was divided into two kinds of financial feasibility: financial feasibility in the sense that a Basic Income scheme could be funded, and financial feasibility in the sense that a Basic Income scheme would not impose significant losses on low-income households; and 'political feasibility' was divided into 'political feasibility' and 'policy process feasibility'.

References

Adam, S., et al. (2011). *Tax by design: The Mirrlees Review*. Oxford University Press.

Anglund, S. M. (1999). American core values and policy problem definition. In S. S. Nagel (Ed.), *The policy process* (pp. 147–163). Nova Science Publishers.

Barkai, H. (1998). *The evolution of Israel's social security system*. Ashgate.

Citizen's Basic Income Trust. (2018). *Illustrative draft legislation for a Citizen's Basic Income*. Retrieved March 26, 2022, from https://citizensincome.org/news/illustrative-draft-legislation-for-a-citizens-basic-income/

De Wispelaere, J., & Noguera, J. A. (2012). On the political feasibility of Universal Basic Income: An analytic framework. In R. Caputo (Ed.), *Basic Income Guarantee: International experiences and perspectives on the viability of Income Guarantee* (pp. 17–38). Palgrave Macmillan.

Dictionary.com. (2022). *Dictionary.com*. Retrieved March 26, 2022, from https://www.dictionary.com/

French, J. R. P. Jr., & Raven, B. H. (1959). The bases of social power. In D. Cartwright (Ed.), *Studies in social power* (pp. 150–67). Institute for Social Research. Reprinted in Pugh, D. S. (1984). *Organization theory: Selected readings* (2nd ed., pp. 150–167). Penguin.

Her Majesty's Revenue and Customs. (2022). *Child Benefit if you move to the UK*. Retrieved March 26, 2022, from www.hmrc.gov.uk/childbenefit/start/who-qualifies/new-arrivals-uk.htm

Hill, M. (2009). *The public policy process* (5th ed.). Pearson/Longman.

Jacobs, L. R., & Shapiro, R. Y. (1999). The media reporting and distorting of public opinion towards entitlements. In S. S. Nagel (Ed.), *The policy process* (pp. 135–145). Nova Science Publishers.

James, W. (2012). *The varieties of religious experience: A study in human nature*. Oxford University Press. First published 1902.

Moscovici, S. (1980). Toward a theory of conversion behavior. In L. Berkowitz (Ed.), *Advances in experimental social psychology* (Vol. 13, pp. 209–239). Academic Press.

Pasquali, F. (2012). *Virtuous imbalance: Political philosophy between desirability and feasibility*. Ashgate.

Richardson, J. J. (1969). *The policy-making process*. Routledge and Kegan Paul.

Richardson, J. (1999). Interest group, multi-arena politics and policy change. In S. S. Nagel (Ed.), *The policy process* (pp. 65–99). Nova Science Publishers.

Sargant, W. (1976). *Battle for the mind: A physiology of conversion and brainwashing*. Heinemann.

Smith, M. J. (1993). *Policy networks: Pressure, power and policy*. Harvester Wheatsheaf.

Steiner, I. D. (1972). *Group process and productivity*. Academic Press.

Torry, M. (2012). Research note: A Citizen's Income scheme's winners and losers. *Citizen's Income Newsletter*, issue 3 for 2012, p. 2.

Torry, M. (2013). *Money for everyone: Why we need a Citizen's Income*. Policy Press. The appendices can be found at https://citizensincome.org/money-for-everyone/appendices/

Torry, M. (2016a). *The feasibility of Citizen's Income*. Palgrave Macmillan.

Torry, M. (2016b). *How might we implement a Citizen's Income?* Institute for Chartered Accountants of England and Wales. Retrieved March 26, 2022, from https://www.icaew.com/-/media/corporate/files/technical/sustainability/outside-insights/citizens-income-web---final.ashx?la=en

Torry, M. (2019). *Static microsimulation research on Citizen's Basic Income for the UK: A personal summary and further reflections* (EUROMOD Working Paper EM13/19). Institute for Social and Economic Research. Retrieved March 26, 2022, from https://www.euromod.ac.uk/sites/default/files/working-papers/em13-19.pdf

Torry, M. (2020). *Evaluation of a Recovery Basic Income, and of a sustainable revenue neutral Citizen's Basic Income, with an appendix relating to different Universal Credit roll-out scenarios* (Institute for Social and Economic Research Working Paper EM7/20). Institute for Social and Economic Research, University of Essex. Retrieved March 26, 2022, from https://www.iser.essex.ac.uk/research/publications/working-papers/euromod/em7-20.pdf

Torry, M. (2021). *Three income maintenance options for 2021*. Centre for Microsimulation and Policy Analysis report. Institute for Social and Economic Research, University of Essex. Retrieved March 26, 2022, from https://www.microsimulation.ac.uk/publications/publication-526555/

CHAPTER 9

Objections and Responses

Introduction

Basic Income receives its fair share of objections, mainly in the form 'The rich don't need it', 'People would stop working', and 'We can't afford it'. The objections are often based on misunderstandings. This chapter is made up of three articles, two previously published on the *Social Europe* website and subsequently in a book published by Social Europe, and one published in the journal *Renewal*. The first two articles respond to the 'We can't afford it' objection, the first in general terms, and the second by being clear about the difference between 'Basic Income' and 'Basic Income scheme', which objectors to Basic Income rather too often confuse with each other. A Basic Income is always an unconditional income paid regularly to every individual; a Basic Income scheme is a Basic Income, with the levels for different age groups specified, the funding method specified, and any changes to existing taxes and benefits fully specified. Showing that a particular Basic Income scheme would be unaffordable does not prove that Basic Income is unaffordable. It only requires one Basic Income scheme to be affordable for Basic Income to be affordable (Torry, 2018a, 2018b).

The third article republished here is a response to authors who called something a Basic Income when it was not one. Their criticisms of an

M. Torry, *Basic Income—What, Why, and How?*,
Exploring the Basic Income Guarantee,
https://doi.org/10.1007/978-3-031-14248-2_9

income-tested benefit were entirely reasonable. What was not reasonable was to say that the same criticisms could therefore be made in relation to Basic Income, which they cannot (2018c).

The global Basic Income debate is important, which is why it is important that the debate should benefit from the best available evidence and the best possible logic.

Basic Income: Both Feasible and Useful

There has been much discussion [...] in *Social Europe* posts about a Basic Income: an unconditional and nonwithdrawable income for every individual. My aim here is to respond to one particular point made more than once: that a Basic Income would be unaffordable.

This is a complex question to which a variety of responses might be offered. Several of those responses in terms of alternative funding methods would not be viable in the short or medium term but might be possible in the longer term: for instance, new forms of taxation, such as a financial transaction tax or land value tax, or the creation of new money, along the lines of the quantitative easing practised by central banks since the financial crisis. None of these funding methods would be easy to establish, and the likelihood of being able to implement one of them at the same time as introducing a Basic Income would be close to zero.

A more feasible method for funding a Basic Income in the short to medium term would be adjustments to the current tax and benefits systems. In the UK, such measures might be the reduction of the Income Tax Personal Allowance, adjustments to National Insurance Contribution rates and thresholds, changes to Income Tax rates, and the abolition or adjustment of existing means-tested benefits. A wide variety of different configurations would clearly be possible, but some would be more feasible than others.

In the UK, the value of the combination of the Income Tax Personal Allowance and the National Insurance Contributions Lower Earnings Limit is similar to that of the main out-of-work means-tested benefit, [Universal Credit], suggesting that a Basic Income of the same value could be paid for by reducing to zero the Personal Allowance and the Lower Earnings Limit and abolishing means-tested benefits. This approach might look attractive, but first of all the levels of means-tested benefits related to housing (Housing Benefit, Council Tax Benefit, and the housing component of Universal Credit) are substantial in areas of high housing costs, so those benefits would need to be retained; and secondly, households receiving Working Tax Credits and Child Tax Credits would find that their Citizen's Incomes would replace the lost Income Tax Personal Allowance but not the value of their in-work means-tested benefits. Large numbers of low-income households would therefore suffer substantial losses at the point of implementation of the Basic Income. This would clearly be unacceptable.

The only option in the short to medium term is the retention of means-tested benefits, with each household's means-tested benefits being recalculated on the basis that they would now be receiving Basic Incomes and that their net earnings will have changed. It might be objected—and it has been objected—that this sacrifices the simplicity of Basic Income, which is one of the advantages claimed by its proponents. This is to misunderstand. The Basic Income would still be radically simple. It would be paid at the same rate to everyone of the same age, whatever their income, household structure, or employment status. It would function as a secure foundation on which every individual and every household would be able to build.

The means-tested benefits which some households would still receive would still of course remain as complex and stigmatising as they are now: and households still on means-tested benefits would continue to suffer high marginal deduction rates. However, any household that found itself no longer on means-tested benefits would see reduced marginal deduction rates and higher employment incentives, and would no longer experience the bureaucratic intrusion, sanctions, stigma, insecurity and complexity of means-tested benefits. So what matters is the number of households that would no longer be on means-tested benefits following the implementation of a Basic Income and related tax and benefits changes; and also the number of households within striking distance of coming off means-tested benefits—because any household with means-tested benefits of only a few pounds a week would choose to abandon their claim and instead add to their employment hours, in the knowledge that any additional gross earnings would no longer result in benefits withdrawal.

The Institute for Social and Economic Research has published a number of working papers on costed Basic Income schemes (Torry, 2019, 2020, 2021). These show that a Basic Income scheme that leaves in place and recalculates current benefits, and raises Income Tax rates by only 3 percentage points, can be revenue neutral, can avoid losses at the point of implementation for low-income households, can minimise losses for all households, can reduce poverty, can reduce inequality, can take appreciable numbers of households off means-tested benefits, and can reduce substantially the average levels of payments of most means-tested benefits for those households still receiving them. The fact that such a scheme would reduce both poverty and inequality at zero net cost would be argument enough for implementing it. The fact that it would also take a lot of households off means-tested benefits, and that it would provide every individual and every household with a solid financial floor on which they could build, would be to take the first steps towards a tax and benefits system appropriate to the flexible labour market and household structures of the twenty-first century. The reduction in the number of means-tested benefits claims would deliver an administrative saving greater than the administrative cost of Basic Incomes, which would be simpler to administer than Child Benefit.

The Basic Income debate has evolved rapidly during the past five years or so, from a discussion of Basic Income's advantages and disadvantages, to exploration of its feasibility, and more recently to ideas about implementation. As the debate continues to evolve, the feasibility and possible consequences of illustrative schemes will be increasingly important (Torry, 2018a).

Basic Income and Basic Income Schemes

On the 23 November 2017, *Social Europe* published an article by Bo Rothstein entitled 'UBI: A bad idea for the welfare state' (Rothstein, 2018). It sets out from a definition of 'Unconditional Universal Basic Income' (UUBI) as 'every citizen will be entitled to a basic income that frees them from the necessity of having a paid job'; and it adds the details that the level of UBI would be £800 per month, and that 'all means-tested programs for those who cannot support themselves through paid work can be abolished'.

Rothstein correctly identifies as an advantage of such a reform that it 'would force employers to create more acceptable and less demeaning types of work because people would not take jobs they consider unsatisfactory. Releasing people from the compulsion to have a paid job would, according to the proponents, also mean strengthening the voluntary/civil society sector and cultural life'. He equally correctly identifies as disadvantages that it 'would be unsustainably expensive and would thereby jeopardise the state's ability to maintain quality in public services such as healthcare, education and care of the elderly', that it would lose political legitimacy, and that 'people who can work [would] choose not to work'.

Rothstein's verdict is that 'the basic error with the idea of unconditional basic income is its unconditionality', because that threatens 'the principle of reciprocity [...] Breaking with this principle is most likely to lead to the dismantling of the type of broad-based social solidarity that built [the] welfare state'.

No. The main problem with the Basic Income that Rothstein discusses in his article is not its unconditionality: it is the detail and the flawed definition.

The definition of a Basic Income offered by BIEN (the Basic Income Earth Network) is this: 'A Basic Income is a periodic cash payment unconditionally delivered to all on an individual basis, without means-test or work requirement' (Basic Income Earth Network, 2022); and the definition offered by the UK's Citizen's Basic Income Trust is 'an unconditional and non-withdrawable income paid to every individual as a right of citizenship' (Citizen's Basic Income Trust, 2022). The consensus—and, after all, consensus is what definitions are about—is that a Basic Income is an unconditional income paid to every individual. The definition implies neither a particular amount, nor that means-tested benefits would be abolished, and it does not imply that the Basic Income would free people from paid employment.

So instead of a Basic Income scheme that pays £800 per month to every individual, and that abolishes means-tested benefits, let us instead pay £264 per month to every individual (with different amounts for children, young adults, and elderly people), and let us leave means-tested benefits in place and recalculate them on the basis that household members now receive Basic Incomes. Instead of leaving undefined the funding method for a UK-based Basic Income, as Rothstein does, let us choose to fund it by abolishing the Income Tax Personal Allowance and the National Insurance Contribution (NIC) Primary Earnings Threshold (so that Income Tax and NICs are paid on all earned income), let us apply a flat rate NIC of 12% to all earned income (rather than the current two-tier 12% and 2% structure), and let us increase Income Tax rates by just 3 percentage points.

According to research published by the Institute for Social and Economic Research at the University of Essex (Torry, 2019, 2020, 2021), the effects of such a Basic Income scheme would be interestingly different from the effects of Rothstein's. Far from being 'unsustainably expensive', it would require no additional public expenditure, and so would not affect expenditure on public services. Rothstein cannot show that his scheme would not impose significant losses on low-income households. This alternative scheme would not impose significant losses on these households, it would impose few losses on households in general, and it would still take a lot of households off some of our existing means-tested benefits. Rothstein cannot tell us how his scheme would redistribute disposable income, or how it would affect poverty or inequality indices. This alternative scheme would redistribute from rich to poor, and it would reduce every poverty index and significantly reduce inequality. Rothstein tells us that his scheme would reduce the incentive to seek employment. This alternative scheme would reduce some important marginal deduction rates (the rate at which additional earned income is reduced by taxation and the withdrawal of means-tested benefits) and it would therefore incentivise employment, self-employment, and new small businesses. Far from compromising the reciprocity on which our society is built, it would enhance it. And this alternative scheme would not lose the advantages that Rothstein mentions. Because everyone would have a secure financial platform on which to build, this Basic Income, like Rothstein's, would give workers greater ability to seek the employment or self-employment that they wanted, and would therefore encourage employers to supply better jobs in order to attract workers; and because this Basic Income would give to each household more choice over its employment pattern, it would still encourage both caring and community activity.

Distinctions matter. A Basic Income is always an unconditional income paid to every individual, without means test and without work test. A Basic Income scheme specifies the rate at which the Basic Income would be paid for each age group, and the funding mechanism. There are many possible Basic Income schemes. As Rothstein correctly suggests, his chosen scheme would have many disadvantages. As I have shown, an alternative scheme might exhibit none of those disadvantages, and might offer many additional advantages.

The increasingly mainstream UBI debate is important. It is therefore vital that the debate should be rational. Rationality requires attention to definitions and details. So definitions and details matter (Torry, 2018b).

Speenhamland, Automation, and Basic Income

In the final edition of Renewal for 2017 (volume 25, issue 3–4), Frederick Pitts, Lorena Lombardozzi and Neil Warner suggest that the experience of the Speenhamland reforms of 1795 were 'an experiment in a kind of basic income' (Pitts et al., 2017: 150). It was not. It was an extension of poor relief to the working poor. The supplements paid out of the rates guaranteed a net income. They were definitely not a 'Basic Income'. The difference is crucial. A guaranteed minimum income is a minimum income level below which a household's income is not allowed to fall, and the payment made is designed to bring a household's net income up to the specified level. The modern equivalents are Working Tax Credits and so-called Universal Credit. In Speenhamland the supplement paid out was designed to fill the gap between the worker's earnings and a specified minimum income that was related to the size of the family and to the price of bread. The supplement was a means-tested benefit.

A Basic Income is entirely different. It is an equal payment to every individual of the same age. The difference is clear. The Speenhamland payments fell if earnings rose, and rose if earnings fell. A Basic Income remains the same whatever the individual's earnings. This means that the effects are very different. The Speenhamland supplement functioned as a dynamic subsidy. It rose if wages fell, so employers who cut wages knew that the supplement would make up for the wage cut. A Basic Income would be a static subsidy: that is, it would not rise if wages fell, so both employers and employees would know that if wages fell then employees' families would be worse off. Both collective bargaining and the National Living Wage would be even more important than they are now, and the effort to maintain them would intensify.

Another difference relates to employment incentive. Within the communities that were paying the Speenhamland supplement, for a large family with a single low-wage breadwinner there was no financial advantage to seeking increased wages, or to seek a better-paying job, or to seeking additional skills. Increased wages would mean a lower supplement. But because a Basic Income would never change, anyone currently on means-tested benefits whose Basic Income enabled them to come off them would immediately experience increased incentives to seek higher wages, or to seek additional skills in order to obtain a better-paying job. No longer would an increase in wages result in a loss of benefits, so an increase in earned income would result in a far greater increase in net income (Torry, 2017).

Pitts, Lombardozzi and Warner are quite right to make a variety of criticisms of the Speenhamland approach. Means-tested in-work benefits such as the Speenhamland supplements, Working Tax Credits, and Universal Credit, do 'keep the cost of labour competitive with machines so that employers keep workers hanging on for longer than otherwise would be the case' (Pitts et al., 2017: 149); they do restrict 'the freedom of workers to sell their capacity to labour to employers as equal parties to a contract' (Pitts et al., 2017: 149); and they do 'render impossible the commodification of labour in a world still organised on the basis of the commodification of everything else' (Pitts et al., 2017: 150). A Basic Income, on the other hand, would never compromise 'the bargaining power of labour', and so would not contribute to 'falling or stagnating wages and deteriorating employment prospects' (Pitts et al., 2017: 151). Indeed, by providing a secure financial platform on which individuals and households could build, a Basic Income would increase workers' ability to start their own businesses, to turn down badly paid jobs, and to argue for wage increases.

The Basic Income enthusiasts that Pitts, Lomardozzi, and Warner have in their sights are those who suggest that a Basic Income would be a useful response to an automated economy in which fewer human workers would be required. It needs to be said that we cannot know the future of the employment market. Previous periods of technological change have seen new jobs created at the same time as existing jobs have been destroyed. It is the fact that we cannot know the future shape of the employment market that is the argument for Basic Income. The benefits system that we are running in the UK is still a combination of the Poor Law and Speenhamland—that is, means-tested benefits both in and out of work. It is a system designed for a 1940s employment market characterised by long-term full-time jobs. This is even more true of Universal Credit. But the world has changed, and it will continue to change in ways that we cannot now predict. What we shall need is an income maintenance strategy that makes no assumptions about the future structure of the employment market, that incentivises employment, that provides as much freedom as possible for workers to choose how to deploy their labour, and that does not depress wages. Today's benefits system is precisely what is not required. A Basic Income might be the best option.

The debate about Basic Income is important, so it needs to be rational. Rational debate requires careful definition and attention to detail. A Basic Income is an unconditional and nonwithdrawable income paid to each individual. The Speenhamland supplements were very different. What the current debate requires is not erroneous comparisons but high-quality research and careful logic (Torry, 2018c).

Acknowledgements The first part of this chapter was first published as a post on the 'Social Europe' website, https://socialeurope.eu/, on 10 April 2017, and subsequently as Malcolm Torry (2018), 'Citizen's Income: Both feasible and useful', in Philippe Van Parijs (ed.), *Basic Income and the Left: A European debate*, London: Social Europe Ltd., pp. 97–102. Social Europe's permission to republish the article is gratefully acknowledged.

The second part of the chapter was first published as a post on the 'Social Europe' website, https://socialeurope.eu/, on 11 December 2017, and subsequently as Malcolm Torry (2018), 'What is an Unconditional Basic Income? A response to Rothstein', in Philippe Van Parijs (ed.), *Basic Income and the Left: A European debate*, London: Social Europe Ltd., pp. 110–115. Social Europe's permission to republish the article is gratefully acknowledged.

The third part of this chapter was first published as Malcolm Torry (2018), 'Speenhamland, automation, and Basic Income: A response', in *Renewal*, volume 26, no. 1, pp. 32–35. The editor's permission to republish the article is gratefully acknowledged.

Much of the material in the articles were presented at the BIEN Congress in Tampere in 2018. The congress paper is published as Chapter 4 in this volume.

References

Basic Income Earth Network. (2022). *Basic Income*. Retrieved March 26, 2022, from https://basicincome.org/

Citizen's Basic Income Trust. (2022). *Citizen's Basic Income*. Retrieved March 26, 2022, from https://citizensincome.org/

Pitts, F. H., Lomardozzi, L., & Warner, N. (2017). Speenhamland, automation and the basic income: A warning from history? *Renewal, 25*(3–4), 145–155.

Rothstein, B. (2018). UBI: A bad idea for the welfare state. In P. Van Parijs (Ed.), *Basic Income and the left: A European debate* (pp. 102–109). Social Europe Ltd.

Torry, M. (2017). *A variety of indicators evaluated for two implementation methods for a Citizen's Basic Income* (Euromod working paper EM12/17). Institute for Social and Economic Research, University of Essex. Retrieved March 26, 2022, from https://www.euromod.ac.uk/sites/default/files/working-papers/em12-17.pdf

Torry, M. (2018a). Citizen's income: Both feasible and useful. In P. Van Parijs (Ed.), *Basic Income and the left: A European debate* (pp. 97–102). Social Europe Ltd.

Torry, M. (2018b). What is an unconditional Basic Income? A response to Rothstein. In P. Van Parijs (Ed.), *Basic Income and the left: A European debate* (pp. 110–115). Social Europe Ltd.

Torry, M. (2018c). Speenhamland, automation, and Basic Income: A response. *Renewal, 26*(1), 32–35.

Torry, M. (2019). *Static microsimulation research on Citizen's Basic Income for the UK: A personal summary and further reflections* (EUROMOD Working Paper EM13/19). Institute for Social and Economic Research, University of Essex. Retrieved March 26, 2022, from https://www.euromod.ac.uk/sites/default/files/working-papers/em13-19.pdf

Torry, M. (2020). *Evaluation of a Recovery Basic Income, and of a sustainable revenue neutral Citizen's Basic Income, with an appendix relating to different Universal credit roll-out scenarios* (Institute for Social and Economic Research Working Paper EM7/20). Institute for Social and Economic Research, University of Essex. Retrieved March 26, 2022, from https://www.iser.essex.ac.uk/research/publications/working-papers/euromod/em7-20.pdf

Torry, M. (2021). *Three income maintenance options for 2021.* Centre for Microsimulation and Policy Analysis report. Institute for Social and Economic Research, University of Essex. Retrieved March 26, 2022, from https://www.microsimulation.ac.uk/publications/publication-526555/

CHAPTER 10

Testing Different Routes to a Basic Income Scheme

Introduction

The global debate about Basic Income has experienced a number of changes. Perhaps the most noticeable is the debate's transition from fringe to mainstream. Thirty years ago Basic Income was an idea on the fringe of social policy debate. Now it is at the heart of it. This change has been accompanied by a change in the debate's extent. Whereas thirty years ago it was a debate among a handful of academics and interested others, it now involves politicians, journalists, think tanks, university departments, and activists. Thirty years ago it was possible to count the number of people involved in the debate, and to keep up with the books, papers, and articles being written on the subject. Now it is not. A further change relates to the debate's depth. Thirty years ago the debate was purely about the desirability of Basic Income. Basic Income's desirability was evaluated mainly in three particular ways: on the basis of a narrow range of ideological commitments—mainly 'real freedom for all' and 'equality'; as a response to increasing automation; and as a solution to poverty and unemployment traps. Now Basic Income's desirability is discussed on the basis of multiple ideological commitments, across the whole of the Left/Right spectrum and beyond it; in connection with a more diverse debate about the possible futures of employment; and in relation to broad

M. Torry, *Basic Income—What, Why, and How?*, Exploring the Basic Income Guarantee,
https://doi.org/10.1007/978-3-031-14248-2_10

swathes of the social policy field: ecology, housing policy, employment, social cohesion, and so on. As the debate has evolved, no elements have disappeared from it. The evolution has been one of constant reformulation and addition, resulting in the highly complex global debate that we experience today.

As well as the increasing globalisation of the debate, the major changes during the past ten years have been its extension from the question of desirability to questions about feasibility and implementation: the latter change being particularly noticeable in the UK. This chapter discusses a set of feasibility tests, and applies them to a number of ways for implementing Basic Income schemes and pilot projects. What the schemes and pilot projects might look like in the UK is discussed, and an indication is given as to how the chapter's findings might be applied in Australia. For the purpose of clarity: Basic Income, Citizen's Income, Universal Basic Income, and Citizen's Basic Income all mean the same thing: an unconditional and nonwithdrawable income for every legally resident individual. A 'Basic Income scheme' states the levels of Basic Income for each age group, specifies the funding method, and lists any changes to existing tax and benefits arrangements. There are an infinite number of possible schemes, and different schemes would have different effects.

Financial Feasibility

The question of feasibility has always been a feature of the debate in the UK, as evidenced by some of the literature from the late 1980s and early 1990s (Brittan & Webb, 1990; Parker, 1989): but now that the reasons for establishing a Basic Income are widely understood—even if they are rejected—the question of feasibility has become increasingly important, and objections are now more likely to be framed as arguments for infeasibility than as arguments for undesirability.

A prominent and unique aspect of the Basic Income debate in the UK has been the amount of effort that has been put into researching the question of financial feasibility. Two methods have been employed. For schemes that abolish means-tested benefits, the national accounts and census data can be employed to calculate the net cost of a Basic Income scheme (Citizen's Income Trust, 2007; Miller, 2017; Painter & Thoung, 2015). Unfortunately, this method cannot evaluate the net cost of schemes that retain and recalculate means-tested benefits, nor can it discover how many low-income households might suffer losses at the point of implementation. It has therefore become essential to employ microsimulation: computer programmes into which are coded the regulations of a country's tax and benefits systems, and through which are passed data from the Family Resources Survey, which regularly surveys the financial details of a 0.1% sample of the UK's population. Running the microsimulation programme can generate a variety of statistics, such as poverty and inequality indices, household disposable incomes, and the numbers of households on means-tested benefits. The software can then be reprogrammed to represent changed tax and benefits systems—for instance, by adding Basic Incomes of different amounts for different age groups, changing Income Tax rates and personal allowances, and taking those changes into account when means-tested benefits are recalculated—and the programme can then be run again. The outputs for the Basic Income scheme can then be compared with those for the current tax and benefits system. Martinelli and Reed each choose a variety of Basic Income schemes and test for their effects (Martinelli, 2017a, 2017b, 2017c; Reed & Lansley, 2016). This author takes a different approach. He first sets some initial feasibility criteria (revenue neutrality, reductions in poverty and inequality, Income Tax rates to rise by no more than 3 percentage points, minimal losses for low-income households, only manageable losses for any household, and significant numbers of households leaving means-tested benefits) and then, by changing in turn the different parameters of the Basic Income scheme, tests to see whether there is a scheme that fits the criteria. There is (Torry, 2015, 2016c, 2016d, 2017, 2018, 2019, 2020, 2021).

Feasibility Tests

The feasibility tests that I shall be applying in this chapter are as follows (De Wispelaere & Noguera, 2012; De Wispelaere & Stirton, 2011, 2012; Torry, 2016a):

Financial : There are two kinds of financial feasibility, not just one:

(a) *Fiscal feasibility*: Would it be possible to finance a Basic Income? In today's financial climate it is likely that Basic Incomes will only be thought to be financially feasible if they are funded by making adjustments to the current tax and benefits systems.

(b) *Household financial feasibility*: Would implementation impose significant financial losses on any households or individuals? If low-income households would suffer losses on the implementation of a Basic Income scheme, of if any households would suffer significant losses, then the scheme would not be thought financially feasible.

Psychological: Is the idea readily understood, and understood to be beneficial? Satisfying this feasibility test will never be easy. Most countries' populations, if not all, will contain large numbers of people, and probably majorities, who believe that giving people money without attaching conditions would mean that they would no longer seek employment, and that it would be foolish to give money to the rich who don't need it. There are of course good reasons for doing both of those things—unconditional benefits would not contribute to high marginal deduction rates in the way that means-tested benefits do; and it is efficient and non-stigmatising to give money to everyone and then to tax the rich. It is always possible for individuals to experience paradigm shifts: but population paradigm shift can be a slow business. For good reasons, legislators do not stray too far from majority public opinion: so the psychological feasibility test will probably need to be passed before political and policy process feasibility tests can be attempted.

Behavioural: Would a Basic Income deliver the benefits promised for it? Short-term Basic Income pilot projects and other experiments can give some indication as to how employment market activity would be affected by a permanent Basic Income (Gilbert et al., 2018), but until a permanent Basic Income is implemented, we cannot test properly for behavioural feasibility. The test is listed here because if it is not passed post-implementation then the Basic Income will not last.

Administrative: This is another feasibility test in two parts:

(a) Would it be possible to administer a Basic Income? This is the easiest feasibility test to pass. The answer is Yes.
(b) Would it be possible to manage the transition? This part of the administrative feasibility test would be more challenging: not because there is anything complicated about a Basic Income, but because most countries' current tax and benefits systems are complex. Because it is likely that Basic Incomes would initially need to be funded out of current tax and benefits systems, those systems

would need to be altered as Basic Incomes were implemented. That will never be easy.

Political: Would the idea cohere with existing political ideologies? Because every country's political parties are individual to that country, no generalisations are possible. Only a detailed study of governments' and political parties' ideological commitments and current concerns, and of statements made by members of those governments and parties, will determine whether this test can be passed.

Policy process: Would the policy process be able to process the idea to implementation? This too is a highly country-specific test. Every country's policy process is different, and all of them are complex, being made up of numerous institutions and individuals connected by complex networks of relationships. Navigating the best ideas through the policy process can prove highly problematic, and navigating contested ideas through it can be almost impossible.

But having said all of that: policy accidents can occur, where new policies are implemented without passing all of the tests listed, and sometimes without passing any of them (Torry, 2016a: 238–239)—although of course such policy accidents can be short-lived if the tests are not passed subsequent to implementation.

I shall now outline five routes to the implementation of Basic Income, and I shall then ask whether they might be able to pass the feasibility tests.

Five Routes to Implementation

Different possibilities for Basic Income schemes might be available in the short, the medium, and the longer term. For instance: while it might be possible in the longer term to fund a sizeable Basic Income from a sovereign wealth fund, financial transaction taxes, carbon taxes, and a land value tax, in the short to medium term that would not be administratively, financially, or politically feasible; whereas to implement a small Basic Income funded by rearranging the current tax and benefits system might be entirely feasible within a single parliamentary term. I here list five possible ways of implementing a Basic Income scheme in today's context, recognising that further steps might be possible in the longer term (Torry, 2016b).

(a) *Replacement*: A Basic Income for everyone legally resident in a country, implemented all in one go, with at the same time the abolition of the existing social security system, possibly during the course of a single parliamentary term. In the UK, this would mean the abolition of means-tested benefits, and possibly of social insurance (National Insurance) benefits as well: although the differences between housing costs in different parts of the country would probably require the retention of a means-tested Housing Benefit.
(b) *Alongside*: A Basic Income for everyone legally resident, implemented all in one go, with the existing social security system retained. In the UK, this would mean the retention of the entire means-tested and National Insurance benefits systems, with households' means-tested benefits being recalculated on the basis that household members would be receiving Basic Incomes, and that changes to the tax system would have altered the relationship between gross and net earnings.
(c) *Single age group*: A Basic Income for everyone in a particular age group, followed by other age groups. In the UK, the process could be as follows: enhancing the existing universal Child Benefit (this is still unconditional, although additional Income Tax now has to be paid by high earners living in households that receive Child Benefit); turning the new Single Tier State Pension into a genuine Citizen's Pension, or Basic Income for elderly people (that is, making legal residence rather than the National Insurance Contribution record the criterion for receipt); paying a Basic Income to young adults aged 16–18, or perhaps 18–21; paying a Basic Income to the pre-retired (possibly after a period of inviting volunteers from this age group); and then paying a Basic Income for working age adults.
(d) *Pilot project*: A Basic Income for a representative sample of a country's population, followed by an extension to the whole population. In the UK, a relatively isolated community would be chosen, and a Basic Income scheme (including associated changes to the current tax and benefits systems) would be implemented. The pilot would then be evaluated, preferably against a control community.
(e) *Single age group pilot project*: A Basic Income for a representative sample of one age group, followed by an extension to the whole of the age group, and then to other age groups. In the UK, we might choose 16 to 18-year-olds, or 18 to 21-year-olds, as their

relationships with the current tax and benefits systems tend to be simpler than for older age groups.

Testing the Five Routes to Implementation

(a) A Basic Income for Everyone Legally Resident in a Country, Implemented all in One Go, with at the Same Time the Abolition of the Existing Social Security System

The Basic Income for working age adults would need to be set high enough to replace the main out of work benefits, otherwise far too many low-income households would automatically lose disposable income at the point of implementation; and such a scheme would require substantial increases in Income Tax rates. In a UK context, this kind of scheme would impose substantial losses on a lot of low-income households, and on far too many other households as well (Torry, 2015). If additional funds were to be available from outside the tax and benefits systems, then the scheme could pass all of the feasibility tests except for the fiscal feasibility test: so, with additional funds, and a redrafted fiscal feasibility test to permit a constant injection of additional funding, this route to implementation could be feasible.

Even if additional funding could be found, psychological feasibility would be difficult to secure, particularly among higher earners experiencing sizeable increases in tax rates. Because the psychological feasibility test would be difficult to pass, it would also be difficult to get this implementation route through the political and policy process feasibility tests (Torry, 2016b: 15).

(b) A Basic Income for Everyone Legally Resident, Implemented All in One Go, with the Existing Social Security System Retained

This scheme could be funded from within the current tax and benefits system, it would not generate losses of any significance for low-income households, and it would generate few losses for other households (Torry, 2018, 2019, 2020, 2021), so this scheme could pass the fiscal and household financial feasibility tests. Because the current benefits system would not need to be changed, the administration of the transition would be fairly simple. Because each household on means-tested benefits would have their benefit claim reduced by the Basic Incomes coming into the household, many households would come off means-tested benefits, and many more would be brought closer to coming off them. Every household enabled by their Basic Incomes to escape from means-testing would generate administrative simplification, and because the Basic Income itself would be very simple to administer, the overall effect would be a reduction in administrative complexity.

(c) A Basic Income for Everyone in a Particular Age Group, Followed by Other Age Groups

Feasibility would be highly country-specific, and would depend on the age group. For instance, in the UK context, and possibly elsewhere, an unconditional income for children would be more acceptable than one for working-age adults: so in the UK a start could be made by enhancing the current Child Benefit, and possibly equalising the amounts paid for the first and subsequent children. Where there is not a Citizen's Pension, that could be a priority: so in the UK the new Single Tier State Pension could be turned into a Citizen's Pension. One way of choosing the age group to which the first Basic Incomes would be paid would be to ask which age groups face the greatest challenges in relation to their income strategies. In the UK that might be young adults aged 18 to 21, and the pre-retired, from the late 50s to state pension age.

With a single age group, and particularly one with less complicated relationships with the current tax and benefits systems, neither of the financial feasibility tests would be difficult to pass. By choosing a 'more deserving' age group, and particularly one for which everyone recognises that the ways in which they receive subsistence incomes are far from ideal, a psychological feasibility test should not be too difficult to pass: so political and policy process feasibilities could follow. A Basic Income for every young person between their eighteenth and twenty-second birthdays would be popular with them and with their parents. With a limited age range, behavioural feasibility would be easy to test after implementation, and could help to build the psychological feasibility required for implementation for the next age group.

(d) A Pilot Project: A Basic Income for a Representative Sample of the Population in an Isolated Community

In a developing country, every member of an entire community or communities can be given a small unconditional income without adjustments having to be made to existing tax or benefits systems, and at relatively little cost. Communities can often be sufficiently isolated and stable to enable the same people to remain in the pilot from beginning to end. Such pilot projects have been carried out in Namibia and India, and they have delivered significant results in relation to health, education, democracy, and economic activity, particularly among households with the lowest original disposable incomes (Basic Income Grant Coalition, Namibia, 2009: 72–73; Davala et al., 2014; Haarmann & Haarmann, 2007; Torry, 2009). However, in both cases, there was one sense in which they were not in fact genuine pilot projects. The behavioural effects of a permanent Basic Income scheme would be different from the effects of a scheme established for only two years, particularly in relation to labour market and other economic activity. Both the Namibian and Indian projects were for two years or less. The positive changes that the two projects delivered in terms of economic activity during that short timespan suggest that a permanent scheme would generate even more additional economic activity: but only the establishment of permanent Basic Incomes would be able to prove that.

The construction of pilot projects for Basic Income schemes will always pose more problems in countries with existing complex tax and benefits systems. Any permanent Basic Income established in a more developed country would probably need to be largely funded by making adjustments to existing systems: so a genuine pilot project would need to take a representative sample of the population and change their tax rates, tax allowances, and means-tested benefits, in the same ways in which they would be changed if there were a nationwide Basic Income. This would absorb much government time and energy, and there would be understandable resistance to attempting it. Finding sufficiently isolated and stable communities would also be problematic. If the community was not sufficiently isolated then people would come and go, so decisions would be required as to whether people who left the community should cease to be part of the experiment, and whether people who moved in would become part of it. Cross-border commuting would also be problematic if employers collect income tax on behalf of the government, because someone living in pilot project town A and working in town B would need their employer to relate to the tax and benefits systems according to the rules of the pilot project, and vice versa, meaning that many employers would need to operate two parallel tax collecting systems. A community that was sufficiently isolated to avoid this problem would be unlikely to be representative of the country as a whole.

The experiment that took place in Finland for two years from January 2017 to December 2018 has produced some useful results in relation to employment market behaviour, and those results might inform our understanding of the likely employment market effects of a Basic Income. However, the experiment was of limited duration, and only involved a limited number of randomly selected currently unemployed individuals (Kangas et al., 2020), and not a representative sample of the population: so whether it can be called a Basic Income pilot project is open to question. A randomised selection of an entire population, rather than of unemployed individuals, might be an option for a future pilot project in a developed country, but as with the saturation site option discussed above, adjusting existing tax and benefits systems just for the members of the sample would be a very complicated process.

While a pilot project might theoretically pass the feasibility tests, if it was not in fact a pilot project then it would not represent a Basic Income's effects.

(e) A Single Age Group Pilot Project

This might be less of a problem. Take the four-year cohort of young adults aged 18–21, that is, between their eighteenth and twenty-second birthdays. The first thing to say is that the entire population of this age group could itself be regarded as a pilot project if a genuine Basic Income were to be given to everyone of the appropriate age. This age group generally has quite simple relationships with current tax and benefits systems, so running a tax system just for them would not be difficult if only minor changes were made. For instance, in the UK, all that would be required if we wished to remove the Income Tax Personal Allowance for everyone of the appropriate age would be for employers to apply the basic rate (BR) tax code. If the Basic Income were to be set at or just below the level of out-of-work means-tested benefits, then the majority of current claimants would no longer be claimants. And an ideal aspect of this particular starting point is that it would be easy to extend the Basic

Income to subsequent age cohorts simply by allowing existing participants to retain their Basic Incomes and new tax arrangements beyond their twenty-second birthdays.

An important outcome of a pilot project of this nature would be an understanding of the effect of unconditional incomes on the behaviour of young adults. The Mincome experiment in Dauphin, Canada, was not a Basic Income pilot project, but the income mechanism tested exhibited similarities to a Basic Income. Hence, the increase in educational engagement seen in that experiment might also be seen in a Basic Income pilot project for that age group (Forget, 2012). Furthermore, students' willingness to accrue significant debt in order to obtain an education suggests that an unconditional income would achieve increased engagement in education. The pilot project would be able to test these reasonable assumptions.

If a test of this pilot project were to be required then that would not be difficult to organise. It would be relatively easy to pay a Basic Income, and to make other adjustments, for every one of the appropriate age living in a particular town. If the town were as representative as possible of the nationwide age cohort, then the only respect in which the pilot project would not be a genuine pilot project would be that it would be time-limited. Given the simplicity of the exercise, the project could be run for a number of years, with a new single-year cohort joining, and a single age cohort automatically leaving the project every year as new participants reached their eighteenth birthdays and existing participants reached their twenty-second. Granted, nobody would be in the pilot project for more than four years: but there might soon be pressure to extend the project to higher age groups, and then to other communities, so the pilot project could soon become a nationwide Basic Income for an increasing age range.

This plan for a pilot project of a pilot project for an age group is financially very feasible; it would generate almost no losses at the point of implementation; it could be psychologically feasible—because the young adults and their parents and grandparents would approve; it could therefore be politically feasible; it would not be difficult to get the idea through the policy process; and behavioural feasibility could easily be tested after implementation.

Conclusion

We might summarise the feasibilities relating to the different implementation routes as in Table 10.1.

We can see that implementing a Basic Income for a single age group could be entirely feasible, and at least as feasible as carrying out a pilot project. This suggests that the easiest way to establish a Basic Income would be to establish a Basic Income for a single age group, and in the UK the four-year cohort between the eighteenth and twenty-second birthdays would be a fairly obvious candidate. An important advantage of this particular age group is that it would be easy to extend their Basic Incomes beyond their twenty-second birthdays, thus rolling out a Basic Income for the entire population.

As we have recognised, all of the implementation options that we have discussed relate to Basic Income schemes designed to be implemented in the current context. A further question relates to how those initial first steps might then be followed by developments of the scheme. The first two options represent complete schemes for entire populations, and we can see how, following initial implementation, changes might be made: in

Table 10.1 The feasibilities of five different Basic Income implementation routes

Implementation route *Feasibility type*	*Replacement*	*Alongside*	*Single age group*	*Pilot project*	*Single age group pilot project*
Financial: (a) Fiscal	√	√	√	√	√
Financial: (b) Household financial	x	√	√	√	√
Psychological	?	?	√	√	√
Behavioural	?	√	√	√	√
Administrative: (a) scheme	√	√	√	√	√
Administrative: (b) transition	?	√	√	√	√
Political	x	?	√	√	√
Policy process	x	?	√	?	√

Source Table constructed by the author

relation to route (a) we would need to see changes towards new protections for households suffering losses at the point of implementation, and in relation to route (b) we might want to see changes towards higher levels of Basic Income. Route (c) envisages the addition of further age groups following implementation for a single age group; route (d) envisages subsequent roll-out to an entire population; and route (e) again envisages subsequent roll-out to the entire age group and then to the entire population.

The detail of this chapter is, as stated, specific to the United Kingdom, but much of the content would of course be equally relevant to other countries. The feasibility tests could be applied in any national or regional context, and even if the entire range of implementation methods discussed here might not be applicable, variations of them would be likely to be. The message that researchers and policymakers from any country would be able to take away from this chapter would be that, whatever their context, a careful study of all of the relevant feasibilities, and research on the feasibilities of a variety of different implementation methods, must be essential components of their country's ongoing debate about Basic Income.

Australia

In the case of Australia, we can say more than this, because the current Australian social security system is remarkably similar to the system in the UK. It is predominantly based on means-tested benefits, and it is complex, unfair, arbitrary, harmful, and no longer relevant (Watts, 2016: 75–81) in ways very similar to the complexity, unfairness, arbitrariness, harmfulness, and irrelevance of the UK's current system. This suggests not only that the implementation methods for a Basic Income scheme relevant to the UK might also be relevant to Australia, but also that their relative feasibilities might be similar when judged against the feasibility criteria discussed in this chapter.

And we can go further than this because the income tax system in Australia is similar to that of the UK. The presence of a sizeable Personal Allowance of A$18,200 per annum means that Australia would be able to fund a revenue-neutral initial Basic Income scheme in much the same way as the UK by reducing the Personal Allowance to zero and paying a Basic Income of the same value as the additional tax that the reduction of the Personal Allowance would represent.

The consequence of these similarities is that if an initial Basic Income scheme were to be successfully implemented in the UK, then Australia would be able to predict that a similar scheme could be successfully implemented there, and vice versa. The interesting question then becomes which country will get there first.

Acknowledgements This chapter began as a paper presented at the Basic Income Earth Network (BIEN) 2017 congress in Lisbon, Portugal. The paper was then revised and published as Torry, M. (2019). Testing different routes to a Basic Income scheme. *Social Alternatives*, 38(2), 47–53. Permission to republish the article is gratefully acknowledged.

References

Basic Income Grant Coalition, Namibia. (2009). *Making the difference: The BIG in Namibia: Basic Income Grant pilot project, assessment report*. Basic Income Grant Coalition, Namibia NGO Forum. Retrieved March 26, 2022, from www.bignam.org/Publications/BIG_Assessment_report_08b.pdf

Brittan, S., & Webb, S. (1990). *Beyond the welfare state: An examination of Basic Incomes in a market economy*. Aberdeen University Press.

Citizen's Income Trust. (2007). *Citizen's Income: A brief introduction*. Citizen's Income Trust.

Davala, S., Jhabvala, R., Mehta, S. K., & Standing, G. (2014). *Basic Income: A transformative policy for India*. Bloomsbury.

De Wispelaere, J., & Noguera, J. A. (2012). On the political feasibility of Universal Basic Income: An analytic framework. In R. Caputo (Ed.), *Basic Income Guarantee: International experiences and perspectives on the viability of Income Guarantee* (pp. 17–38). Palgrave Macmillan.

De Wispelaere, J., & Stirton, L. (2011). The administrative efficiency of Basic Income. *Policy and Politics, 39*(1), 115–132.

De Wispelaere, J., & Stirton, L. (2012). A disarmingly simple idea? Practical bottlenecks in implementing a Universal Basic Income. *International Social Security Review, 65*(2), 103–121.

Forget, E. L. (2012). Canada: The case for Basic Income. In M. C. Murray, & C. Pateman (Eds.), *Basic Income worldwide: Horizons of reform*. Palgrave Macmillan.

Gilbert, R., Murphy, N. A., Stepka, A., Barrett, M., & Worku, D. (2018). Would a Basic Income Guarantee reduce the motivation to work? An analysis of labor responses in 16 trial programs'. *Basic Income Studies, 13*(2), 1–12.

Haarmann, C., & Haarmann, D. (2007). From survival to decent employment: Basic income security in Namibia. *Basic Income Studies, 2*(1), 1–7.

Kangas, O., Jauhiainen, S., Simanainen, M., & Ylikännö, M. (2020). *Suomen Perustulokokeilun Arviointi*. Sosiaali-ja terveysministeriö. Retrieved March 26, 2022, from http://julkaisut.valtioneuvosto.fi/bitstream/handle/10024/162219/STM_2020_15_rap.pdf (In Finnish, with English summary).

Martinelli, L. (2017a). *The fiscal and distributional implications of alternative Universal Basic Income schemes in the UK*. Institute for Policy Research. Retrieved March 26, 2022, from https://www.bath.ac.uk/publications/the-fiscal-and-distributional-implications-of-alternative-universal-basic-income-schemes-in-the-uk/

Martinelli, L. (2017b). *Exploring the distributional and work incentive effects of plausible illustrative Basic Income schemes*. Institute for Policy Research. Retrieved March 26, 2022, from https://www.bath.ac.uk/publications/exploring-the-distributional-work-incentive-effects-of-plausible-illustrative-basic-income-schemes

Martinelli, L. (2017c). *Assessing the case for a Universal Basic Income in the UK*. Institute for Policy Research. Retrieved March 26, 2022, from www.bath.ac.uk/publications/assessing-the-case-for-a-universal-basic-income-in-the-uk

Miller, A. (2017). *A Basic Income handbook*. Luath Press.

Painter, A., & Thoung, C. (2015). *Report: Creative citizen, creative state: The principled and pragmatic case for a Universal Basic Income*. Royal Society of Arts. Retrieved March 26, 2022, from www.thersa.org/reports/basic-income.

Parker, H. (1989). *Instead of the dole: An enquiry into integration of the tax and benefits systems*. Routledge.

Reed, H., & Lansley, S. (2016). *Universal Basic Income: An idea whose time has come?* Compass.

Torry, M. (2009). Can unconditional cash transfers work? They can: A report of a seminar. *Citizen's Income Newsletter*, issue 2 for 2009. Citizen's Income Trust, pp. 1–3.

Torry, M. (2015). *Two feasible ways to implement a revenue neutral Citizen's Income scheme* (EUROMOD Working Paper EM6/15). Institute for Social and Economic Research, University of Essex. Retrieved March 26, 2022, from https://www.iser.essex.ac.uk/research/publications/working-papers/euromod/em6-15

Torry, M. (2016a). *The feasibility of Citizen's Income*. Palgrave Macmillan.

Torry, M. (2016b). *How might we implement a Citizen's Income?* Institute for Chartered Accountants of England and Wales.

Torry, M. (2016c). *An evaluation of a strictly revenue neutral Citizen's Income scheme* (EUROMOD Working Paper EM 5/16). Institute for Social and Economic Research, University of Essex. Retrieved March 26, 2022, from https://www.iser.essex.ac.uk/research/publications/working-papers/euromod/em5-16

Torry, M. (2016d). *Citizen's Income schemes: An amendment, and a pilot project: An addendum to EUROMOD Working Paper EM 5/16* (EUROMOD Working Paper EM 5/16). Institute for Social and Economic Research, University of Essex. Retrieved March 26, 2022, from https://www.iser.essex.ac.uk/research/publications/working-papers/euromod/em5-16a

Torry, M. (2017). *A variety of indicators evaluated for two implementation methods for a Citizen's Basic Income* (EUROMOD Working Paper EM 12/17). Institute for Social and Economic Research, University of Essex. Retrieved March 26, 2022, from https://www.iser.essex.ac.uk/research/publications/working-papers/euromod/em12-17

Torry, M. (2018). *An update, a correction, and an extension, of an evaluation of an illustrative Citizen's Basic Income scheme—Addendum to EUROMOD working paper EM12/17* (EUROMOD Working Paper EM 12/17a). Institute for Social and Economic Research, University of Essex. Retrieved March 26, 2022, from https://www.iser.essex.ac.uk/research/publications/working-papers/euromod/em12-17a

Torry, M. (2019). *Static microsimulation research on Citizen's Basic Income for the UK: A personal summary and further reflections* (EUROMOD Working Paper EM13/19). Institute for Social and Economic Research. Retrieved March 26, 2022, from https://www.euromod.ac.uk/sites/default/files/working-papers/em13-19.pdf

Torry, M. (2020). *Evaluation of a Recovery Basic Income, and of a sustainable revenue neutral Citizen's Basic Income, with an appendix relating to different Universal Credit roll-out scenarios* (Institute for Social and Economic Research Working Paper EM7/20). Institute for Social and Economic Research, University of Essex. Retrieved March 26, 2022, from https://www.iser.essex.ac.uk/research/publications/working-papers/euromod/em7-20.pdf

Torry, M. (2021). *Three income maintenance options for 2021.* Centre for Microsimulation and Policy Analysis report. Institute for Social and Economic Research, University of Essex. Retrieved March 26, 2022, from https://www.microsimulation.ac.uk/publications/publication-526555/

Watts, R. (2016). 'Running on Empty': Australia's neoliberal social security system, 1988–2015. In J. Mays, G. Marston, & J. Tomlinson (Eds.), *Basic Income in Australia and New Zealand: Perspectives from the neoliberal frontier* (pp. 69–91). Palgrave Macmillan.

CHAPTER 11

Minimum Income Standards in the Basic Income Debate

Introduction

The now lively debate about Basic Income—an unconditional income for every individual—is seeing the term 'Basic Income' used in a variety of ways. The diversity that this chapter will explore relates to the diversity between those usages that state or imply unconditional incomes paid at particular levels, and those that do not. The feasibilities of different levels will be discussed, and in particular the feasibility of paying Basic Incomes at levels defined by published Minimum Income Standard (MIS) reports.

Basic Income

A Basic Income (sometimes called a Citizen's Income, a Universal Basic Income, or a Citizen's Basic Income) is an unconditional income paid to every individual. Sometimes explanatory additions will be found. For instance, 'nonwithdrawable' might be added to the definition (Citizen's Basic Income Trust, 2022), in the sense that as earned income rises, the Basic Income is not withdrawn. 'Unconditional' already implies that: except that unfortunately 'unconditional' has been used by some participants in the debate to mean simply 'not work-tested' rather than 'without any conditions' (Young, 2018: 16, 22), which is why it is now wise to

M. Torry, *Basic Income—What, Why, and How?*, Exploring the Basic Income Guarantee, https://doi.org/10.1007/978-3-031-14248-2_11

add 'nonwithdrawable' to the definition. Further additions are sometimes made in order to clarify aspects of Basic Income that might or might not be assumed by readers: for instance, that the income is 'in cash' and 'periodic ... paid at regular intervals (for example, every month)', according to the Basic Income Earth Network (BIEN) (Basic Income Earth Network, 2022), the former addition ensuring that the Basic Income is understood as money and not services, and as cash and not vouchers with restricted spending options, and the latter distinguishing Basic Income from the annual and varying Alaskan Permanent Fund Dividend (Widerquist & Howard, 2012).

While it is of course true that any individual or organisation has every right to employ a phrase to mean exactly what they wish it to mean, for a debate to be rational there has to be some kind of agreement over definitions. The Citizen's Basic Income Trust (CBIT) was established in the UK in 1984 with the sole purpose of promoting research and debate on Basic Income (when it was founded it was called the Basic Income Research Group); and in 1986 BIEN was established with the same purpose (BIEN was originally the Basic Income European Network, but then, as the debate became more global, the organisation was renamed the Basic Income Earth Network in 2004). CBIT and BIEN are the longest-standing still-functioning organisations with the sole purpose of promoting research and debate on Basic Income, so if any definitions have the right to be regarded as definitive then there would be a strong case for CBIT's and BIEN's very similar definitions to be regarded as such. BIEN's definition reads as follows: 'A Basic Income is a periodic cash payment unconditionally delivered to all on an individual basis, without means-test or work requirement' (Basic Income Earth Network, 2022), and CBIT's says this: 'A Citizen's Basic Income is an unconditional, automatic and nonwithdrawable income for each individual as a right of citizenship' (Citizen's Basic Income Trust, 2022). Definitions matter. A recently aborted experiment in Ontario was described as a 'Basic Income' experiment, but the incomes paid were means-tested and household-based (Ontario, 2021), which is not how 'Basic Income' would normally be understood. Such eccentric use of terminology does the Basic Income debate no favours.

Having explained that a Basic Income is always unconditional, what also needs to be said is that one particular conditionality is both permitted and expected: that the level of the Basic Income will vary with the recipient's age. The reason for this particular condition being acceptable is that there are two kinds of conditionality: those that we can affect to some extent, and those that we cannot. Examples of the former kind of conditionality would be household structure, earned income, and employment status. An example of the latter would be someone's age. The practical administrative difference between the two kinds of conditionality is that once the computer knows someone's date of birth, the amount of someone's Basic Income can be seamlessly adjusted as they grow older, without any additional enquiry having to be made. Conversely, enquiry always has to be made to discover someone's household structure, employment status, or earned income—the kinds of enquiry that blight means-tested benefits. The different kinds of conditionality have different social and economic effects as well. For an income to be household-tested will interfere with people's most intimate relationships; for it to be income-tested will cause payments to be reduced as earned income rises, thus keeping the individual and their household in a poverty trap; and for it to be employment-status-tested will result in the kind of benefits sanctions that are now all too familiar. For an income to be simply age-tested would have none of these effects, but would without any enquiry provide incomes appropriate to someone's age—generally less for a child, more for a working age adult, and more than that for older people.

For the avoidance of doubt: in this chapter, 'Basic Income' will mean an unconditional and nonwithdrawable income paid regularly in cash to every legally resident individual. The income can vary with someone's age, but not in relation to any other contingency.

The Amount of the Payment

Organisations that facilitate debate on Basic Income within their own countries or regions can ask to affiliate to BIEN. BIEN is constituted as a Charitable Incorporated Organisation in the UK with individual members, and has no management or financial links with any of its affiliated organisations, so the relationship between BIEN and its affiliated organisations is simply one of mutual recognition. BIEN's affiliated organisations are expected to conform to BIEN's educational objectives, and there is also an expectation that they will conform to BIEN's definition of Basic Income: 'A Basic Income is a periodic cash payment unconditionally delivered to all on an individual basis, without means-test or work requirement' (Basic Income Earth Network, 2022). However, within that definition diversity is permitted. Research conducted by this author for BIEN, and discussed at the 2017 BIEN Congress in Lisbon, showed that there is just one issue over which the definitions published by different national affiliated organisations disagree: whether or not the definition of Basic Income should include the amount of the payment. Some affiliated organisations do not mention the issue, suggesting that the amount to be paid is not integral to the definition; some say that a democratic process would be used to decide the amount; one mentions a particular amount; and a number of others offer descriptions of the kinds of life that the Basic Income would be expected to fund, or the level at which the Basic Income would be paid—'subsistence', 'dignity', 'participation', 'poverty line'—but without specifying the relevant level of Basic Income (Torry, 2017b).

Minimum Income Standards

How should we decide what constitutes a 'poverty line', 'subsistence', 'participation', or a life characterised by 'dignity'?

The meanings of these different terms are different from each other, but there are connections. 'Poverty line' and 'subsistence' suggest a level of income and other services below which a household will find itself in poverty, or unable to subsist. This could either mean insufficient to survive physically, or it could mean what a society might mean when it thinks about poverty. 'Participation' and a life characterised by 'dignity' suggest something more complex, and look as if they might require resources in addition to those required for subsistence: but once we begin to discuss how these levels of income and services are to be discovered, we find that the different terms can end up meaning much the same thing.

In the UK, the 'Breadline Britain' approach, which today includes the process employed to set the Minimum Income Standards researched by Loughborough University and published by the Joseph Rowntree Foundation, is to ask a representative sample of a population what resources they think are required to enable someone to live a minimally decent life (Davis et al., 2018; Lansley & Mack, 1983, 2015). A second approach is that of John Rawls, who proposes a level of income that 'together with the whole family of social policies, maximises the life prospects of the least advantaged over time' (Rawls, 2001: 129–130; cf. Barrientos, 2016: 154–156). A third approach is to start from the concept of 'human need', with 'need' defined in a rather normative fashion Maslow, 1943: 376–382; Townsend, 1979: 32–34). A fourth option is Amartya

Sen's 'capabilities' approach, which asks about the resources required to enable someone to exercise capabilities (Alkire, 2007: 91; Reader, 2006). The last three approaches suggest that human need is in some way normative, whereas once resources have reached the level of those required for bare survival, need is to a large extent socially constructed (Dean, 2010: 46–47). This means that all of these approaches approximate the level of resources required for subsistence and for the avoidance of poverty to those required for participation in society and a life of dignity. This in turn means that we can treat the 'Breadline Britain' method—that is, the construction of 'Minimum Income Standards' via surveys of representative samples of a population—as a proxy for the other approaches.

Basic Income, and Basic Income Schemes

A 'Basic Income' is always an unconditional and nonwithdrawable income for every individual. A 'Basic Income scheme' states the levels of Basic Income for each age group, and also specifies the funding method, and any changes to existing tax and benefits arrangements. There is an infinite number of possible schemes, and different schemes would have different effects. For instance, if in the UK a small Basic Income were to be funded by increasing Income Tax rates at the lower end of the earnings range, and at the same time existing means-tested benefits were to be abolished, then low-income households could suffer losses at the point of implementation, and poverty and inequality could both increase: whereas if means-tested benefits were retained and recalculated when the Basic Income was implemented, and the scheme was funded by increasing Income Tax rates higher up the earnings range, then low-income households could avoid losses at the point of implementation, and poverty and inequality could both be reduced (Torry, 2015). Because the tax and benefits systems of different countries are different, similar schemes in different countries could have different effects: but it will always be generally true that different schemes in the same country would have different effects, and sometimes very different effects.

An Adequate Basic Income, or an Adequate Basic Income Scheme?

The question then arises: Do we need an adequate Basic Income, or an adequate Basic Income *scheme*? In relation to Minimum Income Standards—for instance, those for the UK published by the Joseph Rowntree Foundation—are we asking for the Basic Income to be paid to every individual at Minimum Income Standard levels, or are we asking that the Basic Income scheme as a whole should raise households to the levels of the Minimum Income Standards?

Before answering that question, we have to discuss the problem that Basic Incomes are by definition paid to individuals, whereas, because people living together in a household can live more cheaply than individuals living alone, Minimum Income Standards are always calculated on the basis of the household (Davis et al., 2018: 39). If we were to expect the Basic Income itself to enable every household to reach the relevant Minimum Income Standard, then a Basic Income would have to be paid to every adult at the level of the Minimum Income Standard for an individual adult living alone. This would of course provide a level of income above the Minimum Income Standards for households containing more than one adult, but to pay less than this would leave adults living alone with less than their relevant Minimum Income Standard. This means that if the Basic Income alone were to provide a level of income that would match Minimum Income Standards, then in 2018 the working age adult Basic Income level for the UK would have needed to be £304.71 per week. A lone parent with one young child would have required £395.68 (excluding child care costs), suggesting that the additional costs of the child would be £90.97 per week. This is higher than the cost of each child in a family with two children, which means that the standard Child Basic Income would have needed to be in the region of £90 per week if the lone parent with a child were to reach the relevant Minimum Income Standard (Davis et al., 2018: 39, 55–56). Because such figures have always looked entirely out of reach, it has been routinely assumed by those researching the levels at which Basic Incomes might be paid that Minimum Income Standard figures that exclude housing costs would need to be employed, rather than those that include them. This would mean a continuing need for a means-tested housing benefit of some kind, but this was always regarded as a small price to pay for Basic

Income levels that might be feasible (Torry, 2013: 268–270; 2018b: 197–198). On this basis, the Basic Income for a working age adult would have needed to be £213.59 per week (Davis et al., 2018: 39, 55–56). Research in 2015 again showed these figures to be infeasible, so the adult working age Basic Income was cut to half of the Minimum Income Standard for a couple. This made the working age adult Basic Income £160 per week in 2015 (the figure in 2018 would have been £176 per week) and the Child Basic Income was set at £80 per week rather than £90. The basis of the funding method for the scheme was the reduction to zero of the Income Tax Personal Allowance and the National Insurance Contribution Primary Earnings Threshold, and the charging of National Insurance Contributions at 12 per cent on all earned income (rather than at 12 per cent below an Upper Earnings Limit and at 2 per cent above it, as now). The assumption was made that the Basic Incomes would have to be funded entirely from within the current tax and benefits system. The results of the research on these twice-cut levels of Basic Income (along with Citizen's Pensions at the level of half the Minimum Income Standard for pensioner couples for each individual) were not encouraging. The Basic Rate of Income Tax would have needed to rise from 20 per cent to 48 per cent. An additional problem was that the Basic Income scheme assumed that, in the context of such high Basic Incomes and a continuing Housing Benefit, other means-tested benefits could be abolished in order to keep the Basic Rate of Income Tax as low as 48 per cent. Unfortunately, this was found to cause a serious problem. The research showed that 29 per cent of households in the lowest disposable income decile would have experienced reductions in disposable income of over 10 per cent as a result of losing Working Tax Credits and Child Tax Credits at the same time as increased taxation of earnings was reducing the net income from employment. Neither the large increase in the Basic Rate of Income Tax, nor the sizeable household disposable income losses, could possibly be regarded as acceptable (Torry, 2015).

At the same time, research was carried out on the possibility of paying Basic Incomes with levels aligned with the levels of existing means-tested benefits. This enabled the Basic Rate of Income Tax rate to rise by only five percentage points to 25%, but unfortunately this scheme produced losses in disposable income of over 10 per cent for 28 per cent of households in the lowest disposable income decile (Torry, 2015).

These research results were generated by microsimulation research, which employs a computer programme into which are coded the regulations of the tax and benefits systems, and through which is passed data from the Family Resources Survey: a regular survey of the financial details of a 0.1 per cent sample of the UK's population. All of those conducting such research (Martinelli, 2017a, 2017b, 2017c; Reed & Lansley, 2016; Torry, 2015, 2016a, 2016b, 2017a, 2018a, 2019, 2020a, 2021) now know that in order to abolish existing means-tested benefits and at the same time avoid disposable income losses for low-income households, additional funding from outside the tax and benefits system would be required. At the present time this does not seem very likely[: and in any case it is now also clear that funding from outside the current tax and benefits system would nullify the microsimulation results as the additional funding would have to come from somewhere, and wherever it came from would impact household disposable incomes]. There are still illustrative schemes published that assume that a low net cost Basic Income scheme can still be constructed that would enable means-tested benefits to be abolished without imposing losses on low-income households (Miller, 2017; Painter & Thoung, 2015), but as those schemes have not been submitted to microsimulation testing it is not clear that such disposable income losses can in fact be avoided.

The failure of the attempt to find a revenue-neutral Basic Income scheme that would provide Basic Incomes at either Minimum Income Standard levels or at the levels of current means-tested benefits, and that would enable means-tested benefits to be abolished without imposing losses on low-income households, has resulted in attention being turned to Basic Income schemes that retain means-tested benefits and recalculate them by taking into account household members' Basic Incomes and the changes in earned income resulting from changes to the tax system. Two approaches are employed. Martinelli (2017a, 2017b, 2017c) and Reed (Reed & Lansley, 2016) select a variety of such schemes and then test them for their effects on poverty, inequality, household losses, numbers of households coming off means-tested benefits, and so on. The current author sets a number of criteria and then tests a large number of schemes by a trial and error method to see if a scheme exists that fits the criteria. By this method he has shown that a Basic Income scheme exists that reduces both poverty and inequality; that requires no additional funding from outside the tax and benefits system (a net cost within £2bn per annum of zero can be regarded as revenue neutral); that takes a significant number of households off means-tested benefits, and brings a lot more households within striking distance of coming off them; that imposes almost no significant losses on low-income households, and only manageable losses on other households; and that raises Income Tax rates by only 3 percentage points (Torry, 2018a, 2020a, 2021). While the disposable incomes of low-income households reach nowhere near Minimum Income Standards levels, simply because in the 2021 illustrative scheme that fits the criteria the affordable working age adult Basic Income is only £60 per week, existing Child Benefit is increased by only £10 per week per child, and the retained means-tested benefits get households nowhere near to Minimum Income Standard levels, the scheme does raise the mean disposable income (before housing costs) of households in the lowest disposable income decile by a full 25 per cent[, and the mean disposable income (after housing costs) of households in the lowest disposable income decile by a full 50 per cent], and so on average gets the lowest household incomes a lot nearer to Minimum Income Standard levels than they are now (Torry, 2018a).

Conclusion

This chapter has shown that in the UK, in the current financial climate, Basic Incomes at Minimum Income Standard levels are nowhere near feasible, but that a Basic Income scheme that would bring household incomes closer to Minimum Income Standard levels would be entirely feasible if means-tested benefits were retained and recalculated. Different countries would be implementing Basic Incomes in different tax and benefits contexts, so for each country the kind of microsimulation research reported here would need to be undertaken to discover whether there might exist feasible Basic Income schemes for that country that would bring the lowest household incomes closer to its Minimum Income Standard levels.

The question then arises as to whether a small Basic Income, funded by the feasible method outlined here, would be of sufficient value to be worth pursuing. The answer to that is unreservedly yes. Take a family of two adults and two children. If they were on low earned incomes and in-work means-tested benefits, then their net disposable incomes might rise only slightly, but an additional £140 per week, or £607 per month, on top of existing unconditional Child Benefit, would be totally secure, when currently Child Benefit is the only income on which the family can absolutely rely. Such a new secure financial platform could transform the choices available to that family, particularly if it enabled them to escape from means-tested benefits. The particular illustrative Basic Income scheme described here would take 6 per cent of households currently on means-tested benefits off them[, and would decrease by 18 per cent the number of households receiving more than £200 per week in means-tested benefits]. Any households which did come off means-tested benefits would no longer be subject to the high withdrawal rates anyone on means-tested benefits currently suffers (currently in the region of 75 per cent, meaning that an additional £1 of earned income results in about 25p of additional disposable income) but would instead be subject only to the combination of Income Tax and National Insurance Contributions, making a total of 35 per cent, so £1 of additional earned income would result in an additional 65p of additional disposable income—and no longer would that family's lives be afflicted by intrusive, stigmatising, and time-consuming benefits administration. And as for social impact: the fact that every individual in the country would be receiving Basic Incomes would substantially enhance social cohesion. Such effects would cause pressure for Basic Income levels to rise, and if additional funding could then be secured then levels closer to Minimum Income Standards might be possible. Whether Basic Income levels could ever reach the Minimum Income Standards published by the Joseph Rowntree foundation I rather doubt. That is not important. What is required is that household net incomes should get as close as possible to Minimum Income Standard levels, and the ability that even quite low Basic Incomes might give to households to reap additional net income from additional earned income would enable far more households to get a lot closer to Minimum Income Standard levels, and possibly to exceed them. That is what matters.

Acknowledgements This chapter was originally published as Malcolm Torry (2020b), 'Minimum Income Standards in the Basic Income debate', in Christopher Deeming (ed.), *Minimum Income Standards and Reference Budgets: International and comparative policy perspectives*, Bristol: Policy Press, pp. 319–329 (Torry, 2020b). Republished with permission of Policy Press (an imprint of Bristol University Press, UK). The publisher's permission to republish this chapter is gratefully acknowledged.

References

Alkire, S. (2007). Choosing dimensions: The capability approach and multidimensional poverty. In N. Kakwani & J. Silber (Eds.), *The many dimensions of poverty* (pp. 89–119). Palgrave Macmillan.

Barrientos, A. (2016). Justice-based social assistance. *Global Social Policy, 16*(2), 151–165.

Basic Income Earth Network. (2022). *Basic Income*. Retrieved March 26, 2022, from www.basicincome.org

Citizens Basic Income Trust. (2022). *Citizen's Basic Income*. Retrieved March 26, 2022, from www.citizensincome.org

Davis, A., Hirsch, D., Padley, M., & Shepherd, C. (2018). *A minimum income standard for the UK 2008–2018: Continuity and change*. Joseph Rowntree Foundation.

Dean, H. (2010). *Understanding human need: Social issues, policy and practice*. Policy Press.

Lansley, S., & Mack, J. (1983). *Breadline Britain*. London Weekend Television.

Lansley, S., & Mack, J. (2015). *Breadline Britain*. Oneworld.

Martinelli, L. (2017a). *The fiscal and distributional implications of alternative Universal Basic Income schemes in the UK*. Institute for Policy Research. Retrieved March 26, 2022, from https://www.bath.ac.uk/publications/the-fiscal-and-distributional-implications-of-alternative-universal-basic-income-schemes-in-the-uk/

Martinelli, L. (2017b). *Exploring the distributional and work incentive effects of plausible illustrative Basic Income schemes*. Institute for Policy Research. Retrieved March 26, 2022, from, https://www.bath.ac.uk/publications/exploring-the-distributional-work-incentive-effects-of-plausible-illustrative-basic-income-schemes

Martinelli, L. (2017c). *Assessing the case for a Universal Basic Income in the UK*. Institute for Policy Research. Retrieved March 26, 2022, from www.bath.ac.uk/publications/assessing-the-case-for-a-universal-basic-income-in-the-uk

Maslow, A. (1943). A theory of human motivation. *Psychological Review, 50*(4), 370–396.

Miller, A. (2017). *A Basic Income handbook*. Luath Press.

Ontario. (2021). *Ontario Basic Income pilot*. Retrieved March 26, 2022, from https://www.ontario.ca/page/ontario-basic-income-pilot

Painter, A., & Thoung C. (2015). *Report: Creative citizen, creative state: The principled and pragmatic case for a universal basic income*. Royal Society of Arts. Retrieved March 26, 2022, from https://www.thersa.org/reports/basic-income

Rawls, J. (2001). *Justice as fairness: A restatement*. The Belknap Press of Harvard University Press.

Reader, S. (2006). Does a basic needs approach need capabilities? *The Journal of Political Philosophy, 14*(3), 337–350.
Reed, H., & Lansley, S. (2016). *Universal basic income: An idea whose time has come?* Compass.
Torry, M. (2013). *Money for everyone: Why we need a citizen's income*. Policy Press.
Torry, M. (2015). *Two feasible ways to implement a revenue neutral Citizen's Income scheme* (Euromod working paper EM6/15). Institute for Social and Economic Research, University of Essex. Retrieved March 26, 2022, from https://www.iser.essex.ac.uk/research/publications/working-papers/euromod/em6-15
Torry, M. (2016a). *An evaluation of a strictly revenue neutral Citizen's Income scheme* (Euromod Working Paper EM 5/16). Institute for Social and Economic Research, University of Essex. Retrieved March 26, 2022, from https://www.iser.essex.ac.uk/research/publications/working-papers/euromod/em5-16
Torry, M. (2016b). *Citizen's Income schemes: An amendment, and a pilot project: an addendum to (EUROMOD Working Paper EM 5/16)* (Euromod Working Paper EM 5/16a). Institute for Social and Economic Research, University of Essex. Retrieved March 26, 2022, from https://www.iser.essex.ac.uk/research/publications/working-papers/euromod/em5-16a
Torry, M. (2017a). *A variety of indicators evaluated for two implementation methods for a Citizen's Basic Income* (Euromod working paper EM 12/17). Institute for Social and Economic Research, University of Essex. Retrieved March 26, 2022, from https://www.iser.essex.ac.uk/research/publications/working-papers/euromod/em12-17
Torry, M. (2017b). *What's a definition? And how should we define 'Basic Income'?* A paper presented at the 2017b BIEN Congress in Lisbon. Retrieved March 26, 2022, from https://basicincome.org/wp-content/uploads/2015/01/Malcolm_Torry_Whats_a_definition_And_how_should_we_define_Basic_Income.pdf. Published as Chapter 2 in this volume.
Torry, M. (2018a). *An update, a correction, and an extension, of an evaluation of an illustrative Citizen's Basic Income scheme—Addendum to (EUROMOD working paper EM12/17)* (Euromod working paper EM 12/17a). Institute for Social and Economic Research, University of Essex. Retrieved March 26, 2022, from https://www.iser.essex.ac.uk/research/publications/working-papers/euromod/em12-17a
Torry, M. (2018b). *Why we need a Citizen's Basic Income: The desirability, feasibility and implementation of an unconditional income*. Policy Press.
Torry, M. (2019). *Static microsimulation research on Citizen's Basic Income for the UK: A personal summary and further reflections* (EUROMOD working paper EM13/19). Institute for Social and Economic Research. Retrieved

March 26, 2022, from https://www.euromod.ac.uk/sites/default/files/working-papers/em13-19.pdf

Torry, M. (2020a). *Evaluation of a Recovery Basic Income, and of a sustainable revenue neutral Citizen's Basic Income, with an appendix relating to different Universal Credit roll-out scenarios*. (Institute for Social and Economic Research Working Paper EM7/20). Institute for Social and Economic Research, University of Essex. Retrieved March 26, 2022, from https://www.iser.essex.ac.uk/research/publications/working-papers/euromod/em7-20.pdf

Torry, M. (2020b). Minimum Income Standards in the Basic Income debate. In C. Deeming (Ed.), *Minimum Income Standards and reference budgets: International and comparative policy perspectives* (pp. 319–329). Policy Press.

Torry, M. (2021). *Three income maintenance options for 2021*. Centre for Microsimulation and Policy Analysis report. Institute for Social and Economic Research, University of Essex. Retrieved March 26, 2022, from https://www.microsimulation.ac.uk/publications/publication-526555/

Townsend, P. (1979). *Poverty in the United Kingdom*. Allen Lane.

Widerquist, K., & Howard, M. (2012). *Alaska's permanent fund dividend*. Palgrave Macmillan.

Young, C. (2018). *Realising Basic Income experiments in the UK: A typology and toolkit of Basic Income design and delivery*. Royal Society of Arts.

CHAPTER 12

Eurodividend: The Idea and the Details

Introduction

> A Basic Income is an unconditional, automatic and nonwithdrawable income for each individual as a right of citizenship. (Citizen's Basic Income Trust, 2018: 3)

There is some debate as to when the concept of a Basic Income was first formulated: but whenever that was, ever since the eighteenth century the idea has occasionally emerged and been discussed, only to fall back into obscurity. 1982 saw a brief flurry of interest in the United Kingdom when a Member of Parliament, Brandon Rhys Williams, submitted a Basic Income proposal to a parliamentary committee. In order to promote further discussion, and to provide the research that would be required for that discussion to be intelligent, the Basic Income Research Group

Note: A chapter about the legal aspects of a Eurodividend is planned to appear in a new edition of the *Research Handbook of European Social Security Law* to be edited by Frans Pennings and Gijsbert Vonk and published by Edward Elgar Publishing Ltd.

M. Torry, *Basic Income—What, Why, and How?*,
Exploring the Basic Income Guarantee,
https://doi.org/10.1007/978-3-031-14248-2_12

(now the Citizen's Basic Income Trust) was established in 1984. And then in 1986 the Basic Income European Network (BIEN) was founded to bring together interested individuals from across Europe. In 2004 BIEN became the Basic Income Earth Network in recognition of the debate spreading to most of the other continents; and a sign of the current extent of the debate is that thirty-four different countries were represented at the 2019 BIEN congress in India (Torry, 2013: 37; Van Parijs and Vanderborght, 2017: 98).

The Definition of Basic Income

When there were just a few individuals involved in the Basic Income debate, and most of us knew each other, mutual comprehension was relatively easy to achieve. In particular, it was possible to maintain some kind of consistency in relation to the meaning of 'Basic Income', generally understood to be an unconditional income for every individual. However, as early as 1982 the terminology used permitted room for interpretation. Brandon Rhys Williams had called his Basic Income a 'Basic Income Guarantee', by which he and his research assistant Hermione Parker meant that 'every citizen would be entitled to a personal basic income ... These guaranteed basic incomes would replace virtually all existing benefits and allowances ...' (House of Commons Treasury & Civil Service Committee Sub-committee, 1982: 425). Here it is clear that what is guaranteed is the Basic Income: an unconditional income for every individual. But the term 'Basic Income Guarantee' was ambiguous, because it could mean either that the Basic Income was guaranteed, or that the government guaranteed that an income of a certain level would be reached by each individual or household, which could imply a means-tested benefit: and because of that ambiguity, 'guarantee' was dropped in the UK, and by 1985 the less ambiguous 'Basic Income' was being used (Parker, 1985: 5). However, the United States Basic Income Guarantee Network (USBIG Network, 2021), established in 1999, continues to employ 'guarantee' terminology, and it defines a 'Basic Income Guarantee' as a 'government ensured guarantee that no one's income will fall below the level necessary to meet their most basic needs for any reason' (USBIG Network, 2021). A stated level of income can be ensured by paying a means-tested benefit with a one hundred per cent taper rate: that is, as other income rises, the Basic Income Guarantee is withdrawn pound for pound. This is the very opposite of a Basic Income, which would never be withdrawn. USBIG goes on to define ‘Basic Income’: ‘Basic Income gives every citizen a check for the full basic income every month, and taxes his or her earned income …’. Although ‘Basic Income’ is understood as an unconditional income, and ‘Basic Income Guarantee’ is understood as a guaranteed income level, the fact that the two words ‘Basic Income’ appear together in both terms makes it too easy to confuse the two. The Basic Income Canada Network’s definitions pose an even bigger problem. The network defines both Basic Income and Basic Income Guarantee as income level guarantees, which imply means-tested benefits: and a study of the detail of their publications confirms this understanding (Basic Income Canada Network, 2022). A particularly unfortunate outcome of this eccentric definition of Basic Income is that a short-lived experiment in Ontario with household-based and income-tested payments was called a Basic Income pilot project, which it clearly was not (Ontario, n.d.).

This matters. Two individuals or organisations conversing with each other can only communicate accurately if they mean the same thing by the same words. If there is no agreed definition of Basic Income, and different individuals and organisations are using the term differently, then rational debate cannot occur, research results cannot be correctly interpreted, and misunderstanding is inevitable. The problem is that there is no authoritative organisation that can legitimately claim to be the sole guardian of the definition of Basic Income, so every individual and organisation can define the term as it wishes, particularly if it adds the word ‘guarantee’ to ‘Basic Income’. A consequence is that experiments with income-tested benefits can be erroneously interpreted as predicting the effects of Basic Income schemes, which of course they cannot.

But having said that there is no authoritative organisation that can impose a definition of Basic Income, the modern debate’s longest-standing organisation is the Citizen’s Basic Income Trust, and its definition of Basic Income, which it calls a Citizen’s Basic Income, might therefore be a useful place to start:

> A Citizen’s Basic Income is an unconditional, automatic and nonwithdrawable income for each individual as a right of citizenship.
>
> [A Citizen’s Basic Income (CBI) is sometimes called a Basic Income (BI) or a Citizen’s Income (CI)]

- 'Unconditional': A CBI would vary with age, but there would be no other conditions: so everyone of the same age would receive the same CBI, whatever their gender, employment status, family structure, contribution to society, housing costs, or anything else.
- 'Automatic': Someone's CBI would be paid weekly or monthly, automatically.
- 'Nonwithdrawable': CBIs would not be means-tested. Whether someone's earnings or wealth increased, decreased, or stayed the same, their Citizen's Basic Income would not change.
- 'Individual': CBIs would be paid on an individual basis, and not on the basis of a couple or household.
- 'As a right': Everybody legally resident in the UK would receive a CBI, subject to a minimum period of legal residency in the UK, and continuing residency for most of the year. (Citizen's Basic Income Trust, 2018: 3)

A definition published by BIEN is worded in a slightly different way—'A Basic Income is a periodic cash payment unconditionally delivered to all on an individual basis, without means-test or work requirement ' (Basic Income Earth Network, 2022)—but the underlying meaning of the term is much the same as that implied by the Citizen's Basic Income Trust's definition.

The one conditionality universally permitted is that the Basic Income can vary with an individual's age, with usually smaller amounts being paid for children, and possibly for younger adults, and larger amounts for elderly people. The reason that this conditionality can be permitted is that once the administration's computer knows someone's date of birth, it can automatically alter someone's Basic Income as their age changes, so no active administration is required; and because we cannot affect our age, moral hazard is impossible: that is, there are no human activities that require investigation, as there would be in relation to employment status, income, wealth, household structure, and so on. The Basic Income keeps on coming, from birth to death, as a secure platform on which to build. It is that that generates the many advantages of Basic Income over other forms of income maintenance: a sense of financial security, social cohesion, work motivation, human dignity, mental health, and so on (Torry, 2013: 81–186).

The definitions of Basic Income published by national organisations affiliated to BIEN confirm this consensus in relation to the definition. The only area of contention is whether the definition of Basic Income should include a statement of the level at which it should be paid (Torry, 2017; Chapter 11 in this volume). We shall return to the issue of the level of the payment later in this chapter.

The Definition of Eurodividend

At what territorial level might we expect a Basic Income, understood as an unconditional, automatic and nonwithdrawable income for every individual, to be implemented? The ability to pay incomes to individuals, and to raise the revenue for doing so, lies generally at the national level, or sometimes at state level in federal states. It is therefore at the level of the nation state that we are likely to see Basic Incomes implemented in the first instance: and it is not insignificant that the first territory-wide income that was something like a Basic Income was established (largely by accident) in Iran in 2010 (Karshenas & Tabatabai, 2019). However, as the debate about Basic Income has globalised, alternative options have been proposed, the two most prominent being a Global Basic Income and a Eurodividend. A Global Basic Income, or World Basic Income, would pay to every resident of the planet an unconditional income, possibly funded by taxing the proceeds of private exploitation of such global commons as the atmosphere, land, and the radio spectrum (World Basic Income, 2022). As a long-term aim, a Global Basic Income could be both feasible and useful: but given the current absence of a global government with tax-raising powers, a Global Basic Income cannot be a short-term or medium-term objective. What might be possible, however, would be a Eurodividend: a Basic Income for the European Union, or perhaps just for nations in the Eurozone: because although the European Union institutions do not currently function as a tax-raising authority, it is not impossible that they might become one in a limited sense if the Union's nation states chose to permit that; or it might be possible for a Eurodividend to be established as a nationally funded and administered exercise with European Commission coordination and European Parliament legitimacy.

In 2013 Philippe Van Parijs wrote a proposal for a Eurodividend: an unconditional income for every citizen in either the European Union or the Eurozone. As usual with a Basic Income, a Eurodividend would vary with the individual's age, but there would be no other conditionalities—except perhaps that it might vary in amount with the country of residence: an issue to which we shall return (Van Parijs, 2013).

As we have seen, clarity of definition is required if debate about a Eurodividend is to be rational. It might therefore be useful to employ an existing definition, and to decide that, assuming that the Eurodividend would be paid throughout the European Union, a Eurodividend would be an 'unconditional, automatic and nonwithdrawable income for each individual as a right of European citizenship'.

- 'Unconditional': A Eurodividend would vary with age, but there would be no other conditions: so everyone of the same age would receive the same Eurodividend, whatever their gender, employment status, family structure, contribution to society, housing costs, or anything else.
- 'Automatic': Someone's Eurodividend would be paid weekly or monthly, automatically.
- 'Nonwithdrawable': Eurodividends would not be means-tested. Whether someone's earnings or wealth increased, decreased, or stayed the same, their Eurodividend would not change.
- 'Individual': Eurodividends would be paid on an individual basis, and not on the basis of a couple or household.
- 'As a right': Everybody legally resident in the European Union would receive a Eurodividend, subject to a minimum period of legal residency, and continuing residency for most of the year (Citizen's Basic Income Trust, 2018: 3, adapted).

Reasons for Establishing a Eurodividend

Van Parijs gives four reasons for implementing a Eurodividend (Van Parijs, 2013). To paraphrase and in places develop his arguments:

1. Nation states with different currencies maintain their economic stability both internally and in relation to other nation states by adjusting exchange rates through an open market in currencies,

through government action, or both. The United States is a federation of states with often very different economies, but because they share the same currency they do not have the option of varying the rates of exchange between the currencies of different states. Instead, stability is maintained by (a) interstate migration, and (b) interstate transfers constituted by federal funding of the welfare state. In Europe, the diversity of languages mitigates against widespread interstate migration, and interstate transfers are almost non-existent, so in the Eurozone, which is attempting to operate with a single currency, there are no means available to maintain economic stability either within or between different countries. In the short term there is not a lot that can be done about linguistic diversity, and untangling the single currency ought not to be an option, so the only mechanism available to maintain the necessary economic stability is an increase in interstate transfers. One means of achieving this would be to pay to every Eurozone citizen a Basic Income, or Eurodividend, and to pay for it by taxing consumption by increasing Value Added Tax.

2. Income differentials between different European Union countries are a significant driver of migration from poorer countries to wealthier ones, causing problems for both. Because the tax take from a wealthy country would be higher than for a less wealthy country, the Eurodividend, paid equally to every Eurozone citizen, could reduce the differentials between countries and thus reduce migration flows, making immigration more manageable for wealthier countries, and reducing the brain drain currently suffered by poorer countries.
3. The increasingly free movement of capital, goods and services across national boundaries forces national governments to compete for capital investment, and also to compete in a global employment market, thus reducing the tax base and making it more difficult to sustain welfare states. The European Union, by establishing a large internal market, is to some extent able to resist such global pressures, so it would be both possible for it establish the whole of that market as a tax base, and useful for it to establish an income floor that would enable it more easily to compete in the global employment market.
4. The European Union can too easily be regarded as the possession of an unaccountable élite that does little for its citizens, even though what it does do is of significant benefit to everyone who lives in

the European Union. To establish a Eurodividend would constitute a tangible engagement of every European citizen with the European Union, resulting in widespread psychological ownership of the European project.

Because the second, third and fourth reasons apply to every European Union country, and the stability of the Eurozone is of interest to every European Union country, the above four arguments constitute an argument for the payment of a Eurodividend to every European Union citizen, and not just to those living in the Eurozone.

How Should the Eurodividend Be Funded?

Van Parijs has suggested that an increase in Value Added Tax should be employed to fund the proposed Eurodividend, and has calculated that an increase in VAT rates of 20 percentage points would pay for a Eurodividend of €200 per month: although, as he says, because national government social expenditures would be able to be reduced because every citizen would be receiving a Eurodividend, existing VAT rates and other taxation as well could be reduced, meaning that the resulting VAT rates would not necessarily be 20 percentage points above current rates. Van Parijs discounts using carbon taxes or financial transaction taxes to fund Eurodividends because these would result in much smaller amounts being paid (Van Parijs, 2013).

While Van Parijs has been able to calculate the additional Value Added Tax required to fund a Eurodividend of a particular level for every European Union citizen—a calculation that requires him to know only the population of the European Union and the Union's VAT tax base—this is not the only calculation required if we are to be sure that the scheme is financially feasible. In 2012 we discovered that a revenue-neutral UK Basic Income scheme that the Citizen's Basic Income Trust had confidently published in 2006 would in fact have imposed substantial disposable income losses on a large number of low-income households (Torry, 2019: 3). The complexity of current tax and benefits systems means that nothing can be taken for granted. The Trust now only publishes illustrative Basic Income schemes that do not impose significant disposable income losses on significant numbers of low-income households: which means that it can no longer publish schemes that abolish current means-tested benefits, but instead has to publish schemes that leave means-tested benefits in place and take a significant number of households off them (Torry, 2019: 22–46). We are fortunate that we have available to us EUROMOD, a microsimulation programme into which are coded the tax and benefit regulations of every European Union country. Passing data on the financial situations of a statistically significant sample of the population through the programme can generate a wide range of statistics: poverty and inequality levels, household and individual disposable incomes, the numbers of households on different social security benefits, and so on. New benefits can then be constructed in the programme (including of course a Basic Income), and existing taxes and benefits can be altered, in order to simulate a different world in which a Basic Income is the foundation of the benefits system. The programme is then run again to generate a new set of statistics, which can then be compared with the statistics for the present tax and benefits system. This enables us to discover the real-world financial effects of introducing a wide variety of different Basic Income schemes, and to test the schemes against prechosen sets of feasibility criteria. For instance, the process can tell us whether it would be possible to implement a Basic Income scheme that would reduce both poverty and inequality, be revenue neutral (that is, not require additional funding from outside the current benefits and income tax systems), not impose significant losses on low-income households, and take a significant number of households off means-tested benefits (Torry, 2019: 22–46; 2020, 2021).

The Institute for Social and Economic Research, with partners from elsewhere in Europe, is now developing an Indirect Tax Tool (ITT) as a new application in EUROMOD, so for the first time it will be possible to simulate the effects of changes to Value Added Tax (Institute for Social and Economic Research, 2022). As soon as the tool becomes available, it will be possible to test the effects of increases in VAT rates on households, and in particular to discover whether VAT-funded Basic Incomes of different levels would reduce the living standards of low-income households. As with the microsimulation research already conducted in the UK, a trial and error method would determine whether a Basic Income paid for by raising VAT rates might be financially feasible, and if conducted for every European Union country the method would tell us at what level the Eurodividend would have to be paid in order for financial feasibility to be secured, or whether for financial feasibility we would need to pay Eurodividends at different levels in different countries.

It might be true that carbon taxes and financial transaction taxes would not generate sufficient funds for a sizeable Eurodividend, but that is no reason for not considering them as useful funding methods. We are going to need to tax carbon use if the climate is not to become uncontrollable, but because such a tax would increase the costs of keeping homes warm, and of both public and private transport, household incomes would need to be protected. Where fuel price increases have not been accompanied by increases in the incomes of low-income households, understandable public resentment has been the result, as in France, where protests led to the abandonment of the new tax (Willsher, 2018). A different approach has been taken by some Canadian states: carbon use is taxed, and an income-tested Climate Action Tax Credit is paid to certain household types (British Columbia, 2022). Canada has not experienced protests. Because low-income households generally cause lower carbon emissions than higher income households, a Basic Income or Eurodividend paid for by taxing carbon use and distributed equally to every individual would be progressive: that is, it would benefit low-income households more than higher income households (Howard et al., 2019: 113–114).

In 1978, James Tobin recommended a tax on financial transactions (Tobin, 1978: 155). He suggested that this would discourage speculative financial transactions designed purely to profit from changes in exchange rates, and would therefore stabilise exchange rates and benefit the real economy. The problem is that financial transactions are highly mobile, and in the absence of an authority capable of imposing a global financial transactions tax, any individual nation state that imposed such a tax would risk driving financial transactions abroad. However, the UK already taxes the trading of shares in UK companies at 0.5%, and New York imposes a similar tax, and these taxes have not driven transactions away from the UK or New York. A low Financial Transaction Tax would not drive business abroad, and it could raise some of the funds required to pay for a Basic Income or Eurodividend. A Financial Transaction Tax imposed throughout the European Union might be sustainable at a higher rate than a purely national tax because there are good reasons—such as robust contract and legal structures—for enacting currency transactions within Europe.

Currency transactions are not the only financial transactions. A variety of other kinds could also be taxed (Adam et al., 2011: 151–153,

195–215), and taxed more effectively at a European level. Financial Transaction Taxes could be more useful than we might think.

There would therefore seem to be good reasons for examining a variety of means of funding a Eurodividend. Careful microsimulation research would be required to ensure that a combination of the Eurodividend and its funding methods would not impose unacceptable household disposable income losses on low-income households, but that would be possible to do, and such research could reveal the optimal mixture of kinds of tax for funding a financially feasible Eurodividend.

Eurodividend and Eurodividend Scheme

The discussion above raises the important question of the difference between 'Basic Income' and 'Basic Income scheme', and therefore between 'Eurodividend' and 'Eurodividend scheme'. A Basic Income is always an unconditional, automatic and nonwithdrawable income for every individual. A Basic Income *scheme* is a Basic Income, along with the levels specified for different age groups, and with the funding method specified, and in particular any changes to the current tax and benefits system. Basic Income is always the same—an unconditional income for every individual: but there is an infinite number of possible Basic Income schemes in any particular jurisdiction (Torry, 2018a; Chapter 4 in this volume), and different schemes can have very different effects.

- One scheme might increase inequality, whereas another might reduce it;
- One scheme might increase poverty, whereas another might reduce it;
- One scheme might impose losses on low-income households at the point of implementation, whereas another might not;
- One scheme might require very high-income tax rates, whereas another might not;
- One scheme might require additional funding from elsewhere, whereas another might not;
- One scheme might increase employment, whereas another might not; and
- One scheme might be politically feasible, whereas another might not.

The same is true for a Eurodividend. A Eurodividend is always an unconditional income for every individual within the European Union or the Eurozone, but there is an infinite number of possible Eurodividend schemes, only some of which would be financially feasible, in the sense that they could be afforded, and that they would not impose significant losses on low-income households; and only some of these would be politically feasible.

Should the Level of the Eurodividend Vary from Country to Country?

An important decision to be made when constructing a Eurodividend scheme would be whether the levels of the Eurodividends for different age groups should be different from country to country. Van Parijs leaves the question open by suggesting that each country's Eurodividend level might relate to the cost of living in that country (Van Parijs, 2013). There would be advantages and disadvantages to either answer to the question. An equal Eurodividend across the European Union or Eurozone would have more of a dampening effect on migration, and would increase the level of state transfers and therefore their effect: but to peg Eurodividend levels to countries' costs of living could make both the idea and the European Union more acceptable to wealthier populations that are too easily persuaded that the European Union is a drain on their national resources. This would suggest that a compromise would be required: that there should be a standard rate of Eurodividend, and a formula that would determine the Eurodividend in each country in relation to the standard rate and the cost of living, with all of the national Eurodividends falling within a fairly narrow band.

An Unconditional Income for Every Individual

To return to the discussion at the beginning of this chapter about the difference between a Basic Income—an unconditional income for every individual—and a minimum income guarantee which guarantees that no household's income will fall below a specified level: a guarantee that can be met by paying a means-tested benefit.

It might be tempting to suggest that the Eurodividend should be an income-tested payment rather than an unconditional one: that is, instead of the same amount being paid to each individual, the amount paid should be reduced as other income rises. The temptation should be resisted. Similarly, basing the payment on the household rather than on the individual, or on a work test, should be resisted even more vigorously. All such conditionalities require bureaucratic intrusion into individuals' personal information, relationships, and motivations, and they impose inevitable consequences: stigma and demotivation for those who receive the means-tested, household-tested, and work-tested incomes; benefit withdrawal as other income increases, which disincentivises earning additional income; and significant levels of administrative cost, fraud, and administrative error (Torry, 2013: 81–160). The whole point of a Basic Income, and therefore of a Eurodividend, is to provide a secure financial foundation on which individuals can build employment, self-employment, community and caring work, and relationships. To test the incomes in any way other than by someone's age would severely compromise that objective; and it would compromise the third and fourth reasons for establishing a Eurodividend listed by Van Parijs. In any case, there is no need to establish the vast Europe-wide administrative bureaucracy that would be required to means test, work test or household-test the Eurodividend. Wealthier countries would be contributing more of the cost, so paying equal amounts to every individual in the European Union or the Eurozone should not be seen as a problem. As with any Basic Income, the rich don't need it, but it is important that the rich should receive it.

It is sometimes suggested that to pay a Negative Income Tax would have the same effect as a Basic Income because it generates the same relationship between earned income and net income. A Negative Income Tax taxes each individual above an income threshold, and below the threshold it pays out a negative tax proportional to the amount that the earned income falls below the threshold. With equal tax rates above and below the threshold it is perfectly true that the relationship between earned income and net income can be the same as for a Basic Income. However, the administration of the two is utterly different. A Basic Income is an unconditional income that arrives every week or every month in the individual's bank account. It might vary with their age, and it might be uprated each year, but it would always be the same, and it would always be the same as the Basic Income paid to everyone else of the same age. It could be turned on at someone's birth, and turned off at their death, and would require no active administration in between. A Negative Income Tax, on the other hand, would require constant and complicated administration, because either the employer or the government agency would require real-time information on all of someone's income in order to calculate any Negative Income Tax that needed to be paid out. The fact that on a graph with earned income and net income on its axes the line relating earned and net incomes is the same for both Basic Income and Negative Income Tax is irrelevant (Torry, 2018b: 181–187).

Conclusion

For the different participants in a debate to be able to communicate comprehensibly with each other there needs to be a substantial level of agreement as to the definitions of terms. There also needs to be a widespread understanding of important distinctions and why the distinctions matter. So in relation to the Basic Income debate, particularly now that it is global in character, there needs to be agreement that a Basic Income is an unconditional, automatic and nonwithdrawable income for every individual within a jurisdiction; and there needs to be an understanding that a Basic Income and a minimum income guarantee are anything but the same; that there is a significant difference between a Basic Income and a Negative Income Tax; and that a Basic Income is always an unconditional income for every individual, but that there is an infinite number of possible Basic Income schemes, only some of which would be financially feasible.

So in relation to the rather more recent debate about a Eurodividend, there needs to be agreement that a Eurodividend is an unconditional, automatic and nonwithdrawable income for every individual within the European Union; and there needs to be an understanding that a Eurodividend and a minimum income guarantee are anything but the same; that there is a significant difference between a Eurodividend and a Negative Income Tax; and that a Eurodividend is always an unconditional income for every individual, but that there is an infinite number of possible Eurodividend schemes, only some of which would be financially feasible.

Acknowledgements This chapter publishes for the first time a slightly revised version of a paper presented at a conference held at the University of Freiburg on 11 and 12 October 2018 on *Basic Income and the Euro-Dividend as sociopolitical pillars of the EU and its member countries*.

References

Adam, S., et al. (Eds.). (2011). *Tax by design: The Mirrlees Review*. Oxford University Press.

Basic Income Canada Network. (2022). *Basic Income Canada Network*. Retrieved March 27, 2022, from https://www.basicincomecanada.org/about_basic_income

Basic Income Earth Network. (2022). Retrieved March 27, 2022, from https://basicincome.org/basic-income

British Columbia. (2022). *Climate action tax credit*. Retrieved March 27, 2022, from https://www2.gov.bc.ca/gov/content/taxes/income-taxes/personal/credits/climate-action

Citizen's Basic Income Trust. (2018). *Citizen's Basic Income: A brief introduction*. Citizen's Basic Income Trust. Retrieved March 27, 2022, from https://citizensincome.org/news/citizens-basic-income-a-brief-introduction

House of Commons Treasury and Civil Service Committee Sub-committee. (1982). *The structure of personal income taxation and income support: Minutes of evidence, Wednesday 21 July 1982*. HC331-ix. Her Majesty's Stationery Office.

Howard, M., Pinto, J., & Schachtschneider, U. (2019). Ecological effects of Basic Income. In M. Torry (Ed.), *The Palgrave international handbook of Basic Income* (pp. 111–132). Palgrave Macmillan.

Institute for Social and Economic Research. (2022). *Tax benefit microsimulation platform*. Retrieved March 27, 2022, from https://www.microsimulation.ac.uk/euromod/

Karshenas, M., & Tabatabai, H. (2019). Basic Income by default. Lessons from Iran's 'Cash Subsidy' programme. In M. Torry (Ed.), *The Palgrave international handbook of Basic Income* (pp. 339–355). Palgrave Macmillan.

Ontario. (n.d.). *Ontario's Basic Income pilot: Studying the impact of a basic income*. Retrieved March 27, 2022, from https://files.ontario.ca/170508_bi_brochure_eng_pg_by_pg_proof.pdf

Parker, H. (1985). The debate about costings. *BIRG Bulletin*, no. 4, Autumn 1985, pp. 5–7.

Tobin, J. (1978). A proposal for international monetary reform. *Eastern Economic Journal*, *4*(3–4), 153–159.

Torry, M. (2013). *Money for everyone: Why we need a Citizen's Income*. Policy Press.

Torry, M. (2017). *What's a definition? And how should we define 'Basic Income'?* A paper presented at the 2017 BIEN Congress in Lisbon. Retrieved March 27, 2022, from https://basicincome.org/wp-content/uploads/2015/01/Malcolm_Torry_Whats_a_definition_And_how_should_we_define_Basic_Income.pdf. Published as Chapter 2 in this volume.

Torry, M. (2018a). *Basic Income and Basic Income schemes: Definitions and details*. A paper prepared for the 2018a BIEN congress in Tampere, Finland. Retrieved March 27, 2022, from https://basicincome.org/wp-content/uploads/2018a/09/Basic-Income-and-Basic-Income-schemes-definitions-and-details.pdf

Torry, M. (2018b). *Why we need a Citizen's Basic Income: The desirability, feasibility and implementation of an unconditional income*. Policy Press.

Torry, M. (2019). *Static microsimulation research on Citizen's Basic Income for the UK: A personal summary and further reflections* (EUROMOD Working Paper EM13/19). Institute for Social and Economic Research. Retrieved March 27, 2022, from https://www.euromod.ac.uk/sites/default/files/working-papers/em13-19.pdf

Torry, M. (2020). *Evaluation of a Recovery Basic Income, and of a sustainable revenue neutral Citizen's Basic Income, with an appendix relating to different Universal Credit roll-out scenarios* (Institute for Social and Economic Research Working Paper EM7/20). Institute for Social and Economic Research, University of Essex. Retrieved March 27, 2022, from https://www.iser.essex.ac.uk/research/publications/working-papers/euromod/em7-20.pdf

Torry, M. (2021). *Three income maintenance options for 2021*. Centre for Microsimulation and Policy Analysis report. Institute for Social and Economic Research, University of Essex. Retrieved March 27, 2022, from https://www.microsimulation.ac.uk/publications/publication-526555/

USBIG Network. (2021). *What is Basic Income Guarantee*. https://usbig.net/about-big/. Accessed 6 October 2021.

Van Parijs, P. (2013). *The Eurodividend: Why the EU should introduce a basic income for all*. London School of Economics. Retrieved March 27, 2022, from https://eprints.lse.ac.uk/75819/1/blogs.lse.ac.uk-The%20Eurodividend%20Why%20the%20EU%20should%20introduce%20a%20basic%20income%20for%20all.pdf

Van Parijs, P., & Vanderborght, Y. (2017). *Basic Income: A radical proposal for a free society and a sane economy*. Harvard University Press.

Willsher, K. (2018, December 5). Macron scraps fuel tax rise in face of gilets jaunes protests. *The Guardian*. Retrieved March 27, 2022, from https://www.theguardian.com/world/2018/dec/05/france-wealth-tax-changes-gilets-jaunes-protests-president-macron

World Basic Income. (2022). *World Basic Income*. Retrieved March 27, 2022, from https://www.worldbasicincome.org.uk

CHAPTER 13

Do We Need Basic Income Experiments?

Introduction

In this chapter terms will be defined, the difference between 'Basic Income' and 'Basic Income scheme' will be clarified, the feasibility of Basic Income schemes will be explored, a variety of past, current, and future Basic Income experiments will be discussed, methods for evaluating the financial feasibility of Basic Income schemes will be compared, and the question that constitutes the title of this chapter will be answered.

'Basic Income'

The UK's Citizen's Basic Income Trust (CBIT) defines a Citizen's Basic Income or Basic Income as

> an unconditional, automatic and nonwithdrawable income for each individual as a right of citizenship. (Citizen's Basic Income Trust, 2018: 3)

And the Basic Income Earth Network (BIEN) defines it as

M. Torry, *Basic Income—What, Why, and How?*,
Exploring the Basic Income Guarantee,
https://doi.org/10.1007/978-3-031-14248-2_13

> a periodic cash payment unconditionally delivered to all on an individual basis, without means-test or work requirement. (Basic Income Earth Network, 2022)

These definitions represent a consensus among BIEN's affiliated organisations (Torry, 2017; Chapter 11 in this volume), and they reflect common usage of the term 'Basic Income'. For the purposes of this chapter, I shall employ a working definition based on the two definitions above: A Basic Income is

> an equal and regular payment of the same amount, varying only by an annual uprating, to every individual of the same age legally resident in the jurisdiction in question.

National organisations affiliated to BIEN disagree over whether the definition of 'Basic Income' implies payment of Basic Incomes at a 'subsistence' level, somehow defined (Torry, 2017; Chapter 11 in this volume): but neither CBIT's nor BIEN's definition assumes that a Basic Income will be paid at a particular amount, and our working definition similarly does not assume that it will be. For the purposes of this essay, a regular, unconditional, and individual income of any amount counts as a Basic Income.

The definitions do not require the incomes to be permanent in order to be called Basic Incomes. We would expect the social and economic effects of short-term unconditional incomes to be different from those of long-term ones: in particular in relation to employment market behaviour, because if the Basic Income is only short term then behaviour will be largely determined by the situation that will follow the experiment, whereas with a permanent Basic Income behaviour will be determined by the new Basic Income scheme. However, that difference does not compromise the fact that both short-term unconditional incomes as well as long-term ones can properly be called Basic Incomes; and that consequence means that short-term experiments with unconditional incomes can properly be called Basic Income pilot projects or experiments.

In this chapter, the definition of Basic Income will be strictly applied. If an income fails to fulfil any of the elements of the definition, then it is not a Basic Income.

'Basic Income' and 'Basic Income Scheme'

A Basic Income is 'an equal and regular payment of the same amount … to every individual of the same age …'. A Basic Income *Scheme* is a Basic Income with its levels for different age groups specified, along with the funding method specified in detail, and any changes to existing tax and benefits systems also specified in detail. A Basic Income is always the same: 'an equal and regular payment of the same amount … to every individual of the same age …': but for any country, there is an infinite number of possible Basic Income schemes.

The distinction is important. Arguments against any particular Basic Income scheme are not arguments against Basic Income (Torry, 2018b; Chapter 9 in this volume); and if in any country just one particular Basic Income scheme is feasible, then Basic Income is feasible in that country.

The distinction is also important because it draws our attention to precisely what must be tested if a genuine Basic Income pilot project is to be carried out. The whole idea of a pilot project is to test something that could be done. This means that simply paying a Basic Income to a pilot community does not necessarily constitute a Basic Income pilot project. Only if the Basic Income *scheme* tested in the pilot community could be rolled out as a national scheme should the project be termed a Basic Income pilot project. This requires a scheme to be tested for national financial and administrative feasibility before the pilot project is carried out, and that a view has been taken that the scheme would potentially meet psychological, political, behavioural, and policy process feasibility tests (Torry, 2016).

'Experiment' and 'Pilot Project'

In *The Palgrave International Handbook of Basic Income*, a distinction is made between Basic Income experiments and Basic Income pilot projects:

> Only if a project is testing a genuine Basic Income is it right to call the project a 'Basic Income pilot project'. A project that tests anything else should be called an 'experiment' from which useful lessons might be learnt. (Torry, 2019: 10–13)

The title of this chapter contains the phrase 'Basic Income experiments', which suggests that genuine Basic Incomes are being tested: so for the purpose of this chapter I shall assume that 'Basic Income experiment' means 'Basic Income pilot project', and the two phrases will be used interchangeably. The title is not asking a question about experiments that are not Basic Income pilot projects: so the main subject of this essay will be genuine Basic Income pilot projects: that is, experiments with entirely unconditional, equal, and regular payments of the same amount to everyone of the same age. Where other kinds of experiments are being discussed, the differences from Basic Income pilot projects will be made clear.

Basic Income Pilot Projects

There have been two genuine Basic Income pilot projects, in Namibia and India. In Namibia, everyone in the chosen community was paid a Basic Income for a period of two years, and in India the residents of a number of villages were paid Basic Incomes for shorter periods. The 'jurisdictions' were small, and the periods of payment were short, but those characteristics of the experiments do not invalidate the payments as Basic Incomes. Every individual of the same age in those jurisdictions was paid an income of the same amount, unconditionally. There were differences between the projects: the Namibian project took place in a single community, whereas the larger Indian project took place in a large number of communities of three distinct kinds; and for the Namibian pilot community there was no control community that did not receive the Basic Income, whereas in India the pilot communities were matched with control communities that did not receive the Basic Income so that the effects of the Basic Income could be properly evaluated (Widerquist, 2018: 19–25). These differences did not invalidate the Namibian project's right to be properly termed a Basic Income pilot project.

In both cases, the outcomes were significant. The pilot communities developed democratic structures to control aspects of the local economy; women, people with disabilities, and elderly people, experienced emancipation; economic activity increased, especially among low-earning households; no unwanted economic effects occurred; new businesses were established; money was pooled to enable such infrastructure as toilets and a post office to be built; school attendance and results improved; the community's health improved; nutrition improved; greater social cohesion was experienced; and crime was reduced (Basic Income Grant

Coalition, 2009; Davala, 2019; Davala et al., 2015; Haarmann & Haarmann, 2007, 2012; Haarmann et al., 2019; Torry, 2013: 69–73; 2018a: 134–135; Widerquist, 2018: 58–59).

The income recently tested in the aborted Ontario experiment was income-tested and household-based (Ontario, n.d.; Widerquist, 2018: 65), so it was not a Basic Income: so although the project was an interesting one, it ought not to have been called a Basic Income experiment or pilot project.

The recent Finland experiment (De Wispelaere et al., 2019; Widerquist, 2018: 64–65) selected two thousand unemployed individuals throughout the country and made their unemployment benefit unconditional for a period of two years. The important question is whether we can count widely dispersed individuals as a community or jurisdiction. Because this question can be answered either way, we have to conclude that the Finland experiment fell between being a Basic Income experiment and not being one.

Experiments during the 1970s in the USA and Canada were Minimum Income Guarantee experiments: that is, they ensured that household annual disposable incomes did not fall below prescribed annual minimum income levels. In order to reach the prescribed minima, income-tested benefits were paid to households: so these were not Basic Income experiments, and the extent to which the significantly useful results of the experiments (in terms of improved health and other outcomes) can be used to predict the effects of genuine Basic Incomes must remain an open question (Forget, 2011; Widerquist, 2018: 43–55).

As far as I know, no genuine Negative Income Tax (NIT) experiments have ever taken place (that is, experiments that weekly or monthly pay with each individual's salary an amount of money proportional to the extent to which earned income falls below a tax threshold): but if any such experiments were to take place, then we would have to say the same as we have said in relation to Minimum Income Guarantee experiments: that because of the substantial administrative differences between a Negative Income Tax and a Basic Income, results from the NIT experiments could not necessarily predict the effects of a Basic Income scheme (Widerquist, 2018: 15–17).

The major difference between all these experiments—whether with unconditional individual incomes or not—and a genuine nationwide Basic Income, is that the experiments were all short term, which means that results must be treated carefully. But that is probably not a problem.

Take, for instance, employment market behaviour. In Namibia and India, economic activity increased, and the employment market changed in character, with shifts away from employment and towards own-account economic activity. If the Basic Incomes had become permanent during the experiment, then we can theorise that because everyone's economic activity would then have been determined entirely by the new Basic Income situation, and no longer partially by the situation that would transpire at the end of the two-year experiment, the employment market effects might have been more pronounced than they were, and were unlikely to have been less than they were. Similarly with the Finnish experiment. No employment market effects were noticed during the first year of the experiment[, and there was a small increase during the second year], which means that any employment market withdrawal was balanced by new employment market engagement (Kangas et al., 2020). With a permanent scheme, in which a permanent Basic Income would not be affected by additional earned income, we can theorise that there would be less incentive to leave employment, and more incentive to engage with it, suggesting that employment market activity would be higher with a permanent Basic Income than during the experiment. Clearly, only permanent Basic Incomes can test this: but those would no longer be pilot projects. Similarly, all of the projects delivered enhanced wellbeing, so we can theorise that permanent Basic Incomes would deliver even more of it.

As discussed, an essential test as to whether an experiment is a genuine Basic Income experiment is only passed if the Basic Income scheme tested would be feasible to roll out nationwide. The small amounts paid in Basic Incomes in the Namibian and Indian projects would constitute small proportions of the countries' Gross Domestic Products (GDPs), and so would be financially feasible; and in India that feasibility would be enhanced by the abolition of a variety of current schemes intended to reduce poverty. The schemes would clearly be administratively feasible to roll out across their respective countries, and although neither is currently politically feasible, it is possible to envisage situations in which they might become so. The Finnish scheme made unemployment benefits unconditional for two thousand randomly selected individuals, without changing existing tax and benefits systems. The scheme would not be financially feasible if rolled out nationwide: yet another reason for denying that the experiment should have been called a Basic Income pilot project.

The Conditions for Running a Genuine Basic Income Pilot Project in a Developed Country

Both of the genuine pilot projects were conducted in developing countries. They were possible because, even though such projects are never without their difficulties, there were no complex tax and benefits systems that had to be changed just for the pilot communities if the experiments were to mirror Basic Income schemes that could be rolled out nationwide.

The situation is very different in more developed countries with existing complex tax and benefits systems. Take the United Kingdom (UK) as an example. For a nationwide Basic Income scheme to be feasible, the existing Income Tax Personal Allowance—the amount of someone's income that is not taxed—would have to be removed or reduced; Income Tax rates might have to rise; National Insurance Contributions (the UK's social insurance contributions) rates and thresholds might have to change; and means-tested benefits claims would have to be reduced. For a genuine pilot project to take place, these changes would have to take place just for the pilot community or for randomly selected individuals. The problem is that it is exceedingly difficult to alter complex tax and benefits systems just for a single community or individual. A number of Scottish boroughs and English cities have expressed a wish to run Basic Income community-wide pilot projects, but so far none of them have worked out how to run a genuine Basic Income pilot project. If there was a UK government that wished pilot projects to take place, then it could ask the Department for Work and Pensions (which runs means-tested benefits) and Her Majesty's Revenue and Customs (which runs Income Tax and National Insurance Contributions) to make the necessary changes for pilot communities: but that would still be remarkably difficult to achieve. Equally difficult to achieve would be a pilot project for a Basic Income scheme that redistributed from rich to poor, even if only mildly (Widerquist, 2018: 37–42). Because of the complexity of tax and benefits systems in more developed countries, an experiment in which revenue neutrality or something close to it was required (because a nationwide scheme would probably require that) would need to prevent losses to low-income households, and so at least some wealthier households would have to lose money. Given that wealthier households are likely to enjoy political influence, it is easy to see that only experiments that did not require *any* household to lose money would be likely to be politically feasible, which would of course mean that no genuine Basic Income pilot projects could take place.

But that is not necessarily the end of the story. Two possibilities have been researched and have been found to be feasible were a UK government wishing to run pilot projects (perhaps because policymakers were sympathetic towards Basic Income as an idea, but were worried about possible press reactions to a decision to establish one) (Widerquist, 2018: 74–75, 131–139). The definition of Basic Income does not require every age group to be provided with an unconditional income for every individual: what it requires is that every one of the same age should be paid an equal and unconditional individual income. In the UK, it would be feasible to pay Basic Incomes to younger adults—for instance, 18 to 21-year-olds—and to allocate to each of them a 'BR' (basic rate) tax rate, which automatically removes the Income Tax Personal Allowance for each of those individuals. Because young adults are usually not already enmeshed in the worst complexities of the UK's tax and benefits systems, there would be very few anomalies to negotiate. It is of course debatable whether such a nationwide experiment should be regarded as a pilot project. First of all, there would be no control community (Widerquist, 2018: 19–25); and secondly, it would be difficult to take the Basic Income away once it had been implemented, so the experiment might turn out not to be an experiment at all. The extent to which evaluation would be possible is debatable.

Further research has shown that a more ambitious UK government would be able to employ a similar approach for an entire community. It would not be able to make every change that would be required for the pilot project community's Basic Income and associated tax and benefits changes to match those that would be required for a nationwide Basic Income scheme, but it could get close enough to enable valid conclusions to be reached as to some of the likely effects of a national Basic Income scheme (Torry, 2021b).

Every country is different in relation to its tax and benefits systems, so research would have to be undertaken separately for each country to determine whether it would be possible to make the tax and benefits changes for a single community that would enable a Basic Income pilot project to be run that would be close enough in character to a scheme that it would be feasible to roll out nationwide for valid conclusions to be reached as to the likely effects of a nationwide scheme.

We rarely experiment with changes to tax and benefits systems before making the changes across an entire population. First of all, as we can now see, it is always difficult to run such experiments; and secondly, decisions about reforms are taken on the basis of political ideology and a variety of common presuppositions as much as on the basis of the kinds of effects that a pilot project might be able to measure (Widerquist, 2018: 87–91). A Basic Income scheme can be viewed in two different ways: as minor administrative changes to current tax and benefits systems (Torry, 2019; 2020; 2021b), or as wholesale reform of the benefits system. If the former assumption is made, then a pilot project would seem to be an unnecessary adjunct to normal policy reform processes; if the latter assumption is made, then a pilot project might be thought appropriate: and if there might be widespread demand for one, or policymakers were hesitant about implementing what they might see as a major reform (a not unlikely eventuality given the problems that successive governments have had with the roll-out of the UK's means-tested Universal Credit), then a carefully planned pilot project could be useful.

Methods for Testing a Basic Income Scheme's Financial Feasibility

If we are to ensure that we only run pilot projects that mirror a Basic Income scheme that could feasibly be rolled out nationwide, then we shall need to test schemes for feasibility, and in particularly for financial feasibility. This is by no means the only feasibility test that a scheme would have to pass, nor the most difficult. The others would be tests for administrative feasibility (easy to pass), psychological feasibility (whether people understand the idea of Basic Income and understand it to be beneficial), behavioural feasibility (would it have the predicted effects?), political feasibility (do current political ideologies support it?), and policy process feasibility (could the scheme navigate its way through the country's complex policy process from idea to implementation?) (Torry, 2016): and different countries might find that additional feasibility tests needed to be passed. But however many tests there might be in a particular context, proving financial feasibility would always be essential, and in two respects: first of all, would it be possible to pay for the Basic Incomes; and secondly, would low-income households be made worse off by the combination of their Basic Incomes and the changes that would have to be made to the tax and benefits system to pay for it. (It is sometimes suggested that if alternative funding mechanisms were to be employed, then this problem would not arise. That is not true. For instance, a carbon tax would increase the costs of heating homes and of transport, and therefore of food and other commodities. The overall effect could be net disposable income losses for low-income households. The same could occur if Basic Incomes were to be financed by increasing consumption taxes.)

So what is required is a method for ensuring that the net cost of the Basic Income scheme as a whole is low to zero, and that no significant losses would be suffered by low-income households. We might also wish to ensure that the scheme would reduce all poverty indices, inequality indices, and by a substantial proportion the number of households receiving means-tested benefits.

During the earlier years of the modern Basic Income debate, the question being asked was whether schemes were affordable. If the scheme abolished existing means-tested benefits, then a 'national accounts' method could be employed. This used the national accounts, census data, and other national statistics, to calculate the cost of giving to every member of the population a Basic Income, the money saved by abolishing tax allowances and means-tested and other benefits, and the additional revenue that would be collected from increased tax rates. The net cost of the Basic Income scheme was the total cost of the Basic Incomes, less the money saved by abolishing benefits, and less the additional tax revenue collected. If a revenue-neutral scheme was required, then by a process of trial and error the net cost could be reduced to zero. This was the method that used to be used in the UK (House of Commons Work and Pensions Committee, 2007: Ev.84–90) and that is still sometimes used by researchers (Citizen's Income Trust, 2016; Miller, 2017; Painter & Thoung, 2015). The problem with this method is that it cannot tell us about losses that households would experience at the point of implementation: a serious problem because research in 2012 and 2014 showed that those losses were likely to be substantial for low-income households (Torry, 2014). A further problem was that if means-tested benefits were retained and recalculated rather than abolished, then the national accounts method could not tell us how much additional revenue would be available to fund the Basic Incomes.

Because the 'national statistics' method is inadequate in the context of today's more demanding debate, in which detailed questions are often asked about the financial feasibility of illustrative Basic Income schemes, and in which the possibility of net disposable income losses at the point of implementation is well understood, we are fortunate to have available an additional research method: microsimulation. This can provide all of the information that we need: the net cost of a scheme; household losses at the point of implementation, including for low-income households; changes in poverty and inequality indices; redistribution patterns; and the numbers of households taken off retained and recalculated means-tested benefits. Two different strategies are available. Some researchers propose illustrative Basic Income schemes and then research their financial effects. Another approach is to set criteria for a financially feasible Basic Income scheme and then test multiple illustrative schemes until one is found that fits the criteria (Torry, 2019, 2020, 2021b).

Microsimulation is constituted by (a) a computer programme into which are coded all of the tax and benefits regulations of a country, and (b) financial data obtained from a survey of a statistically significant sample of the population. The data is run through the programme to discover a wide variety of statistics; new benefits are then written into the programme (for instance, Basic Incomes at different levels for different age groups), along with changes to existing taxes and benefits, and the programme is run again. The new set of statistics generated can then be compared to those generated by the current tax and benefits system, and conclusions can be drawn about changes in poverty and inequality indices, numbers of households that would be taken off means-tested benefits by the Basic Income scheme, household net disposable income losses, and the net cost of the scheme (Morgan et al., 2019).

Because the data that the programme uses is real-world data from a statistically significant sample of the country's population, microsimulation is effectively a pilot project run on the entire population of the country. This means that in order to discover a large number of the financial effects of an illustrative Basic Income scheme, there is no need to run a pilot project: microsimulation can do the job for us; and it can also, by a trial and error method, find an illustrative scheme that fits prechosen criteria for a feasible scheme, if such a scheme exists; and it can generate a lot of information about the effects that that scheme would have.

However useful microsimulation might be—and it is very useful—there are of course things that it cannot do. For instance, it can calculate marginal deduction rates (MDRs)—that is, the proportion of additional earned income that is withdrawn by income taxes and the withdrawal of means-tested benefits—but it cannot tell us what effect MDR changes would have on employment incentives; and neither can it tell us the ways in which household members might rearrange their employment patterns if they all had Basic Incomes, and how such pattern changes might alter employment incentives. For all of that, a real on-the-ground pilot project is required. Similarly, microsimulation offers only a static 'morning-after' evaluation of the implementation of a Basic Income scheme. It cannot tell us about the dynamic effects: for instance, if employment patterns were to change, then earned incomes and therefore tax revenues would change, thus changing the Basic Income scheme. Nor can microsimulation tell us about levels of wellbeing or social cohesion, and those are factors in which we might be interested. It is possible that in the future there will be a more dynamic microsimulation programme available that would use an employment model to tell us about likely employment market changes and the effects that those changes would have on the scheme, and so on: but such an extension of microsimulation would rely on a set of presuppositions relating to how changes to household economies might affect households' employment market behaviour, so we would not have the same confidence that results obtained would reflect what would happen in the real world if the Basic Income scheme were to be implemented. With current static microsimulation, we can be fairly sure that the morning after the implementation of a Basic Income scheme we would see the effects that the microsimulation research tells us that it would have.

Widerquist suggests that it is important for those running Basic Income experiments to be clear about the questions that the project needed to answer (Widerquist, 2018: 1–12, 93–98), and also to be clear about the questions that experiments cannot answer or can only answer in a partial fashion (Widerquist, 2018: 99–129). We are now clearer about the financial feasibility questions that an experiment in a more developed country would not have to answer, and the questions to which answers might still be required.

What (If Anything) Justifies Basic Income Experiments?

We are now in a position to answer the question set by the title of this chapter.

In countries with less developed economies, and therefore without existing complex tax and benefits systems, pilot projects that test genuine Basic Income schemes can reveal some of the effects that a nationwide Basic Income scheme might generate, and they can facilitate active public debate about Basic Income: although we must recognise that the limited length of the pilot project will mean that results must be treated carefully, and that detailed reasoning will be required to work out the extent to which the pilot project results might or might not reflect the effects that the scheme tested would deliver if it were to be rolled out nationwide and permanently.

In more developed countries, microsimulation functions as a pilot project, but there are some things that it cannot tell us. To discover the likely effects that a microsimulation programme cannot tell us about would require an on-the-ground pilot project, and although it might not be easy to establish one in a more developed country, compromise might be possible (as it is in the UK), meaning that it might be possible to construct a pilot project for a Basic Income scheme sufficiently like a scheme that could be rolled out nationwide that the results from the pilot project would give us useful information about the effects that a national version of the scheme might deliver. Such an experiment would provide useful information and stimulate public debate about Basic Income, as the ambiguous experiment undertaken in Finland has shown. In both situations, a Basic Income experiment would appear to be justified.

This leaves two issues to be addressed:

First of all, how useful are experiments that test things other than Basic Income schemes?—for instance, projects that test Minimum Income Guarantee schemes that establish household-based minimum income levels and then pay means-tested benefits to enable household incomes to reach the guaranteed levels, such as the experiments in Canada researched by Evelyn Forget. Generalisation is impossible, but what we might be able to say is that the closer an experiment gets to being a Basic Income experiment, the more useful the results might be.

Secondly: Precisely what is being requested by the general public needs to be carefully evaluated. If there is public demand for a Basic Income pilot project *rather than* for a Basic Income, and there are questions in the minds of the general public that an experiment might be able to answer, then holding a Basic Income experiment would be fully justified, and the experiment should be held. But if policymakers are motivated to hold a pilot project because demand for a Basic Income is growing, but they fear how the media might react to a proposal to establish a nationwide Basic Income scheme, then if they are convinced of the desirability and feasibility of Basic Income, it might be better for them to make the argument for establishing a Basic Income and then do that (Widerquist, 2018: 141–144). Under these circumstances the justification for holding a Basic Income experiment is reduced.

Conclusion

The outcome of our discussion is that in any country a genuine Basic Income experiment might be useful, at least to some extent, in telling us what some of the effects of a nationwide Basic Income scheme might be. Such experiments might be either a distraction from the policy process (because they might mean nationwide Basic Income schemes missing political opportunities); detrimental to it (because the results might be poorly communicated or misinterpreted, whether purposely or not) (Widerquist, 2018: 43–59, 77–85, 145–149); or useful adjuncts to other policy reform processes, providing useful information to policymakers. The decision to hold a pilot project should only be made following consideration of these factors, and the other factors discussed in this chapter; and because it would only be possible to hold a Basic Income experiment in collaboration with a willing national government, there would need to be evidence that the government would be happy to assist before the planning process got very far.

We have seen some excellent pilot projects in the developing world. If in a more developed country the factors discussed in this essay were to suggest that a Basic Income experiment might be justified, then if at all possible it should be carried out. Holding a carefully planned Basic Income experiment in a more developed country could be of enormous benefit to the global Basic Income debate.

Acknowledgements This chapter was first published as Malcolm Torry, 'Do we need Basic Income experiments?' *Basic Income Studies*, vol. 16, no. 1, 2021, pp. 39–54, https://doi.org/10.1515/bis-2021-0020 (Torry, 2021a). The publisher's permission to republish the article is gratefully acknowledged.

References

Basic Income Earth Network. (2022). *Basic Income*. Retrieved March 27, 2022, from https://basicincome.org

Basic Income Grant Coalition. (2009). *Making the difference: The BIG in Namibia: Basic Income Grant Pilot Project, assessment report*. Namibia NGO Forum. Retrieved March 27, 2022, from http://www.bignam.org/Publications/BIG_Assessment_report_08b.pdf

Citizen's Basic Income Trust. (2018). *Citizen's Basic Income: A brief introduction*. Citizen's Basic Income Trust.

Citizen's Income Trust. (2016). London: Royal Society of Arts [Review of London: Royal Society of Arts by A. Painter and C. Thoung (2015)]. *Citizen's Income Newsletter*, (2) for 2016, 20–21. London: Citizen's Income Trust. Retrieved March 27, 2022, from http://citizensincome.org/research-analysis/the-royal-society-of-arts-report-on-citizens-income/

Davala, S. (2019). Pilots, evidence and politics: The Basic Income debate in India. In M. Torry (Ed.), *The Palgrave international handbook of Basic Income* (pp. 373–387). Palgrave Macmillan.

Davala, S., Jhabvala, R., Kapoor Mehta, S., & Standing, G. (2015). *Basic Income: A transformative policy for India*. Bloomsbury.

De Wispelaere, J., Halmetoja, A., & Pulkka, V.-V. (2019). The Finnish Basic Income Experiment: A primer. In M. Torry (Ed.), *The Palgrave international handbook of Basic Income* (pp. 389–406). Palgrave Macmillan.

Forget, E. (2011). The town with no poverty: The health effects of a Canadian guaranteed annual income field experiment. *Canadian Public Policy/Politiques Canadienne, 37*(3), 283–305.

Haarmann, C., & Haarmann, D. (2007). From survival to decent employment: Basic Income security in Namibia. *Basic Income Studies, 2*(1), 1–7.

Haarmann, C., & Haarmann, D. (2012). Namibia: Seeing the sun rise—The realities and hopes of the Basic Income Grant Pilot Project. In M. C. Murray & C. Pateman (Eds.), *Basic Income worldwide: Horizons of reform* (pp. 33–58). Palgrave Macmillan.

Haarmann, C., Haarmann, D., & Nattrass, N. (2019). The Namibian Basic Income Grant pilot. In M. Torry (Ed.), *The Palgrave international handbook of Basic Income* (pp. 357–372). Palgrave Macmillan.

House of Commons Work and Pensions Committee. (2007). *Benefit simplification: The seventh report of session 2006–2007*. HC 463, vol. 2. The Stationery Office. Retrieved March 27, 2022, from www.publications.parliament.uk/pa/cm200607/cmselect/cmworpen/463/463ii.pdf

Kangas, O., Jauhiainen, S., Simanainen, M., & Ylikännö, M. (2020). *Suomen Perustulokokeilun Arviointi*. Sosiaali-ja terveysministeriö. Retrieved March 27, 2022, from http://julkaisut.valtioneuvosto.fi/bitstream/handle/10024/162219/STM_2020_15_rap.pdf. (In Finnish, with English summary).

Miller, A. (2017). *A Basic Income handbook*. Luath Press.

Morgan, G., Reed, H., & Torry, M. (2019). Analysis of the financial effects of Basic Income. In M. Torry (Ed.), *The Palgrave international handbook of Basic Income* (pp. 191–211). Palgrave Macmillan.

Ontario. (n.d.). Ontario's Basic Income Pilot: Studying the impact of a basic income. Retrieved March 27, 2022, from https://files.ontario.ca/170508_bi_brochure_eng_pg_by_pg_proof.pdf

Painter, A., & Thoung, C. (2015). *Creative citizen, creative state: The principled and pragmatic case for a Universal Basic Income*. Royal Society of Arts.

Torry, M. (2013). *Money for everyone: Why we need a Citizen's Income*. Policy Press.

Torry, M. (2014). *Research note: A feasible way to implement a Citizen's Income* (EUROMOD Working Paper EM17/14). Institute for Social and Economic Research, University of Essex. Retrieved March 27, 2022, from https://www.iser.essex.ac.uk/research/publications/working-papers/euromod/em17-14

Torry, M. (2016). *The feasibility of Citizen's Income*. Palgrave Macmillan.

Torry, M. (2017). What's a definition? And how should we define 'Basic Income'? A paper for the Basic Income Earth Network (BIEN) Congress in Lisbon, 2017. Retrieved March 27, 2022, from http://basicincome.org/wp-content/uploads/2015/01/Malcolm_Torry_Whats_a_definition_And_how_should_we_define_Basic_Income.pdf

Torry, M. (2018a). *Why we need a Citizen's Basic Income: The desirability, feasibility and implementation of an unconditional income*. Policy Press.

Torry, M. (2018b). What is an Unconditional Basic Income? A response to Rothstein. In P. Van Parijs (Ed.), *Basic Income and the Left: A European debate* (pp. 110–115). Social Europe.

Torry, M. (2019). *Static microsimulation research on Citizen's Basic Income for the UK: A personal summary and further reflections* (EUROMOD Working Paper EM13/19). Institute to Social and Economic Research, University of Essex. Retrieved March 27, 2022, from https://www.iser.essex.ac.uk/research/publications/working-papers/euromod/em13-19.pdf

Torry, M. (2020). *Evaluation of a Recovery Basic Income, and of a sustainable revenue neutral Citizen's Basic Income, with an appendix relating to different Universal Credit roll-out scenarios*. Institute for Social and Economic Research (Working Paper EM7/20). Institute for Social and Economic Research, University of Essex. Retrieved March 27, 2022, from https://www.iser.essex.ac.uk/research/publications/working-papers/euromod/em7-20.pdf

Torry, M. (2021a). Do we need Basic Income experiments? *Basic Income Studies, 16*(1), 39–54. Retrieved March 27, 2022, from https://doi.org/10.1515/bis-2021-0020

Torry, M. (2021b). *Three income maintenance options for 2021*. Centre for Microsimulation and Policy Analysis report. Institute for Social and Economic Research, University of Essex. Retrieved March 27, 2022, from https://www.microsimulation.ac.uk/publications/publication-526555/

Widerquist, K. (2018). *A critical analysis of Basic Income experiments for researchers, policymakers, and citizens*. Palgrave Macmillan.

PART V

What, Why and How in the United Kingdom

CHAPTER 14

Factors Influencing Political Decisions About Social Security Benefits in the UK

Introduction

> The policy process is a complex and multi-layered one. It is … a complex political process in which there are many actors: politicians, pressure groups, civil servants, publicly employed professionals, and even sometimes those who see themselves as the passive recipients of policy. (Hill, 2009: 4)

Some suggestions for reforming the UK's income maintenance system are implemented. Some are not. This chapter enquires into the characteristics and histories of some of the proposals for reforming the UK's

In this chapter 'National Living Wage' should be taken to mean a compulsory Living Wage. The original conference paper was written before the UK's Chancellor of the Exchequer renamed the National Minimum Wage a National Living Wage and increased it to less than the Living Wage, thus compromising the Living Wage campaign. The Chancellor's actions do not compromise either the argument or the conclusions of the paper, so it has not been revised before being published here.

M. Torry, *Basic Income—What, Why, and How?*,
Exploring the Basic Income Guarantee,
https://doi.org/10.1007/978-3-031-14248-2_14

benefits system (Torry, 2013a) and into the characteristics and histories of the National Minimum Wage and the Living Wage, in order to ask whether it might be possible to bring some sense of order into our understanding of the somewhat haphazard policy process (Hill, 2009: 159, 164), and whether we might be able to predict the success or otherwise of two current proposals: a statutory version of the Living Wage—defined as a wage 'explicitly tied to the purchasing power deemed necessary ... to provide workers and their families with a basic but acceptable standard of living rather than estimates of what the market can bear without impacting on employment' (Pennycook, 2012: 4–5); and a Basic Income: an unconditional, nonwithdrawable income for every individual as a right of citizenship, and here understood as funded by reducing tax allowances and means-tested and contributory benefits.

Histories and Characteristics

Family Allowance

By the beginning of the Second World War, the payment of an allowance to mothers to help them to care for their children was by no means a new idea. During the First World War child allowances had been paid to mothers of soldiers at the front; and child allowances were being paid in addition to wages at the London School of Economics, where William Beveridge, the Director, had been persuaded of the wisdom of the idea by reading Eleanor Rathbone's 1924 *The Disinherited Family* (Beveridge, 1949: 270; Rathbone, 1924/1986: 139, 167, 353). Rathbone had argued that a worker's wage could be expected to support a small family, but not a large one, so mothers needed an income of their own to enable them to care for their children (Macnicol, 1980: 5–10, 20–23; Thane, 1996: 63–64, 202). When Beveridge was asked to chair a war-time committee to plan for post-war social security benefits, he was not asked to discuss child allowances, so he wrote the idea into the report as a presupposition.

Child allowances were already being paid with Unemployment Benefit, so a worker with a large family could find that when they moved from unemployment to employment they could be worse off. Not only was this bad for labour market incentives, but employers were also concerned that after the war full employment would create the conditions for unsustainable wage rises, and that the subsistence needs of workers with large families would exacerbate the resulting wage inflation. The only solution to these problems was to provide child allowances both in and out of employment. In 1945 Parliament passed the Family Allowance Act, and the first Family Allowances were paid in 1946. While no allowance was paid for the first child in a family, and the allowance was set lower than Beveridge had wished, an unconditional Family Allowance was implemented because 'little money can be saved by any reasonable income test' (Beveridge, 1942: 154, 157, 163, 177).

Family Allowances were an attack on poverty, but they were also an attack on the poverty trap. Because Family Allowances were not means-tested, and were paid whatever the household's employment status, the scheme meant that a worker who moved from Unemployment Benefit to paid employment no longer experienced a drop in net income. Other possible causes for the success of Rathbone's proposal were that the plan had a champion in William Beveridge; there was substantial public approval of the scheme, particularly among women; MPs could support it, either because they wanted to keep a lid on wages (Harris, 1981: 249), because they approved of the scheme's equal treatment of every family, or because they did not wish to be seen to disapprove of a clearly popular measure (Land, 1975: 169, 173–179, 195–196, 205, 221, 227); trades unions were able to approve (because by the end of the Second World War there were more women in trades unions than there had been before the war); the civil service was able to approve the plan once a lower allowance than was at first intended had been achieved, and presumably because a new department would be needed to administer the Family Allowances; the scheme exhibited clear continuities with previous schemes, both with child allowances paid with Unemployment Benefit and with child allowances paid to soldiers' families; the London School of Economics experience was a useful pilot project; administration of the non-means-tested benefit was uncomplicated; the scheme presented no transitional problems; and the benefit's recipients were clearly a deserving social group: that is, children, and the mothers who cared for them.

National Insurance and National Assistance

William Beveridge's report, *Social Insurance and Allied Service*, published in 1942 (Beveridge, 1942), proposed National Insurance benefits in return for regular National Insurance contributions, and means-tested

National Assistance to top up contributory benefits if they were insufficient—for instance, for working age adults whose contributory Unemployment Benefit had expired, or whose Unemployment Benefit did not provide a high enough income to cover housing costs (Beveridge had intended contributory benefits to be sufficiently high to cover housing costs, but the Government set the rates too low for this and more families than originally intended found themselves having to apply for National Assistance) (Atkinson, 1969: 24; Bradshaw & Bennett, 2011; Thane, 2011). The combination of contributory and means-tested benefits was one that people already knew about, because contributory benefits already existed for some industries, Friendly Societies and other organisations were already paying benefits if contributions conditions were met, and for many households means-testing was either a difficult memory or a present experience. The plan assumed full employment for households' male breadwinners, and because for all but the largest families a male wage provided more than the benefits system, and for families with children Family Allowances were not withdrawn as earnings increased, no poverty trap was expected to materialise.

In 1946 an Act of Parliament established National Insurance (contributory) Retirement Pensions, Unemployment Benefit, and Sickness Benefit; and in 1948 an Act gave birth to means-tested National Assistance.

The scheme was in continuity with the somewhat chaotic system that had preceded it (elements of which could be regarded as pilot projects); it was publicly understood; it tackled poverty; it did not generate an appreciable poverty trap; it met with substantial public understanding and approval; it was difficult for MPs of any party to find fault with it; it promised an expansion of the civil service; administration of contributory benefits was relatively simple; it was not thought that there would be many people claiming the more administratively complex National Assistance; and transition into the scheme was undertaken with enthusiasm and relatively little difficulty. While the scheme was universal in coverage, only the contingencies of illness, disability, unemployment, and old age, triggered benefits claims, so in an era of almost full employment the vast majority of the population had no contact with the scheme apart from their employer fixing the weekly National Insurance stamps onto their cards.

Universal Credit

In 1965 Peter Townsend and Brian Abel-Smith published *The Poor and the Poorest*, which showed that almost one in five families were on incomes below half the average (Abel-Smith & Townsend, 1965; Titmuss, 1962). Many of those families were in work. In 1971 the Government responded by implementing the means-tested in-work benefit Family Income Supplement (Banting, 1979: 89), renamed 'Family Credit' in 1985. Unfortunately, the freezing of Child Benefit (Barr & Coulter, 1991: 282) and the more generous nature of Family Credit exacerbated an existing poverty trap. The 1997 Labour Government renamed Family Credit 'Working Families Tax Credit', and in 2003 replaced it with 'Child Tax Credits' and 'Working Tax Credits' (available for the first time to households without children). The more generous nature of Tax Credits reduced child poverty, but at the same time it increased the earnings range across which households experienced a poverty trap (Field, 2002: 54, 57).

'Universal Credit' is now being implemented. Universal Credit combines in-work and out-of-work means-tested benefits into a single means-tested benefit in order to ease the transition into employment. By reducing the rate at which means-tested benefits are withdrawn (Centre for Social Justice, 2009: 265; Department for Work and Pensions, 2010: 21; 2011a: 13) Universal Credit will reduce child poverty and also the depth of the poverty trap, but in doing so it will increase the earnings range across which households will experience benefits withdrawal. The benefit will therefore embed means-testing at the heart of millions of households' income maintenance strategies, and in particular will make it less worthwhile for second earners to seek employment.

The plan had a champion in Iain Duncan Smith [then Secretary of State for Work and Pensions]; there is a level of public understanding of the general idea, but not of the detail; the plan is in continuity with previous means-tested benefits; MPs of all parties have been able to support the general idea, whatever they might think about its detail and implementation; the civil service is content to try to make it work; and trades unions have been largely absent from the debate, which is somewhat surprising given that the scheme integrates in-work with out-of-work benefits and therefore risks extending the stigma relating to out-of-work means-tested benefits to families receiving in-work means-tested benefits (Dean, 2012; Dean & Mitchell, 2011). Administration of the new benefit requires accurate real time communication between employers', Her Majesty's Revenue and Customs, and Department for Work and Pensions computer systems, and is proving to be a problem, so transition from the existing to the new system has been somewhat fraught. If the transition fails then it will be because of the administrative problems. The plan's other characteristics have been no barrier to legislation and attempted implementation.

Child Benefit

A further result of Peter Townsend's and Brian Abel-Smith's research, and of the 1966 play *Cathy Come Home*, about a family's slide into unemployment and homelessness, was the new Child Poverty Action Group's campaign for higher Family Allowances, and for the benefit to be paid for every child, including the first, the money to be found by abolishing Child Tax Allowances (Hill, 1990: 41). In 1974 a new Labour Government recognised that the proposed extension of Family Allowance to the first child, and the proposed increase in value, would ameliorate the poverty trap, because more of an unemployed or low income family's income would not be means-tested (Barr & Coulter, 1991: 291), and parliament passed legislation to turn Family Allowance into Child Benefit. However, nothing happened until in 1976 Malcolm Wicks, a young civil servant who later became a Member of Parliament (Wicks, 2014), leaked cabinet minutes to Frank Field, the Director of the Child Poverty Action Group (CPAG), who published them. The minutes revealed that implementation had been postponed out of concern that the abolition of Child Tax Allowances would fuel wage inflation. CPAG's 'Child Benefit Now' campaign, and Barbara Castle MP's support in Parliament, resulted in Child Benefit being phased in over a three year period, although at a level lower than originally intended (Walley, 1986).

Child Benefit was an attack on child poverty (because mothers were more likely to spend the Family Allowance on their children than were fathers to spend the value of their child tax allowances on them), and, as we have seen, it was an attack on the poverty trap. The scheme had some significant champions in Barbara Castle and Frank Field; it was in continuity with the highly popular Family Allowance, of which there had been twenty years' experience; the general public, and especially mothers, were in favour; enough MPs had good reasons for voting for Child Benefit; and after the scandal of the Government's attempt to block implementation there were plenty of MPs who wanted to see it happen. The civil service was content, and possibly happy, to implement the scheme; trades unions were in favour (women constituted an increasing proportion of members); administration and transition were easy to manage; and again the benefit's recipients were clearly a deserving social group: children, and the mothers who cared for them.

A National Minimum Wage

In spite of the implementation of Family Income Supplement, by the early 1980s in-work poverty remained a problem (Pond & Winyard, 1983: 8). Two solutions vied for attention: a National Minimum Wage (NMW), of which there was already experience in other countries (Pond & Winyard, 1983: 42–44); and an increase in the value of in-work means-tested benefits, which, as we have seen, was the policy chosen by the Conservative Government when Family Income Supplement became Family Credit. But the problem with that strategy was that because Family Credit was withdrawn as earnings rose, and there was now more to withdraw, the poverty trap was deepened. As proponents of a NMW pointed out, a higher wage would reduce the amount of means-tested benefit required and would therefore reduce the depth of the poverty trap; and as Chris Pond and Steve Winyard pointed out in their *Case for a National Minimum Wage*:

> Even if it were possible to devise a social policy which would compensate for the effects of low wages without stigma and without the problem of the poverty trap, this would not overcome the feelings of injustice and humiliation which are associated with the receipt of low wages. (Pond & Winyard, 1983: 24)

In 1970 the Trade Union Congress (TUC) suggested a 'guideline' NMW, because there were some trade unionists who wanted to resist government interference in wage-setting; but although during the 1980s this argument was still heard (Metcalf, 1999: 2), in 1982 the TUC passed a resolution committing itself to consult with a future Labour Government over the establishment of a NMW (Pond & Winyard, 1983: 36–37), and in 1995 the TUC itself published *Arguments for a National Minimum Wage*:

> A National Minimum Wage which raised pay levels in the poorest paid occupations and industries would clearly reduce the extent to which Family Credit currently subsidises low pay. (Trade Union Congress, 1995: 19)

The 'widespread assumption that raising wages will automatically lead to a loss of jobs' (Pond & Winyard, 1983: 51) was intuitive: but the counterarguments were increasingly heard: that wage-setting is a political activity (Edwards & Gilman, 1998); that the wage paid does not necessarily equate to the marginal product of labour (Pond & Winyard, 1983: 17, 51–52); that the impact of a NMW would only increase the total wage bill by about 5%, because raising the lowest wages to an agreed or statutory minimum has only a small effect on wage levels above that minimum (Dickens & Manning, 2002: 9; Edwards & Gilman, 1998; Trade Union Congress, 1995: 54); that therefore a NMW would lead to very little additional unemployment, if any (Robson et al., 1997: 20); that only minor reductions in the return to capital and minor increases in prices would be the result; and that higher wages for the lowest paid would lead to increased consumption of goods and services and would therefore increase demand and thus employment (Edwards & Gilman, 1998; Pond & Winyard, 1983: 53; Robson et al., 1997: 20). As for the argument that the Government should stay out of wage-setting: the Government regulated working conditions, so why not wages? (Pond & Winyard, 1983: 21).

In 1995 the Confederation of British Industry (CBI) declared itself opposed to a National Minimum Wage, but by 1997 it was recommending one on the basis that it would create a floor to the market (Metcalf, 1999: 2). Crucial to the debate was the expressed view of many business leaders who resented being forced to pay low wages and to reduce investment in both human and physical capital by competitors who reduced their production costs by paying low wages (Pond & Winyard, 1983: 13, 19; Trade Union Congress, 1995: 20). An additional argument more often thought than expressed was that a general rise in wage rates would put some of the least efficient businesses out of business, thus improving the general efficiency of the industries concerned.

The Labour Party's manifesto for the 1997 General Election included a pledge to establish a National Minimum Wage, and in 1998 the National Minimum Wage Act was passed. It was implemented in April 1999 with NMW levels set by the new Low Pay Commission at £3.60 per hour for workers aged over 21, and £3.00 per hour for workers aged between 18 and 20 (Robson et al., 1997: 19). The Treasury, the Bank of England, the TUC and the CBI all declared themselves happy with the calculation (Metcalf, 1999: 7, 12). In 2003 a new lower rate was established for 16 and 17 year olds.

The idea of a National Minimum Wage was not entirely new. In 1909 the Government, with Winston Churchill's enthusiastic support, had established Trades Boards (Pond & Winyard, 1983: 13, 53) to set minimum wages for particular industries. These later became the Wages Councils: and although these had been abolished by the time of the 1997 election, they provided an important precedent and pilot project. A NMW could therefore be seen as in direct continuity with almost one hundred years of experience of national wage-setting.

The NMW was an attack on poverty, and, as we have seen, it was also an attack on the poverty trap. The Prime Minister and the Cabinet were in favour, so there were plenty of parliamentary champions: but also important was sustained work on the issue by the Low Pay Unit, and particularly by its Director, Chris Pond, who became a member of parliament in 1997 (Metcalf, 1999: 1). There was substantial public understanding of the problem of low pay, and of the proposal for a NMW; there were clear arguments for the proposal; and eventually there was sufficient understanding that evidence did not support the intuitive arguments against it (Pond & Winyard, 1983: 51). The legislation established a new Low Pay Commission to set NMW levels, an inspectorate to enforce them, and tribunals to hear cases, thus increasing the number of public servants. Administration of the scheme is relatively simple, and implementation was not difficult. Recipients were a clearly deserving group of people: the working poor.

Future Possibilities

The Campaign for a Living Wage

The Low Pay Commission established by the 1998 National Minimum Wage Act studied a variety of possible levels for the initial NMW, and decided on a relatively low wage that would have only a minor impact on employment levels. The NMW was never going to be enough to live on, meaning that in-work benefits would continue to be needed. Already in 1996 The East London Communities Organisation (TELCO) had brought US-style community organising to London (Citizens UK, 2022), and in 2001 a Living Wage—a wage level based on a Minimum Income Standard calculated to provide a decent standard of living (Torry, 2020; Chapter 11 in this volume)—became an important campaign for what had by then become London Citizens. In 2005 the Greater London Authority established its Living Wage Unit to encourage London's employers to pay a Living Wage; and in 2011 the national community organising organisation Citizens UK gave birth to the Living Wage Foundation, which validates Living Wage employers: that is, employers who pay the Living Wage rates established by the Foundation on the basis of research into Minimum Income Standards by the Centre for Research in Social Policy at Loughborough University (Centre for Research in Social Policy, 2022; Living Wage Foundation, 2022). The number of Living Wage employers continues to grow both because local campaigning has been effective and because a Living Wage makes good business sense. In the early days of mass car production Henry Ford more than doubled his workers' wages in order to increase motivation and reduce absenteeism, staff turnover, and training costs. Counterintuitively, doubling the wages saved the company money (Ford, 1934: 43). Living Wage employers discover similar effects when they increase wages from the National Minimum Wage to the Living Wage (Living Wage Foundation, 2022).

The question for us is this: What is the likelihood that we shall see the establishment of a National Living Wage (NLW)?—that is, of a statutory National Minimum Wage that rises sufficiently to become a statutory National Living Wage? (and in this case, like the Living Wage and unlike the National Minimum Wage, a higher rate would need to be set for London than for the rest of the country). One way to tackle this question is to ask the related question: If a NLW were to be established, what would we then say were the causes of its implementation? This is to treat a not yet implemented proposal in the same way as we have treated the implemented proposals studied above. For the purpose of this chapter, I shall use the past tense.

The voluntary Living Wage had plenty of champions: the Prime Minister, other party leaders, the Mayor of London, the vast majority of MPs and local councillors, and numerous public, private, voluntary, and religious sector organisations. Initially, it was not clear how much of this support for a voluntary Living Wage would translate into support for an NLW, but public support for National Minimum Wages was rising in a variety of OECD countries, and the value of National Minimum Wages in other OECD countries was rising (apparently without adding to unemployment) (Manning, 2014), and the number of validated Living Wage employers in the UK continued to rise: so increasing numbers of organisations and individuals felt able to support an NLW. Living Wage employers were particularly vociferous in support of an NLW because they were being undercut by firms that were paying only the National Minimum Wage.

The NLW was an attack on poverty, and also an attack on the poverty trap, for the same reasons that the NMW was an attack on them in 1998. There was substantial experience and public understanding of an NMW, a growing appreciation of the importance of the idea, and increasing awareness that the NMW had made very little difference to employment levels (Plunkett et al., 2014: 25). Research had shown that the National Minimum Wage had raised the average wage bill by 0.5% (Metcalf, 1999: 12), that in many industries the payment of a Living Wage would increase the wage bill by just 1%, and that in the lowest paid sectors companies' wage bills would rise by about 5%, but that phased implementation would reduce up-front costs and would enable businesses to adapt (Pennycook, 2012: 2–3). Companies found this to be the case. The NLW was in direct continuity with the NMW, and the same mechanisms were employed to enforce it. The legislation permitted transition from the NMW into an NLW over a three-year period, and businesses found that this was sufficient time in which to adjust, and in which to appreciate the higher motivation and lower absenteeism and staff turnover that the policy had delivered. Implementation was enthusiastically handled by the public authorities involved; and the press was behind the change because recipients were a clearly deserving group: the working poor.

A particularly interesting characteristic of the journey towards a National Living Wage was the strong relationship between research and practice. The Greater London Authority both researched and paid a Living Wage; and, to take just one example from a London borough: Matthew Pennycook, who had conducted important research on the Living Wage for the Resolution Foundation, as a Greenwich local councillor was a major influence on the Council becoming a Living Wage employer.

Universal Benefits

> One of the reasons why the rate and intensity of poverty are relatively insensitive to the level of the NMW is that many low paid workers who are in poor households, are in families who are in receipt of means-tested benefits. Entitlements to these fall if incomes rise, and rise if incomes fall. (Sutherland, 2001: 9)

Because means-tested benefits are withdrawn as earnings rise, many families in poverty see only minor differences in disposable income if their earned incomes rise substantially. The structure of the benefits system is therefore an important cause of people's inability to earn their way out of poverty. The non-means-tested Child Benefit does not have this disincentive effect, and so has inspired a long-standing campaign to extend unconditional and nonwithdrawable benefits to working age adults.

Juliet and Brandon Rhys Williams

In 1942, Juliet Rhys Williams, a member of the commission that issued the report *Social Insurance and Allied Services*, wrote a minority report which she then expanded and published as *Something to Look Forward To*. She believed that the time-limited nature of the proposed National Insurance benefits, and the fact that National Assistance would be withdrawn as earnings rose, would create too much of a disincentive to seek paid employment, meaning that coercion would be required (Beveridge, 1942; Harris, 1981: 258; Rhys Williams, 1943: 13, 45, 139–147; Torry, 2013a, 2013b: 34–36). She believed that justice required that

> the State owes precisely the same benefits to all of its citizens, and should in no circumstances pay more to one than to another of the same sex and age, except in return for services rendered ... Therefore the same benefits [should be paid] to the employed and healthy as to the idle and sick. ... The prevention of want must be regarded as being the duty of the State to all its citizens and not merely to a favoured few. (Rhys Williams, 1943: 139, 145)

For every worker to receive 'the whole benefit of wages (less taxation)' (Rhys Williams, 1943: 147) it was essential that benefits should not be withdrawn as earnings rose. This did not mean, however, that the income should be entirely unconditional. Although Rhys Williams believed that the nonwithdrawable nature of the benefit would mean that there would always be sufficient incentive to seek employment, she also wanted unemployed workers to have to visit the Labour Exchange and to have to accept any employment offered (Rhys Williams, 1943: 167).

If implemented, Rhys Williams' scheme for nonwithdrawable benefits would have abolished the poverty trap, increased employment incentives, and reduced poverty. It would have been simple to administer, and it would have improved women's status (Rhys Williams, 1953: 138). But the scheme was not implemented. Beveridge's scheme achieved immediate public acceptance (it was the scheme that people already knew, although extended and somewhat tidied up), and this left very little social space within which Rhys Williams' scheme could be considered. A further major problem with Rhys Williams' scheme was that it would have 'abolished bureaucrats' and that it therefore 'met with an official wall of silence' (Harris, 1981: 258).

Forty years later, Juliet Rhys Williams' son, Sir Brandon Rhys Williams, a Conservative MP, gave evidence to the House of Commons Treasury and Civil Service Committee Sub-Committee on a similar scheme for a universal benefit, but this time the proposal was for a benefit entirely unconditional as well as nonwithdrawable:

> Every citizen would be entitled to a personal basic income or PBI. These guaranteed basic incomes would replace virtually all existing benefits and allowances. (House of Commons Treasury & Civil Service Committee Sub-Committee, 1982: 423; cf. Parker, 1989: 224–253; Rhys Williams, 1989)

The final exchange between Sir Brandon and the committee Chair expressed clearly the scheme's advantages:

> *Chair*: There seem to me to be many benefits of this system.
> *BRW*: There are.
> *C*: Clearly you are expressing them very eloquently. Clearly they would go a long way toward easing the unemployment and poverty traps.
> *BRW*: There would not be any unemployment under these schemes. You would not need to register as unemployed. There would be people who were not in full-time work but they would not need to have themselves labeled as unemployed. If they got an opportunity of work or casual work they could take it and nobody would have to know.

> *C*: Are you saying that the unemployment benefit trap would be virtually eradicated by this?
> *BRW*: Certainly.
> *C*: Also it would be administratively much simpler.
> *BRW*: Yes, it would.
> *C*: I wonder what degree of redistribution of resources there would be or is that one of the matters that could be flexible within the system?
> *BRW*: This is optional. This is why I have not put figures in my paper because you could make the scheme do what you liked. If you want to help people on low wages or low incomes you can tilt the tax and benefit structure in such a way that it is redistributive in certain directions (House of Commons Treasury & Civil Service Committee Sub-Committee, 1982: 459).

The committee recommended that the Government should consider an unconditional and nonwithdrawable benefit as a serious option for reform, that more work should be done on the scheme, and that

> meanwhile, it is desirable that changes to the present system should be compatible with an eventual move to an integrated structure of tax and social security. (Parker, 1989: 100)

In 1983 a General Election prevented the matter from being taken any further.

A year later the Basic Income Research Group was founded, with a brief to promote both research and debate on Basic Income. Ten years later the organisation was renamed the Citizen's Income Trust, and the 'unconditional and nonwithdrawable income for every individual as a right of citizenship' (Citizen's Income Trust, 2013) was renamed a Citizen's Income. For nearly forty years the Trust and numerous others, in the UK and around the world, have promoted debate and research on an idea that would be feasible to implement without additional public expenditure being required. (In the UK a Basic Income could be funded entirely by reducing tax allowances and means-tested and contributory benefits.)

Arguments for Basic Income

A Basic Income would not be withdrawn as earnings rose, so individuals and households on low earnings taken off means-tested benefits by their Basic Incomes would keep all of any additional earnings (minus tax) and would find it much easier than they do now to earn their way out of poverty (Citizen's Income Trust, 2013; Torry, 2013a: 116–117, 119–120, 131–147). A Basic Income would therefore be an attack on poverty as well as an attack on the poverty trap.

We already have a Basic Income for children in Child Benefit, and something like a Basic Income for pensioners is being rolled out. The Single Tier State Pension (STSP) planned by the Minister for Pensions, Steve Webb, will be almost a Citizen's Pension: it will not be withdrawn as earnings or savings rise, although the payment of the maximum pension will be conditional on a complete contributions record (Department for Work and Pensions, 2011b: 10, 29–35; Torry, 2013a: 38–42).

The reasons for the successful implementation of the Single Tier State Pension are similar to those that propelled Family Allowance onto the statute book: it will tackle poverty; it will tackle a poverty trap (in this case the savings trap); it has a ministerial champion; there is sufficient public understanding of the idea; MPs of all parties can support it; there are no intuitive arguments against it; the retention of contributory conditions will mean that no civil service departments will be lost (although there will eventually be some reduction in the numbers of Department for Work and Pensions staff managing means-tested pension top-ups); trades unions will have no problems with the plan; there is clear continuity with the Basic State Pension (which can be regarded as a large pilot project); recipients are clearly a deserving group (the elderly); the plan is administratively feasible; and transition will be relatively simple (as transitional arrangements will be in place for pensioners who have contributed to the State Second Pension).

A Basic Income for every citizen (with the amount varying according to the recipient's age but for no other reason) would be in continuity with Child Benefit and the Single Tier State Pension, which could also be regarded as pilot projects, as could be the Basic Income pilot projects in Namibia and India which showed such significant results, particularly in relation to economic activity among the lowest earners (Torry, 2013a: 69–75; 2013b). A Basic Income's administration would be simple; the error rate would be negligible; and the benefit would attract almost no fraud (Torry, 2013a: 81–98). Transition to a Basic Income would, however, be somewhat complex, not because a Basic Income would be complex, but because our current system is. The main complexity is that some households might experience losses at the point of implementation: but these would be more easily made up by earning additional income than would be possible under the current system because the Basic Income would not be withdrawn as earnings rose (Torry, 2013a: 245–248). Residual means-tested benefits would still be needed if the Basic Income was not paid at subsistence level, but the means-tested benefits still received by households would be of far smaller amounts than they are now, and escaping from means-testing by earning additional income would be far more of an option than it is now and would therefore be an attractive option for households to pursue.

As with some of the provisions that we have already discussed, the intuitive counterarguments can all be answered. It is no problem to pay a Basic Income to the wealthy because they pay more in tax than they would receive as their Basic Income. People would be more likely to work than they are now, and not less, because the Basic Income would not be withdrawn as earnings rose (Torry, 2013a: 277–278). And there would be additional advantages attached to a Basic Income [for any household taken off means-tested benefits] in terms of social cohesion (because everyone would receive a Basic Income), household formation (because no longer would officials need to discover the detail of people's personal relationships, as they do now), and employment patterns (because coercion would no longer be required to persuade people to take employment, and part-time and occasional employment would be more feasible than they are now).

The arguments for a Basic Income are persuasive. It really is a good idea: it needn't cost an extra penny of public money [; and if means-tested benefits are left in place and recalculated, then significant household net disposable income losses due to the complexities of the current system can be avoided for low-income households at the point of implementation].

So let us do as we have done with the Living Wage proposal: that is, in imagination, let us locate ourselves at a time after a Basic Income has been established and look back to see the causes of implementation.

Scenarios

To begin with, we shall explore a scenario in which implementation was seriously considered but did not in the end occur (Torry, 2013a: 50):

The Basic Income would have tackled both poverty and the poverty trap; it would have been in continuity with Child Benefit and the Single Tier State Pension; and they, and time-limited projects in Namibia and India, would have functioned as pilot projects. Administration would have been simple, and transition would have been possible (and a great deal more possible than the transition into Universal Credit). Trades unions had come round to the idea because their members would lose less of any negotiated pay rises through benefits withdrawal (although some still worried about the effect on collective bargaining of an unconditional benefit). But there were problems to face: there was little public understanding of Basic Income; the press peddled intuitive objections ('People won't work', 'the rich don't need this') rather than discussing the idea's merits or listening to counterarguments to the intuitive objections; no minister was willing to champion the idea in the Cabinet or in Parliament; and the civil service would have suffered substantial cuts because no longer would so many people have been needed to administer means-tested benefits, so it is no surprise that civil servants briefed against the proposal, both to ministers and elsewhere. In the end, although a Basic Income could have been implemented by turning tax allowances into cash payments, Basic Income was just too different from what we were used to. We knew where we stood with contributory and means-tested benefits, and transition to a Basic Income looked like too much of a leap in the dark.

But another scenario is possible (Torry, 2013a: 51–52):

After the Chancellor and Prime Minister had failed to fulfil their 2010 promise to means test Child Benefit, and instead withdrew its value from higher rate taxpayers through the tax system, thus establishing for the first time a tax on children, and after Steve Webb MP had established the Single Tier State Pension, and we had begun to appreciate the fact that no longer would pensioners be penalised for earning additional income or for saving for their old age, the Secretary of State for Work and Pensions put together a Pre-Retirement Income (PRI) for men and women aged between 55 and the state pension age. The plan was to remove personal tax allowances and means-tested and contributory benefits from this group (easy to do), and instead provide them with an unconditional and nonwithdrawable income of the same value as their tax allowance. In order to create a pilot project, volunteers were invited to swap their tax allowances and means-tested and contributory benefits for an unconditional benefit (again, easy to organise). The volunteer scheme was overwhelmed with applications, so legislation for a permanent scheme for everyone in the age range soon followed.

The result of this was that people in the pre-retirement age bracket found themselves able to be more flexible about their employment patterns; and it meant that no longer did they have to sign on regularly but could instead accept occasional employment, and at other times they could offer more time to their communities and families. Administration of the scheme was really simple; and nobody minded much if they lost money on the day it all started, because they soon managed to make it up. Administrative error became a distant memory. Two problems remained: housing costs and Council Tax. Those without sufficient income for their housing costs and Council Tax had to apply for continuing means-tested benefits to help with these: but their increased ability to accept occasional and part-time employment, and the fact that some people took their occupational and private pensions earlier than they might otherwise have done, meant that the number of people in the pre-retirement age bracket receiving means-tested benefits fell rapidly.

So it was not long before students and trainees began to see how useful an unconditional and nonwithdrawable income could be for them. Again a voluntary scheme was tried. Volunteers between the ages of 18 and 21 happily gave up their personal tax allowances and any claim on means-tested benefits, and received an Education and Training Income (ETI)—unconditionally and nonwithdrawably—instead. They then earned what they could to top it up. A nice outcome was that academic results improved, and more young adults sought training places and apprenticeships.

So again it was not long before working age adults were asking about the rationale for the rather artificial age boundaries to the pre-retirement and young adult schemes; and it was not long before we had a Working Age Income. Child Benefit rose in value, the Education and Training Income was extended back to sixteen-year-olds: and we found that we had a Basic Income for everyone, the amounts differing only in relation to someone's age. We have already seen the advantages that we were promised. There is less poverty; the poverty trap has largely disappeared (there is still a problem with housing costs, but that is not the fault of the Basic Income); administration is simple (in fact, there really isn't any, because the Basic Income just keeps on coming); we feel much more together as a society; we can negotiate the employment patterns that we want, and the ways in which our household finances are organised; and we wonder why the plan wasn't tried a lot sooner than it was.

Eventually, of course, the number of public servants needed to run the benefits system fell substantially, but not straight away. Because they no longer needed to police the benefits system, Job Centres were able to model themselves on local job broking and training organisations, and public servants were still required for this more satisfying work. Housing costs remained a problem, particularly in London, so a continuing Housing Benefit was still needed, so again public servants were required. The Child Benefit administration was expanded to handle the Basic Income scheme, and administration of disability, maternity, and a variety of other contingency benefits continued: but by the end of the transition the number of public servants administering the benefits system had fallen by three quarters. No compulsory redundancies were required.

Trades unions had started out rather sceptical of the Pre-Retirement Income, but so many of their members volunteered for the scheme that their scepticism didn't last. The National Union of Students was an enthusiastic supporter of the Education and Training Income. Trades unions began to see that a Working Age Income would make it more possible for their members to refuse low-wage jobs: and enthusiastic trade union support for the Working Age Income meant that an all-through Basic Income became irresistible.

Feasibility

Michael Hill has pointed out that one of the major characteristics of the UK's pensions policy is that it has always been incremental (Hill, 2009: 164). Successful implementation of a Basic Income will probably need to be incremental as well. A consequence of the intuitive arguments against implementing a Basic Income being so firmly lodged in the public mind ('The rich don't need it', 'People won't work') is that evidence to the contrary is difficult for most people to even begin to comprehend. As Michael Hill suggests, only evidence that least challenges the status quo, and that conforms to current public opinion, can be received (Hill, 2009: 159). This means that a new status quo, and a new public opinion, will have to be painstakingly prepared by establishing unconditional and nonwithdrawable benefits on the basis of more easily heard arguments, and on the basis of evidence relating to particular clearly deserving groups of people.

Julia Unwin, the Chief Executive Officer of the Joseph Rowntree Foundation, would agree with this. On 4 April 2014, she gave a lecture entitled 'A recipe for social change' (Unwin, 2014). She outlined the ingredients required for social change: a sense of crisis; a shared narrative; emotion; vocal supporters; proven solutions; surprising friends; movements of people; and public acceptance. These criteria have much in common with the criteria around which I have structured this chapter. In the context of the benefits system, the chronic crises are poverty and the poverty trap; shared narrative, emotional and vocal supporters, movements of people, surprising friends, and public acceptance, together represent public and parliamentary understanding; and continuity and pilot projects will identify proven solutions. Employing Unwin's criteria: There is certainly a sense of crisis about the benefits system. There is already a shared narrative, and a proven solution, in the sense that Child Benefit is an integral part of our understanding of ourselves as members of society. A Single Tier State Pension will fulfil the same function. Emotion, vocal supporters, and movements of people are emerging, both in the UK and around the world. A Basic Income has always had surprising friends. What an unconditional and nonwithdrawable income for working age adults does not have is public acceptance. For one demographic group at a time to receive a Basic Income would generate such public acceptance, and thus complete the set of success criteria outlined by Unwin.

Conclusions

All of the schemes that we have studied in this chapter, apart from National Assistance, were designed to reduce both poverty and the poverty trap. They all claimed some level of continuity with what had gone before, and they could all claim to have been piloted in one way or another. They were all administratively feasible (Universal Credit barely so), and for all of them, transition was a possibility (the jury is still out on Universal Credit).

The differences between the schemes that were implemented and those that have not been would appear to be in the areas of public understanding, civil service size and enthusiasm, and recipient group. Juliet and Brandon Rhys Williams' schemes did not have ministerial champions (although this is not a crucial factor, as the implementation of Family Allowance shows); there was little public understanding of the proposals; and, crucially, they were attempting to encompass the entire population in a single reform, thus precluding the development of a public understanding that a clearly deserving group of people would benefit. While we might regret that this might be a criterion for the success of a scheme, it would appear to be.

I am not a betting man, but if I were then I would be willing to put money on a National Living Wage being implemented within ten years. It fulfils all of the criteria for successful legislation and implementation.

A further conclusion is that however good the arguments for a Basic Income—and they are very good—it is probably pointless to pursue the implementation of a Basic Income as a single project. The two imaginary scenarios that I have outlined above suggest that a phased implementation could well succeed, and could deliver the public understanding and enthusiasm that would propel the process towards eventual implementation of an unconditional, nonwithdrawable income for every individual as a right of citizenship.

Table 14.1 represents the different factors relating to the feasibility of implementing a variety of implemented and proposed tax and benefits reforms.

Basic Income appears twice, once before the Pre-retirement Income and the Education and Training Income have been established, and again after their implementation. The implementation of the pre-retirement Income and the Education and Training Income would encourage public, parliamentary, and trade union understanding of Basic Income.

Table 14.1 A representation of the different factors relating to the feasibility of implementing a variety of implemented and proposed tax and benefits reforms

	Tackles poverty	*Tackles the poverty trap*	*Ministerial champion or similar*	*Public understanding*	*Reasons for the policy understood in Parliament*	*Intuitive arguments against proposal answerable*	*Civil service expansion*	*Trades Unions*	*Continuity (path dependency)*	*Pilot project*	*'Deserving' recipients*	*Administratively feasible*	*Transition feasible*
Family Allowance	√	√	√	√	√	√	√	√	√	√	√	√	√
National Insurance/ National Assistance	√	√ X	√	√	√	√ X	√	√	√	√	√ ?	√ ?	√
Universal Credit	√	√	√	√	√	√	?	?	√	X	?	?	?
Child Benefit	√	√	√	√	√	√	√	√	√	√	√	√	√
National Minimum Wage	√	√	√	√	√	√	√	√	√	√	√	√	√
National Living Wage	√	√	√	√	√	√	√	√	√	√	√	√	√
Basic Income	√	√	?	X	X	√	X	?	√	√	?	√	√
Single Tier State Pension	√	√	√	√	√	√	?	√	√	√	√	√	√

	Tackles poverty	*Tackles the poverty trap*	*Ministerial champion or similar*	*Public understanding*	*Reasons for the policy understood in Parliament*	*Intuitive arguments against proposal answerable*	*Civil service expansion*	*Trades Unions*	*Continuity (path dependency)*	*Pilot project*	*'Deserving' recipients*	*Administratively feasible*	*Transition feasible*
Pre-retirement Income	√	√	√	√	√	√	?	√	√	√	√	√	√
Education and Training Income	√	√	√	√	√	√	?	√	√	√	√	√	√
Working Age Income	√	√	√	√	√	√	?	√	√	√	√	√	√
Basic Income	√	√	√	√	√	√	X	√	√	√	√	√	√

Acknowledgements This chapter publishes for the first time a paper presented at the Social Policy Association annual conference in July 2014 in Sheffield.

References

Abel-Smith, B., & Townsend, P. (1965). *The poor and the poorest: A new analysis of the Ministry of Labour's Family Expenditure Surveys of 1953–54 and 1960.* Bell.

Atkinson, A. B. (1969). *Poverty in Britain and the reform of social security.* Cambridge University Press.

Banting, K. G. (1979). *Poverty, politics and policy: Britain in the 1960s.* Macmillan.

Barr, N., & Coulter, F. (1991). Social security: Solution or problem? In J. Hills (Ed.), *The state of welfare: The welfare state in Britain since 1974* (pp. 274–337). Clarendon Press.

Beveridge, W. (1942). *Social insurance and allied services.* Cmd 6404. Her Majesty's Stationery Office.

Beveridge, W. (1949). Epilogue. In E. Rathbone (Ed.), *Family Allowances.* George Allen and Unwin (a new edition of *The disinherited family* with an epilogue by William Beveridge).

Bradshaw, J., & Bennett, F. (2011). National Insurance: Past, present, and future? *Journal of Poverty and Social Justice, 19*(3), 207–209.

Centre for Research in Social Policy (2022). *The Living Wage.* Retrieved March 27, 2022, from https://www.lboro.ac.uk/research/crsp/minimum-income-standard/living-wage/

Centre for Social Justice. (2009). *Dynamic benefits: Towards welfare that works.* Centre for Social Justice.

Citizen's Income Trust. (2013). *Introductory booklet: Citizen's Income.* Citizen's Income Trust.

Citizens UK. (2022). *Welcome to the home of community organising.* Retrieved March 27, 2022, from https://www.citizensuk.org/

Dean, H. (2012). The ethical deficit of the UK's proposed Universal Credit: Pimping the precariat? *Political Quarterly, 83*(2), 353–359.

Dean, H., & Mitchell, G. (2011). *Wage top-ups and work incentives: The implications of the UK's Working Tax Credit scheme: A preliminary report*. London School of Economics.

Department for Work and Pensions. (2010). *21st century welfare*. Cm 7913. The Stationery Office.

Department for Work and Pensions. (2011a). *Universal Credit: Welfare that works*. Cm 7957. The Stationery Office.

Department for Work and Pensions. (2011b). *A state pension for the 21st century*. Cm 8053. The Stationery Office.

Dickens, R., & Manning, A. (2002). *Has the National Minimum Wage reduced UK wages?* Centre for Economic Performance, London School of Economics.

Edwards, P., & Gilman, M. (1998). *A National Minimum Wage: Stimulus to economic efficiency?* Warwick Business School.

Field, F. (2002). *Welfare titans: How Lloyd George and Gordon Brown compare, and other essays on welfare reform*. Civitas.

Ford, H. (1934, April). *Ford News*. Retrieved March 27, 2022, from https://www.thehenryford.org/collections-and-research/digital-resources/popular-topics/henry-ford-quotes/

Harris, J. (1981). Some aspects of social policy in Britain during the Second World War. In W. J. Mommsen (Ed.), *The emergence of the welfare state in Britain and Germany, 1850–1950* (pp. 247–262). Croom Helm.

Hill, M. (1990). *Social security policy in Britain*. Edward Elgar.

Hill, M. (2009). *The public policy process* (5th ed.). Pearson, Longman.

House of Commons Treasury and Civil Service Committee Sub-Committee. (1982). *The structure of personal income taxation and income support: Minutes of Evidence*. HC 331–ix. Her Majesty's Stationery Office.

Land, H. (1975). The introduction of Family Allowances: An act of historic justice? In P. Hall, H. Land, R. Parker, & A. Webb (Eds.), *Change, choice and conflict in social policy* (pp. 157–230). Heinemann.

Living Wage Foundation. (2022). *What is the Real Living Wage?* https://www.livingwage.org.uk/what-real-living-wage. Accessed 14 October 2021.

Macnicol, J. (1980). *The movement for Family Allowances, 1918–1945: A study in social policy development*. Heinemann.

Manning, A. (2014). Minimum wages: The economics and the politics. *CentrePiece, 1*(1), 9.

Metcalf, D. (1999). *The British National Minimum Wage*. Centre for Economic Performance, London School of Economics.
Parker, H. (1989). *Instead of the dole: An enquiry into integration of the tax and benefit systems*. Routledge.
Pennycook, M. (2012). *What price a Living Wage? Understanding the impact of a Living Wage on firm-level wage bills*. The Resolution Foundation.
Plunkett, J., Hurrell, A., & D'Arcy, C. (2014). *More than a minimum: The Resolution Foundation review of the future of the National Minimum Wage: The final report*. The Resolution Foundation.
Pond, C., & Winyard, S. (1983). *The case for a National Minimum Wage*. Low Pay Unit.
Rathbone, E. (1924/1986). *The disinherited family*. Falling Wall Press.
Rhys Williams, B. (1989). *Stepping stones to independence: National Insurance after 1990*. Aberdeen University Press.
Rhys Williams, J. (1943). *Something to look forward to*. MacDonald and Co.
Rhys Williams, J. (1953). *Taxation and incentives*. William Hodge and Co.
Robson, P., Dex, S., & Wilkinson, F. (1997). *The costs of a National Statutory Minimum Wage in Britain*. Judge Institute of Management Studies.
Sutherland, H. (2001). *The National Minimum Wage and in-work poverty*. University of Cambridge.
Thane, P. (1996). *Foundations of the welfare state* (2nd ed.). Longman.
Thane, P. (2011). The making of National Insurance, 1911. *Journal of Poverty and Social Justice, 19*(3), 211–219.
Titmuss, R. (1962). *Income distribution and social change*. Allen and Unwin.
Torry, M. (2013a). *Money for everyone: Why we need a Citizen's Income*. Policy Press.
Torry, M. (2013b). Pilot projects in India. *Citizen's Income Newsletter*, issue 2 for 2013b, pp. 4–5. Citizen's Income Trust.
Torry, M. (2020). Minimum Income Standards in the Basic Income debate. In C. Deeming (Ed.), *Minimum Income Standards and reference budgets: International and comparative policy perspectives* (pp. 319–329). Policy Press.
Trade Union Congress. (1995). *Arguments for a National Minimum Wage*. Trade Union Congress.
Unwin, J. (2014). *A recipe for change*. Joseph Rowntree Foundation. Retrieved March 27, 2022, from https://www.jrf.org.uk/sites/default/files/jrf/migrated/files/YSJ-Lecture-April-2014.pdf
Walley, J. (1986). Public support for families with children: A study of British politics. *BIRG Bulletin*, no. 5, Spring 1986, 8–11.

Wicks, M. (2014, January 19). Malcolm Wicks autobiography: 'I took what I regarded as an ethical decision'. *The Guardian*. Retrieved March 27, 2022, from https://www.theguardian.com/society/2014/jan/19/malcolm-wicks-autobiography-ethical-decision-child-benefit

CHAPTER 15

Research and Education in the UK Basic Income Debate

Introduction

How important is research to the Basic Income debate? In this chapter on the Basic Income debate in the UK, we shall find that research has played a central and positive role. However, when we study three particular incidents, we shall find that Basic Income research can be selectively used to pursue political agendas, and can be misrepresented, selectively employed, and selectively excluded, in order to suggest that Basic Income is not feasible.

The Early History of the UK Basic Income Debate

The three authors normally credited with giving birth to the idea of an unconditional income were British: Thomas More, Thomas Paine, and Thomas Spence—although Thomas Paine was in France by the time he was writing about the idea (Cunliffe & Erreygers, 2004: 3–16, 81–91): and the United Kingdom of Great Britain and Northern Ireland (UK) has always been at the heart of the debate whenever it has reappeared following a period of neglect.

In 1918, as part of its contribution to reconstruction after the First World War, the War and Social Order Committee of the Yearly Meeting

M. Torry, *Basic Income—What, Why, and How?*,
Exploring the Basic Income Guarantee,
https://doi.org/10.1007/978-3-031-14248-2_15

of the Society of Friends (the Quakers) proposed a 'State Bonus': an equal distribution to every member of the UK population of a proportion of the national income. Two members of the Society of Friends, Bertram Pickard and Dennis Milner, then founded the State Bonus League to campaign for a state bonus. Research on the costings and administration of a detailed scheme followed, along with publications and meetings. The Labour Party Executive Committee considered the idea and rejected it in 1921: but the State Bonus League had succeeded in establishing some important characteristics of subsequent UK debate about unconditional incomes: an educational approach, accompanied by careful research (Van Trier, 2018: 1–5, 10).

The British Debate, 1942 to 2014

In 1940, William Beveridge, a former Director of the London School of Economics, and from 1937 the Master of University College, Oxford, was appointed as a temporary civil servant to work on the allocation of recruits to the armed services. In 1941, he was asked to chair a committee established to review the UK's rather patchy social insurance systems: and in 1942 the committee issued the report that gave birth to the UK's welfare state with a shape that survives to the present day: social insurance and means-tested benefits, a National Health Service free at the point of use, and Family Allowances (Beveridge, 1942)—an unconditional income for the second and subsequent children in every family (Macnicol, 1980), which was extended to the first child and renamed Child Benefit thirty years later (Torry, 2013: 22–27). Family Allowance/Child Benefit is the nearest the UK has ever got to the implementation of a Basic Income (Torry, 2012).

In 1943, Lady Juliet Rhys Williams published *Something to Look Forward To* (Rhys Williams, 1943; Torry, 2013: 32–34), which suggested something like a Basic Income (it was subject to a work test). Rhys Williams was a member of the Beveridge Committee, and her book was a personal minority report. And then, in 1982, Rhys Williams's son, Brandon Rhys Williams, a Conservative Member of Parliament, presented to a parliamentary committee a Basic Income scheme constructed by his research assistant, Hermione (Mimi) Parker (House of Commons Treasury & Civil Service Committee Sub-Committee, 1982: 459; House of Commons Treasury & Civil Service Committee, 1983; Parker, 1989: 100). Soon after the hearing a General Election was called, so no action was taken on the committee's suggestion that the Government should research the idea (Torry, 2013: 34–36): but Mimi Parker's research was discussed at a Department for Health and Social Security Summer School in 1982, and by that and other means a small group of individuals convened in 1984 at the headquarters of the National Council for Voluntary Organisations to discuss how to pursue the debate. The group, which called itself the Basic Income Research Group (BIRG), included Mimi Parker, staff members of voluntary organisations (non-governmental organisations), a Church of England priest (this author), and academics, and is now the oldest still-functioning institution with the specific aim of promoting debate and research on Basic Income. In 1986, BIRG sent a delegation to the first meeting of the Basic Income European Network (BIEN: now the Basic Income Earth Network): the second oldest still functioning institution in the field (Basic Income Earth Network, 2022). The Basic Income Research Group is now called the Citizen's Basic Income Trust (Citizen's Basic Income Trust, 2022), and although personnel have changed, the board of trustees still consists mainly of academics and people working for voluntary organisations.

For thirty years the debate remained at a fairly low level. In the UK, BIRG published a journal, the *BIRG Bulletin*, twice a year, and occasional booklets and pamphlets. Around 1990 a flurry of books appeared (Brittan & Webb, 1990; Parker, 1989; Walter, 1989), and then occasional further volumes (Fitzpatrick, 1999; Parker, 1995; Parker & Sutherland, n.d.). The *BIRG Bulletin* became the *Citizen's Income Bulletin*, and then the *Citizen's Income Newsletter*, which is now published three or four times a year; for thirty years occasional conferences and other meetings have been organised; since the mid-nineties a website has been maintained (it was completely redesigned in 2015); monthly email updates have been sent since 2016; and a Twitter account was added in 2016. An increasing number of books have been published, many of them by individuals related to the Citizen's Basic Income Trust. Throughout, the approach might best be described as educational: and a significant element of that approach has been research.

Research on the Financial Effects of Basic Income Schemes

Several of the earlier books (Brittan & Webb, 1990; Parker, 1989; Parker, 1995; Parker & Sutherland, n.d.), and also a number of articles in the *BIRG Bulletin*, included detailed calculations for illustrative Basic

Income schemes (Parker, 1988, 1994; Parker & Dilnot, 1988; Parker, & Sutherland, 1988, 1991, 1994, 1995): and the publication of calculations relating to illustrative Basic Income schemes has continued ever since.

Early on, the only two methods available for researching the effects of illustrative Basic Income schemes in terms of their net costs and their effects on recipients were a method that employs the national accounts and census data to work out the net costs of illustrative schemes that abolished means-tested benefits, and a method that could work out gains and losses for households with specified numbers of children, housing costs, earned incomes, and so on (House of Commons Work and Pensions Committee, 2007). These two methods are still in use (Miller, 2017; Morgan, 2016; Painter & Thoung, 2015), but the serious questions now being asked about the feasibility of Basic Income, and the two methods' inability to answer questions such as those related to the number and extent of net disposable income losses that illustrative schemes would impose on low-income households, means that the two methods on their own are now inadequate to the demands of today's more demanding debate. It is therefore fortunate that we have available to us the more powerful microsimulation research tool EUROMOD: a computer programme into which are coded tax and benefits regulations, and which employs financial data on a statistically significant sample of the population to generate information on such effects of illustrative Basic Income schemes as net costs, gains and losses for different kinds of households, changes in poverty and inequality indices, the numbers of households taken off means-tested benefits, and so on. A particular advantage of microsimulation is that it can handle illustrative Basic Income schemes that leave in place means-tested benefits and recalculate them in relation to the Basic Incomes being received and the changes in net earnings brought about by changes to the tax system (Parker, 1989; Sutherland, 2016; Torry, 2014, 2015a, 2016a, 2016b, 2017, 2018a, 2019, 2020b, 2021).

Researchers' strategies differ. Martinelli and Reed select a variety of schemes and then test them to discover their effects (Martinelli, 2017a, 2017b, 2017c; Reed & Lansley, 2016). The current author sets a number of criteria: the net cost of the scheme has to be within £2bn of zero; poverty and inequality indices should fall; no low-income households should suffer significant losses at the point of implementation; no households should suffer unmanageable losses; Income Tax rates should rise by no more than three percentage points; and significant numbers of households should be removed from means-tested benefits, and more households should be brought within striking distance of coming off them. Then by a trial and error method he tests a wide variety of schemes until he finds one that fits the criteria (Torry, 2017, 2018a, 2019, 2020b, 2021).

The Debate Continues

Although for thirty years books had been written, journals had been published, and occasional conferences had been held, by 2014 no major UK newspaper had carried an article on Basic Income, other media were showing no interest, no other organisation had given serious attention to Basic Income, and in the academic and policymaking worlds Basic Income was regarded as a fringe interest with no practical relevance. Then things began to change. In 2014, Larry Elliott read this author's *Money for Everyone* (Torry, 2013) and wrote an article about Basic Income in *The Guardian* (Elliott, 2014), and since then numerous articles have appeared in the mainstream press and in a wide variety of web-based and other publications.

The previous year, the increasingly global nature of the Basic Income debate had begun to impinge on the UK debate when agreement was obtained for a referendum on Basic Income in Switzerland, and a European Citizens' Initiative was initiated by a group of individuals from a variety of European countries, including the UK (European Commission, 2018). European legislation requires a debate to be held on an issue in the European Parliament if one million European citizens' signatures can be collected on a petition, with specified thresholds being reached in at least seven European Union (EU) countries (European Commission, 2015). The initiative collected an impressive 300,000 signatures, which was not sufficient to trigger a debate in the European Parliament, but the movement to collect them developed into an organisation, Universal Basic Income Europe (UBIE) (Universal Basic Income Europe, 2022), which continues to pursue projects on different ways to implement EU-wide Basic Incomes, and especially Philippe Van Parijs's idea of a Eurodividend (Van Parijs & Vanderborght, 2017: 230–241); to advocate for the EU to fund Basic Income pilots in different regions; and to hold meetings in a variety of European countries (Unconditional Basic Income Europe, 2018). UBIE's affiliated organisations have continued to campaign for Basic Incomes in their own countries, and, in the UK, Basic Income UK

(BI UK), formed in 2013 by a group of people who were collecting UK signatures for the European Citizens' Initiative (Basic Income UK, 2022), was the first new organisation engaged in the Basic Income debate to be established since the Basic Income Research Group was founded in 1984. The two organisations have worked well together, with CBIT fulfilling its educational remit, and BI UK undertaking more active campaigning activity. Good communication is maintained by the Chair of BI UK being also a trustee of CBIT.

An event with a significant impact on the UK debate was the Finnish pilot project that began in January 2017 (Kangas, 2016; Kansaneläkelaitos Kela, 2016). The experiment randomly selected two thousand unemployed individuals from across Finland and made their means-tested and work-tested unemployment benefits unconditional for two years. The message started to circulate in the British media that Finland was about to pay a Basic Income to all of its citizens. This was never the intention, but once erroneous information begins to circulate, it can be difficult to stop it, however much the Citizen's Basic Income Trust might have tried through its publications and website. This author's research of the media at the time suggests that the first article that could be read as an announcement of a nationwide Basic Income rather than as a description of a limited experiment appeared in the *New Statesman* (Penny, 2016), but that might have been picking up ambiguous information from elsewhere. Some of the interesting consequences were one of the Citizen's Basic Income Trust's trustees, Neal Lawson, who is Chair of Compass—a left-leaning think tank that campaigns for a 'more equal, democratic and sustainable society' (Compass, 2022)—appearing on BBC2's *Newsnight* programme to be quizzed about Basic Income; an entire Radio 4 *Money Box Live* programme on the subject; and continuing press enquiries and requests for radio and television interviews. While much of the UK debate on Basic Income has been informed by accurate research, some of it has been driven by the opposite.

More reliable research results that have informed the UK debate are those of the large pilot projects in Namibia and India (Basic Income Grants Coalition, 2009; Davala et al., 2015; Haarmann & Haarmann, 2007, 2012; Osterkamp, 2013; Standing, 2012, 2015). These pilot projects, the Finland experiment, and the personal interest of individual local councillors, have been some of the drivers behind four Scottish boroughs' requests to hold pilot projects; and the boroughs' interest, and the enthusiasm of the Scottish National Party, have been behind the

Scottish Government's agreement to fund a feasibility study. It might not have been easy to run large pilot projects in developing countries, but at least it was possible to do so because there were no complex existing tax and benefits systems that needed to be adjusted to enable genuine pilot projects to be carried out. In more developed countries the situation is entirely different. If a Basic Income scheme were to be implemented across the UK, or in any other developed country, then existing tax and benefits systems would have to be altered: so, for an experiment to be a genuine Basic Income pilot project, the tax and benefits systems would have to be altered just for the pilot communities. Finland avoided this dilemma by selecting only currently unemployed individuals for its experiment—which of course means that the experiment did not mirror what would have to happen if a nationwide Basic Income scheme were to be implemented, thus bringing into doubt the experiment's status as a Basic Income pilot project (Delattre & Torry, 2017; Rolls, 2018). [The Scottish feasibility study has concluded that

> the majority of social security benefits a [Basic Income] would need to interact with are reserved to the UK Government, particularly those in relation to housing, child-care support and other top-up payments. Within current welfare and tax governance arrangements, political will and support across all levels of government (local, Scottish and UK) including the Department for Work and Pensions (DWP) and HM Revenue and Customs (HMRC) would be required to overcome these challenges. Without such support, the feasibility of a pilot, that minimises detriment, would require legislative changes to be made. (Citizens' Basic Income Feasibility Study Steering Group, 2020: 8)]

but [debate about such local pilot projects continues to contribute] to the increasingly widespread debate about Basic Income in the UK.

Increasing amounts of research, increasing evidence from pilot projects, and increasing numbers of press articles, media interviews, books, and so on, have driven the increasingly widespread debate in the UK: but quite as important as all of that has been the increasing number of institutions engaging with the debate. The Citizen's Basic Income Trust has been active for nearly forty years, in 1994 it organised the BIEN Congress in London, and it has assisted BIEN to register as a UK Charitable Incorporated Organisation and to locate its administration in the UK. Basic Income UK works across sectors, particularly with trades unions and faith groups, to build and demonstrate support for

Basic Income at a grassroots level; and it continues to collaborate with other similar organisations across Europe, and to organise campaigning events and meetings, mainly in London, Sheffield, and Birmingham, with increasing numbers of meetings in other parts of the UK. A newer organisation, World Basic Income, a not-for-profit co-operative based in Manchester (World Basic Income, 2021), campaigns for a global Basic Income through its website.

Numerous think tanks and similar organisations have involved themselves in the debate and most of them have continued to engage with it: the left-leaning Compass, mentioned above, has now established a 'Basic Income Conversation' with two members of staff, and both Compass and the more liberal Royal Society of Arts (a two hundred and sixty year old organisation with broad social reform interests) (Royal Society of Arts, 2022), have published reports and organised consultations around them (Painter & Thoung, 2015; Reed & Lansley, 2016; Young, 2018). The Institute for Public Policy Research (another left-leaning 'progressive' think tank) has proposed a universal lump sum payment at the age of twenty-five (Institute for Public Policy Research, 2022; Roberts & Lawrence, 2018); the Adam Smith Institute (a free market neoliberal think tank) (Adam Smith Institute, 2022) has discussed Basic Income and published a report on the similar Negative Income Tax (Story, 2015); the Joseph Rowntree Foundation, which specialises in funding social research, has sponsored Compass's research, and has also contributed its own more critical publications (Hirsch, 2015; Joseph Rowntree Foundation, 2022); and the Fabian Society (a century-old member-based think tank affiliated to the Labour Party) has published reports offering alternatives to Basic Income (Fabian Society, 2022; Harrop, 2016; Harrop & Tait, 2017) at the same time as its Young Fabians networks have engaged enthusiastically with the Basic Income debate. Interestingly, given its name, the New Economics Foundation has hardly engaged at all.

University departments are increasingly involved: the Institute for Social and Economic Research at the University of Essex, which maintains EUROMOD, has published this author's research, and also work on Basic Income by other researchers (Atkinson et al., 2017; Browne & Immervoll, 2018; Levy et al., 2013); the Institute for Policy Research at the University of Bath has conducted its own research (Martinelli, 2017a, 2017b, 2017c); the London School of Economics hosted a whole day on Basic Income in February 2018; and numerous academics and students now study and research Basic Income for their undergraduate and graduate courses and dissertations and for their postgraduate research projects.

As research and other activity increased, and numerous institutions joined in the debate, it became clear that the character of the debate was changing as well as its extent. Before 2014, the debate was largely about whether Basic Income was a good idea: that is, did it compare well with means-tested benefits, would it have useful social and economic effects, and so on. A shift then began towards questions of feasibility, which is why this author was asked for a book on the subject (Torry, 2016c); and then, only a little later, questions were being asked about methods of implementation: for instance, by the Institute for Chartered Accountants of England and Wales, which organised a consultation on the implementation of Basic Income (Torry, 2016e). Questions about desirability and feasibility are still central to the discussion, of course, and this means that the debate is increasingly complex, and is more than ever in need of high-quality research.

There has always been some interest expressed by individual politicians, first in relation to the question of Basic Income's desirability, and now in relation to its feasibility and to implementation methods. We have already discussed the involvement of Conservative Member of Parliament Sir Brandon Rhys Williams. Archy Kirkwood MP, a Liberal Democrat, who from 1997 to 2005 was Chair of the Parliamentary Social Security Committee, and then the Work and Pensions Committee, helped the Citizen's Basic Income Trust to conduct a survey of parliamentary opinion in 2006 (Citizen's Income Trust, 2007); and, from the Labour Party, John McDonnell MP, who became Shadow Chancellor, has a long-standing interest: in 2014 he spoke at the Citizen's Basic Income Trust's own conference, and organised his own public event on the subject in the House of Commons, and as Shadow Chancellor he asked Guy Standing (a co-founder of BIEN, and prolific author of books on Basic Income and related subjects) to write a report for him on the feasibility of organising pilot projects in the UK. The Green Party has for many years expressed interest in the subject, has voted for the proposal at its conferences, and included the idea in its manifesto for the 2015 General Election; and the Scottish National Party has argued for Basic Income in the UK's Parliament, and is supporting the plan for Scottish pilot projects.

A significant element in all of this interest and activity has been the importance of research results. Academics, think tanks, and the Citizen's Basic Income Trust, have generated and disseminated them; politicians have asked for them; and journalists and campaigners have explained them: sometimes accurately, and sometimes not. Increasingly important are opinion polls. A European Social Survey had questions about Basic Income inserted into it by interested academics, and both the Institute for Policy Research at the University of Bath and the Royal Society of Arts have commissioned opinion polls. Public support now reaches 50%: although support drops when people are informed that taxes would need to rise to pay for Basic Incomes (Fitzgerald, 2017; Ipsos MORI, 2017; Young, 2018: 3). John McDonnell MP has suggested that it is when public opinion moves that politicians are willing to do so: so these results from opinion surveys might be the most important research results of all.

So far in this chapter we have recounted *what* has happened in the Basic Income debate in the UK, along with a recognition that research has been a significant element in the process. But *why* has it all happened? Numerous suggestions have been made, and it might be that all that we can say is that a wide variety of factors have together caused the increasing activity and interest recorded here and that we simply cannot decide which factors are significant and which not, and which are causes and which are consequences.

Has the increasing number of books on the subject (Downes & Lansley, 2018; Miller, 2017; Standing, 2017; Torry, 2013, 2015b, 2016c, 2016d, 2018b; Van Parijs & Vanderborght, 2017 …) been causal? At a seminar at the London School of Economics in November 2016, Professor David Piachaud, who is not an advocate of Basic Income, credited this author's books as being a significant factor in the increasing interest in Basic Income. Or has increasing interest in the subject meant that every publisher now feels that they need to publish a book on Basic Income? Have plans for pilot projects generated increasing interest, or has the increasingly widespread interest driven plans for pilot projects?

One factor that could only be causal, and not consequential, might be increasing levels of concern about the effects of automation, computerisation, artificial intelligence, and globalisation, on employment and earned incomes. Clearly, we cannot yet know whether current and future rounds of automation and computerisation will result in net gains or net losses in paid employment: but what we can say with some confidence is that we shall see increasing turbulence, insecurity, and polarisation in employment patterns (Breemersch et al., 2017; Standing, 2011), and it is this that makes the secure financial platform offered by Basic Income an attractive proposition.

A further factor that can only be causal is that we are increasingly aware that means-tested benefits function as a significant employment disincentive, because they are withdrawn as earnings rise, and that the attempt to solve this problem by implementing so-called Universal Credit—yet another means-tested benefit—has caused substantial social damage (Alston, 2018; House of Commons Work and Pensions Committee, 2018). We can confidently predict that a Basic Income would contribute to a solution. We are also more aware than ever of increasing poverty and inequality. Basic Income is sometimes offered as a solution: but here one has to say that a Basic Income scheme would not necessarily reduce poverty and inequality, although there are of course illustrative schemes that would do so (Torry, 2019).

Having surveyed the modern UK debate on Basic Income and found research and an educational approach to have been central to it, we shall now study three incidents from which lessons might be learnt as to how we might usefully approach the relationship between research and the Basic Income debate in the future.

Three Incidents

The Green Party General Election Manifesto, 2015

At its Spring conference in 2014, the Green Party—which started as the Ecology Party forty years ago, and has a single Member of Parliament in the UK Parliament—reaffirmed its long-standing commitment to seeking the implementation of a Basic Income, and it then included the idea in its General Election manifesto in 2015:

> The idea in a nutshell is this. Scrap most of the existing benefits apart from disability benefits and Housing Benefit. Abolish the income tax personal allowance. Then pay every woman, man and child legally resident in the UK a guaranteed, non-means-tested income, sufficient to cover basic needs—a Basic Income. For those who earn, the Basic Income compensates for the loss of the personal allowance. (Green Party, 2015: 54)

The manifesto went on to say that a detailed scheme had been published alongside the manifesto. Unfortunately, that was rather late arriving: but what Natalie Bennett, then Leader of the Green Party, did say about their scheme when questioned in a television interview was that they expected the working age adult Basic Income to be £72 per week and to enable means-tested benefits to be abolished.

The problem that the Green Party then encountered was that the *Guardian*'s political editor, Patrick Wintour, read the Citizen's Income Trust's website and discovered that one of this author's EUROMOD working papers had shown that a Basic Income scheme that paid £72 per week to working age adults, that reduced to zero the Income Tax Personal Allowance, and that abolished all means-tested benefits apart from disability benefits and Housing Benefit, would impose unacceptable losses on low-income households. The working paper had therefore declared that particular scheme to be infeasible (Torry, 2014). In his article on the subject, Wintour accused the Citizen's Income Trust of criticising the Green Party scheme. In a telephone conversation initiated by Wintour this author had carefully not done that: but Wintour was right to draw his own conclusions from the research and to criticise the Green Party's scheme himself on the basis that it would impose losses on low-income households. What Wintour did not say, which he might have done, is that the Citizen's Income Trust had shown that it would have been perfectly possible to implement a genuine Basic Income, with a level for working age adults somewhere in the region of £72 per week, without imposing losses on low-income households, if means-tested benefits were retained and households' Basic Incomes were taken into account when those benefits were recalculated (Torry, 2015c).

At the time, many of us, both those in the Green Party working on its Basic Income policy, and those of us involved in the wider Basic Income debate, were left wondering why *The Guardian* had felt it necessary to be so negative towards the Green Party's Basic Income policy. It would have been perfectly possible to recognise the value of the Basic Income idea, as Larry Elliott had done, and to have pointed out that perfectly feasible Basic Income schemes were available. Many of us shared the suspicion that a number of *Guardian* journalists wanted to see a Labour victory at the General Election and were concerned that the Green Party would attract votes, thereby diminishing Labour's chances in marginal constituencies: so they had set out to denigrate the Green Party's policies. Whatever the truth of that suspicion, Wintour's article, and the many press articles that followed it, stimulated a substantial increase in the extent and depth of the debate, prompted new research on the feasibility of Basic Income, and did nothing to dent the Green Party's enthusiasm for Basic Income.

A Westminster Hall Debate

Westminster Hall debates provide opportunities for UK Members of Parliament to debate issues of interest, though they are not part of the legislative process: nonetheless, such debates can generate continuing discussion that subsequently leads to legislation. When a Member of Parliament is granted permission to introduce a Westminster Hall debate, the resolution is in the form 'This house has considered ...': so when Ronnie Cowan MP—a Scottish National Party Member of Parliament with a long-standing interest in Basic Income—was granted permission to introduce a debate on Basic Income, the resolution was in the form 'This house has considered Universal Basic Income'.

Mr. Cowan's opening address compared Basic Income to the current complex means-tested system, and he closed with the line,

> In the words of Malcolm Torry, the director of the Citizen's Income Trust: 'Technology lying idle, human creativity frustrated, wealth flowing from poor to rich, and finite resources uncontrollably exploited ... we are still waiting for the next new key concept. A Citizen's Income might be just what is required.'

He was followed by Julian Knight, a Conservative Member of Parliament:

> I congratulate the hon. Gentleman on securing this debate. He mentions the EUROMOD report by Mr Torry, and I wonder whether he saw the part of the report in which it is stated that, in order to support a universal basic income, the basic rate of income tax would have to rise to 48 pence in the pound. Can he say how on earth that is supportable in a modern economy? (Hansard, 2016)

Mr. Cowan did not have the relevant working paper in front of him, and so was unable to respond that the paper had been clear that that particular scheme was infeasible, and that further research had shown that a Basic Income scheme that was revenue neutral, and that raised the Basic Rate of Income Tax rates by only three percentage points to 23%, would be entirely feasible.

A varied debate followed, with Members of Parliament discussing recent publications on Basic Income from the Royal Society of Arts and the think tanks Compass and the Joseph Rowntree Foundation; the effects of the current benefits system; the recent Swiss referendum on

Basic Income; and whether a Basic Income would reduce employment incentives. And then Damian Hind MP, the Minister for Employment, contributed this:

> UBI would create too many losers among the poorest families and dramatically increase the number of children living in poverty—a point confirmed through modelling even by the Citizen's Income Trust. (Hansard, 2016)

Again, he had chosen statistics relating to a Basic Income scheme that the working paper that he was quoting had declared to be infeasible, and he had not mentioned the fact that other schemes in that and other working papers both avoided losses for low-income households and reduced child poverty.

As is normal in Westminster Hall debates, the debate ran out of time and no decision was taken on the resolution.

The Work and Pensions Committee Oral Hearing, 2017

In 2016, the House of Commons Work and Pensions Committee asked for applications for invitations to give evidence at a hearing on Basic Income to take place in Birmingham in January 2017. Such hearings provide an opportunity for committee members to study a matter in which they are interested by inviting experts in the field to give evidence and to answer questions. Three of those who had undertaken microsimulation research on Basic Income schemes applied for invitations: Luke Martinelli of the Institute for Policy Research at the University of Bath; Howard Reed of Landman Economics, who had undertaken the research for the report published by Compass earlier that year; and this author, who was offering to explain the results of microsimulation research published by the Institute for Social and Economic Research. None of the three received invitations. Anne Miller, who uses the national accounts method to cost Basic Income schemes, was somewhat surprised to receive an invitation when she had not applied for one. Other members of the panel were academics in a variety of relevant fields, think tank staff, and a trade union officer.

The discussion ranged widely: effects of the current system, possible effects of a Basic Income, employment incentives, the differences between Basic Income and Negative Income Tax, whether Basic Income should replace existing benefits, the different effects of household and individualised incomes, and the costs of Basic Income. A Basic Rate of Income Tax of 55% was mentioned; and then Anne Miller mentioned rates of 50, 60, and 65%. Louise Haagh, the Chair of BIEN, mentioned this author's research, and the research result that a meaningful Basic Income scheme might only need to raise the Basic Rate of Income Tax to 23%: but when committee members asked questions about potential losses for households currently on means-tested benefits, there was nobody able to say that research showed that such a scheme would avoid losses for low-income households (Hansard, 2017).

Peter Alcock, a Professor of Social Policy at the University of Birmingham, and one of the witnesses, offered a summary of the discussion about costs:

> Either you have a very high level of basic income, in which case you are going to have to have massively increased levels of taxation because there is nowhere else for their money to come from, or you do it on the revenue neutral basis that people have been talking about, but if you do it on a revenue neutral basis you do not solve any of the problems because you need to retain all of the means testing and all of the other elements of the benefit system that currently may or may not be causing problems. The problem is you don't solve them like this. It is either too expensive or it isn't worth having. (Hansard, 2017)

None of those called to give evidence were able to respond that a revenue-neutral scheme that offered a Basic Income of £60 per week for working age adults, raised Income Tax rates by only 3 percentage points, and retained and recalculated means-tested benefits, would avoid losses for low-income households, would reduce poverty and inequality, would take a lot of households off means-tested benefits, and would bring a lot more households within striking distance of coming off them.

Following the session, the Work and Pensions Committee published its report, and Frank Field MP, the Chair of the Committee, published a summary:

> A universal Citizen's Income would either require unthinkable tax rises or fail to deliver its objectives of simplification and a guaranteed standard of living. There are problems in the welfare system, but [Basic Income] is not the solution to them. Rather it is a distraction from finding workable solutions. (Work & Pensions Committee, 2017)

Lessons from the Three Incidents

Following the Westminster Hall debate, the trustees of the Citizen's Basic Income Trust decided that the Trust would no longer publish the results of research on Basic Income schemes that would require sizeable tax rises or would impose significant numbers of net disposable income losses on low-income households, and this author has ceased to research them. This is of course entirely unscientific, as an important element in any normal scientific research is the publication of negative results: but the reaction is understandable. The same decision might have been taken following the incident in 2015, but it wasn't, because it was believed that policymakers would treat research results more objectively than journalists had shown themselves able to do. That assumption proved to be mistaken, and it is disappointing that during the same debate both a government minister and a backbench Member of Parliament misrepresented research results. It is equally disappointing that those taking decisions about the evidence that should be available to a parliamentary committee should deny to that committee the results obtained from the best available research methods. To what extent the exclusion of such evidence was purposeful the reader will have to judge.

Some of us have taken it as a compliment that our research results have been both excluded from consideration and misrepresented: but we also recognise that such practices bring the UK's policy process into disrepute.

Conclusions

The Basic Income debate in the UK has been characterised throughout by an educational approach and by research. The history that has been related here has shown that this approach has contributed to the increasing extent and depth of the debate, that education is effective campaigning, that there is no conflict between campaigning and education, and that the boundaries between them might be difficult to determine. The lesson to be drawn is that both in the UK and elsewhere the Basic Income debate will be well served if those involved in it employ the best available research methods, take an educational approach, and ensure that overtly campaigning activity and research-informed educational activity constantly inform each other.

However, the three events recorded at the end of this chapter show that research can be misrepresented, selectively employed, selectively excluded, and employed for political purposes nothing to do with Basic Income. This suggests that how research results are communicated can be as important as the results themselves.

Acknowledgements This chapter was first published as Malcolm Torry (2020), 'Research and Education in the UK Basic Income Debate', in Richard K. Caputo and Larry Liu (eds.), *Political Activism and Basic Income Guarantee: International experiences and perspectives past, present, and near future*, Cham: Palgrave Macmillan, pp. 185–208 (Torry, 2020a). The publisher's permission to republish this chapter is gratefully acknowledged.

References

Adam Smith Institute. (2022). Using free markets to create a richer, freer, happier world. Retrieved March 27, 2022, from https://www.adamsmith.org/

Alston, P. (2018). Visit to the United Kingdom of Great Britain and Northern Ireland: Report of the Special Rapporteur on Extreme Poverty and Human Rights. Retrieved March 27, 2022, from https://digitallibrary.un.org/record/3806308?ln=en

Atkinson, A. B., Leventi, C., Nolan, B., Sutherland, H., & Tasseva, I. (2017). Reducing poverty and inequality through tax-benefit reform and the minimum wage: The UK as a case-study. *Journal of Economic Inequality, 15*, 303–323.

Basic Income Grant Coalition. (2009). *Making the difference: The BIG in Namibia: Basic Income Grant Pilot Project, assessment report*. NGO Forum. Retrieved March 27, 2022, from www.bignam.org/Publications/BIG_Assessment_report_08b.pdf

Basic Income UK. (2022). Basic Income UK. Retrieved March 27, 2022, from https://www.basicincome.org.uk/about_us

Beveridge, Sir W. (1942). *Social insurance and allied services*. Cmd 6404. Her Majesty's Stationery Office.

Basic Income Earth Network. (2022). Basic Income. Retrieved March 27, 2022, from http://basicincome.org/

Breemersch, K., Damijan, J. P., & Konings, J. (2017). *Labour market polarization in advanced countries: Impact of global value chains, technology, import competition from China and labour market institutions* (OECD Social, Employment and Migration Working Papers, No. 197). OECD Publishing. Retrieved March 27, 2022, from https://www.oecd-ilibrary.org/employment/labour-market-polarization-in-advanced-countries_06804863-en

Brittan, S., & Webb, S. (1990). *Beyond the welfare state: An examination of Basic Incomes in a market economy*. Aberdeen University Press.

Browne, J. & Immervoll, H. (2018). *Mechanics of replacing benefit systems with a Basic Income: Comparative results from a microsimulation approach* (EUROMOD Working Paper EM8/18). Institute for Social and Economic Research, University of Essex. Retrieved March 27, 2022, from https://www.iser.essex.ac.uk/research/publications/working-papers/euromod/em8-18

Citizens' Basic Income Feasibility Study Steering Group. (2020). *Assessing the feasibility of Citizens' Basic Income pilots in Scotland*. Basic Income Scotland. Retrieved March 27, 2022, from https://www.basicincome.scot/__data/assets/pdf_file/0024/175371/Draft-Final-CBI-Feasibility_Main-Report-June-2020.pdf

Citizen's Income Trust. (2007). Both the House of Commons and the House of Lords support a Citizen's Income approach to the reform of tax and benefits. *Citizen's Income Newsletter*, issue 2 for 2007, pp. 1–2.

Citizen's Basic Income Trust. (2022). Citizen's Basic Income. Retrieved March 27, 2022, from https://citizensincome.org

Compass. (2022). Progressive Alliance. Retrieved March 27, 2022, from http://www.compassonline.org.uk/

Cunliffe, J., & Erreygers, G. (Eds.). (2004). *The origins of universal grants*. Palgrave Macmillan.

Davala, S., Jhabvala, R., Mehta, S. K., & Standing, G. (2015). *Basic Income: A transformative policy for India*. Bloomsbury.

Delattre, L.,& Torry, M. (2017). Would a Citizen's Basic Income pilot project in the UK be possible? *Citizen's Income Newsletter*, issue 4 for 2017, pp. 2–4.

Downes, A., & Lansley, S. (2018). *It's Basic Income*. Policy Press.

Elliott, L. (2014, August 11). Would a Citizen's Income be better than our benefits system? *The Guardian*. Retrieved March 27, 2022, from https://www.theguardian.com/business/2014/aug/10/tax-benefits-citizens-income-self-employment

European Commission. (2015). *Guide to the European Citizens' Initiative*. European Commission. Retrieved March 27, 2022, from https://publications.europa.eu/en/publication-detail/-/publication/d5c945cb-06ba-11e6-b713-01aa75ed71a1

European Commission. (2018). *Unconditional Basic Income (UBI) - Exploring a pathway towards emancipatory welfare conditions in the EU*. Retrieved March 27, 2022, from https://europa.eu/citizens-initiative/initiatives/details/2013/000001_en

Fabian Society. (2022). Fabian Society. Retrieved March 27, 2022, from https://fabians.org.uk/

Fitzgerald, R. (2017). Survey reveals young people more likely to support Universal Basic Income, but it's not a Left-Right thing. *The Conversation*.

Retrieved March 27, 2022, from https://theconversation.com/survey-reveals-young-people-more-likely-to-support-universal-basic-income-but-its-not-a-left-right-thing-87554

Fitzpatrick, T. (1999). *Freedom and security: An introduction to the Basic Income debate*. Macmillan.

Green Party. (2015). *For the common good: General election manifesto 2015*. The Green Party of England and Wales.

Haarmann, C., & Haarmann, D. (2007). From survival to decent employment: Basic Income security in Namibia. *Basic Income Studies, 2*(1), 1–7.

Haarmann, C., & Haarmann, D. (2012). Namibia: Seeing the sun rise – The realities and hopes of the Basic Income Grant Pilot Project'. In M. C. Murray & C. Pateman (Eds.), *Basic Income worldwide: Horizons of reform* (pp. 35–58). Palgrave Macmillan.

Hansard. (2016). *Universal Basic Income, 14 September 2016*. Retrieved March 27, 2022, from https://hansard.parliament.uk/commons/2016-09-14/debates/1B16BDDC-5BB5-40AB-93E0-A78D0A39BF5B/UniversalBasicIncome

Hansard. (2017). *Work and Pensions Committee. Oral evidence: Universal Basic Income, HC793, Thursday 12 January 2017*. Retrieved March 27, 2022, from http://data.parliament.uk/writtenevidence/committeeevidence.svc/evidencedocument/work-and-pensions-committee/universal-basic-income/oral/45336.html

Harrop, A. (2016). *For us all: Redesigning social security for the 2020s*. Fabian Society.

Harrop, A., & Tait, C. (2017). *Universal Basic Income and the future of work*. Fabian Society.

Hirsch, D. (2015). *Could a 'Citizen's Income' Work?* Joseph Rowntree Foundation. Retrieved March 27, 2022, from www.jrf.org.uk/publications/could-citizens-income-work

House of Commons Treasury and Civil Service Committee Sub-Committee. (1982). *The structure of personal income taxation and income support: Minutes of evidence*. HC 331–ix. Her Majesty's Stationery Office.

House of Commons Treasury and Civil Service Committee. (1983). *Enquiry into the structure of personal income taxation and income support. Third special report, Session 1982–3*, section 13.35. Quoted in Parker, H. (1989). *Instead of the dole: An enquiry into integration of the tax and benefit systems* (p. 100). Routledge.

House of Commons Work and Pensions Committee. (2007). Benefit simplification. The seventh report of session 2006–7. HC 463 (Vol. 2). The Stationery Office. Retrieved March 27, 2022, from https://publications.parliament.uk/pa/cm200607/cmselect/cmworpen/463/463ii.pdf

House of Commons Work and Pensions Committee. (2018). Benefit sanctions. The nineteenth report of session 2017–19. HC 955. The Stationery Office. Retrieved March 27, 2022, from https://publications.parliament.uk/pa/cm201719/cmselect/cmworpen/955/955.pdf.pdf

Institute for Public Policy Research. (2022). IPPR: The progressive policy thinktank. Retrieved March 27, 2022, from https://www.ippr.org/

Ipsos MORI (2017). *Poll conducted for University of Bath – Institute for Policy Research: Universal Basic Income Research.* Ipsos MORI. Retrieved March 27, 2022, from https://www.ipsos.com/sites/default/files/ct/news/documents/2017-09/omnibus-universal-basic-income-topline-2017.pdf

Joseph Rowntree Foundation. (2022). Inspiring Social Change. Retrieved March 27, 2022, from https://www.jrf.org.uk/

Kangas, O. (2016). The Finnish Basic Income Experiment—'A foolish and outrageously expensive travesty'? *Tutkimusblogi*. Kela. Retrieved March 27, 2022, from http://blogi.kansanelakelaitos.fi/arkisto/3316

Kansaneläkelaitos Kela/Social Insurance Institution of Finland Kela. (2016). *From Idea to Experiment. Report on Universal Basic Income Experiment in Finland.* Retrieved March 27, 2022, from https://helda.helsinki.fi/handle/10138/167728?locale-attribute=en

Levy, H., Matsaganis, M., & Sutherland. H. (2013). *Towards a European Union Child Basic Income? Within and between country effects* (EUROMOD Working Paper EM6/13). Institute for Social and Economic Research, University of Essex. Retrieved March 27, 2022, from www.iser.essex.ac.uk/research/publications/working-papers/euromod/em6-13

Macnicol, J. (1980). *The movement for Family Allowances, 1918–1945: A study in social policy development*. Heinemann.

Martinelli, L. (2017a). *The fiscal and distributional implications of alternative Universal Basic Income schemes in the UK*. Institute for Policy Research. Retrieved March 27, 2022, from https://www.bath.ac.uk/publications/the-fiscal-and-distributional-implications-of-alternative-universal-basic-income-schemes-in-the-uk/

Martinelli, L. (2017b). *Exploring the distributional and work incentive effects of plausible illustrative Basic Income schemes*. Institute for Policy Research. Retrieved March 27, 2022, from https://www.bath.ac.uk/publications/exploring-the-distributional-work-incentive-effects-of-plausible-illustrative-basic-income-schemes/

Martinelli, L. (2017c). *Assessing the case for a Universal Basic Income in the UK*. Institute for Policy Research. Retrieved March 27, 2022, from www.bath.ac.uk/publications/assessing-the-case-for-a-universal-basic-income-in-the-uk

Miller, A. (2017). *A Basic Income handbook*. Luath Press.

Morgan, G. (2016). Some typical household effects of a Citizen's Income scheme. *Citizen's Income Newsletter*, issue 3 for 2016, p. 7.

Osterkamp, R. (2013). The Basic Income Grant Pilot Project in Namibia: A critical assessment. *Basic Income Studies, 8*(1), 71–90.

Painter, A., & Thoung, C. (2015). *Report: Creative citizen, creative state – The principled and pragmatic case for a Universal Basic Income*. Royal Society of Arts. Retrieved March 27, 2022, from https://www.thersa.org/discover/publications-and-articles/reports/basic-income. (A review of the report can be found in *Citizen's Income Newsletter*, issue 2 for 2016, pp. 20–21).

Parker, H. (1988, Spring). Are Basic Incomes feasible? *BIRG Bulletin*, (7), 5–7.

Parker, H. (1989). *Instead of the dole: An enquiry into integration of the tax and benefit systems*. Routledge.

Parker, H. (1994, January). Citizen's Income. *Citizen's Income Bulletin*, (17), 4–12.

Parker, H. (1995). *Taxes, benefits and family life: The seven deadly traps*. Institute of Economic Affairs.

Parker, H., & Dilnot, A. (1988, Autumn). Administration of integrated tax/benefit systems. *BIRG Bulletin*, (8), 6–10.

Parker, H., & Sutherland, H. (1988, February). How to get rid of the poverty trap: Basic Income plus National Minimum Wage. *Citizen's Income Bulletin*, (25), 11–14

Parker, H., & Sutherland, H. (1991, August). Child Benefit, Child Tax Allowances and Basic Incomes: A comparative study. *BIRG Bulletin*, (13), 6–13.

Parker, H., & Sutherland, H. (1994, July). Basic Income 1994: Redistributive effects of Transitional BIs'. *Citizen's Income Bulletin*, (18), 3–8.

Parker, H., & Sutherland, H. (1995, February). Why a £20 CI is better than lowering Income Tax to 20%. *Citizen's Income Bulletin*, (19), 15–18.

Parker, H., & Sutherland, H. (1996, February). Earnings top-up or Basic Income and a Minimum Wage. *Citizen's Income Bulletin*, (21), 5–8.

Parker, H., & Sutherland, H. (n.d.). *Child Tax Allowances? A comparison of Child Benefit, Child Tax Reliefs, and Basic Incomes as instruments of family policy*. Suntory-Toyota International Centre for Economics and Related Disciplines, London School of Economics and Political Science.

Penny, L. (2016, April 15). What might society look like with Universal Basic Income? *New Statesman*. Retrieved March 27, 2022, from https://www.newstatesman.com/politics/economy/2016/04/what-would-society-look-universal-basic-income

Reed, H., & Lansley, S. (2016). *Universal Basic Income: An idea whose time has come?* Compass.

Rhys Williams, J. (1943). *Something to look forward to*. MacDonald and Co.

Roberts, C., & Lawrence, M. (2018). *Our common wealth: A citizen's wealth fund for the UK*. Institute for Public Policy Research.

Rolls, J. (2018). State of the pilot projects for CBI. *Citizen's Income Newsletter*, issue 4 for 2018, pp. 5–11.

Royal Society of Arts. (2022). We unite people and ideas. Retrieved March 27, 2022, from https://www.thersa.org/

Standing, G. (2011). *The precariat: The new dangerous class*. Bloomsbury.

Standing, G. (*2012)*. Social insurance is not for the Indian open economy of the 21st century. *Citizen's Income Newsletter*, issue 1 for 2012, pp. 5–7.

Standing, G. (2015). Why Basic Income's emancipatory value exceeds its monetary value. *Basic Income Studies, 10*(2), 193–223.

Standing, G. (2017). *Basic Income: And how we can make it happen*. Penguin Random House.

Story, M. (2015). *Free market welfare: The case for a Negative Income Tax*. Adam Smith Institute. Retrieved March 27, 2022, from www.adamsmith.org/research/free-market-welfare-the-case-for-a-negative-income-tax

Sutherland, H. (2016, November 6). EUROMOD: Introducing the team. *EUROMOD News*. Institute for Social and Economic Research.

Torry, M. (2012). The United Kingdom: Only for children?'. In R. K. Caputo (Ed.), *Basic Income Guarantee and Politics* (pp. 235–263). Palgrave Macmillan.

Torry, M. (2013). *Money for everyone: Why we need a Citizen's Income*. Policy Press.

Torry, M. (2014). *Research note: A feasible way to implement a Citizen's Income* (EUROMOD Working Paper EM17/14). Institute for Social and Economic Research, University of Essex. Retrieved March 27, 2022, from https://www.iser.essex.ac.uk/research/publications/working-papers/euromod/em17-14

Torry, M. (2015a). *Two feasible ways to implement a revenue neutral Citizen's Income scheme* (EUROMOD Working Paper EM6/15). Institute for Social and Economic Research, University of Essex. Retrieved March 27, 2022, from https://www.iser.essex.ac.uk/research/publications/working-papers/euromod/em6-15

Torry, M. (2015b). *101 reasons for a Citizen's Income: Arguments for giving everyone some money*. Policy Press.

Torry, M. (2015c). *Would a Citizen's Income make some people poorer than they are today*? Policy Press. Retrieved March 27, 2022, from https://policypress.wordpress.com/tag/citizens-income/

Torry, M. (2016a). *An evaluation of a strictly revenue neutral Citizen's Income scheme* (EUROMOD Working Paper EM5/16). Institute for Social and Economic Research, University of Essex. Retrieved March 27, 2022, from https://www.iser.essex.ac.uk/research/publications/working-papers/euromod/em5-16

Torry, M. (2016b). *Citizen's Income schemes: An amendment, and a pilot project—addendum to EUROMOD working paper EM5/16* (EUROMOD

Working Paper EM5/16a). Institute for Social and Economic Research, University of Essex. Retrieved March 27, 2022, from https://www.iser.essex.ac.uk/research/publications/working-papers/euromod/em5-16a

Torry, M. (2016c). *The feasibility of Citizen's Income*. Palgrave Macmillan.

Torry, M. (2016d). *Citizen's Basic Income: A Christian social policy*. Darton, Longman and Todd.

Torry, M. (2016e). *How might we implement a Citizen's Income*. ICAEW. www.icaew.com/-/media/corporate/files/technical/sustainability/outside-insights/citizens-income-web---final.ashx; for a report on the consultation. See also Retrieved March 27, 2022, from http://citizensincome.org/news/icaew-report-on-implementing-citizens-income/

Torry, M. (2017). *A variety of indicators evaluated for two implementation methods for a Citizen's Basic Income* (Euromod Working Paper EM 12/17). Institute for Social and Economic Research, University of Essex. Retrieved March 27, 2022, from https://www.iser.essex.ac.uk/research/publications/working-papers/euromod/em12-17

Torry, M. (2018a). *An update, a correction, and an extension, of an evaluation of an illustrative Citizen's Basic Income scheme – Addendum to EUROMOD working paper EM12/17* (EUROMOD Working Paper EM12/17a). Institute for Social and Economic Research, University of Essex. Retrieved March 27, 2022, from https://www.iser.essex.ac.uk/research/publications/working-papers/euromod/em12-17a

Torry, M. (2018b). *Why we need a Citizen's Basic Income: The desirability, feasibility and implementation of an unconditional income*. Policy Press.

Torry, M. (2019). *Static microsimulation research on Citizen's Basic Income for the UK: A personal summary and further reflections* (EUROMOD Working Paper EM13/19). Institute for Social and Economic Research. Retrieved March 27, 2022, from https://www.euromod.ac.uk/sites/default/files/working-papers/em13-19.pdf

Torry, M. (2020a). Research and education in the UK Basic Income debate. In R. K. Caputo & L. Liu (Eds.), *Political activism and Basic Income Guarantee: International experiences and perspectives past, present, and near future* (pp. 185–208). Palgrave Macmillan.

Torry, M. (2020b). *Evaluation of a Recovery Basic Income, and of a sustainable revenue neutral Citizen's Basic Income, with an appendix relating to different Universal Credit roll-out scenarios* (Institute for Social and Economic Research Working Paper EM7/20). Institute for Social and Economic Research, University of Essex. Retrieved March 27, 2022, from https://www.iser.essex.ac.uk/research/publications/working-papers/euromod/em7-20.pdf

Torry, M. (2021). *Three income maintenance options for 2021*. Centre for Microsimulation and Policy Analysis report. Institute for Social and Economic

Research, University of Essex. Retrieved March 27, 2022, from https://www.microsimulation.ac.uk/publications/publication-526555/

Universal Basic Income Europe. (2022). Unconditional Basic Income Europe. Retrieved March 27, 2022, from https://www.ubie.org/

Van Parijs, P., & Vanderborght, Y. (2017). *Basic Income: A radical proposal for a free society and a sane economy*. Harvard University Press.

Van Trier, W. (2018). *Scheme for a State Bonus and the early roots of the basic income idea in the UK*. Paper presented at the 'Basic Income: The past and the present' AEA-ASSA Conference, Philadelphia, 3–5 January 2018. Retrieved March 27, 2022, from https://www.aeaweb.org/conference/2018/preliminary/paper/YQEheHd4

Walter, T. (1989). *Basic Income: Freedom from poverty, freedom to work*. Marion Boyars.

Work and Pensions Committee. (2017). *Citizen's Income not the solution to welfare state problems*. Retrieved March 27, 2022, from https://committees.parliament.uk/committee/164/work-and-pensions-committee/news/97738/citizens-income-not-the-solution-to-welfare-state-problems/

World Basic Income. (2021). http://www.worldbasicincome.org.uk/. Accessed 15 Oct 2021.

Young, C. (2018). *Realising Basic Income experiments in the UK: A typology and toolkit of Basic Income design and delivery*. Royal Society of Arts.

CHAPTER 16

Microsimulation: A Personal Journey

Introduction

A Basic Income, sometimes called a Citizen's Basic Income, a Universal Basic Income, or a Citizen's Income, is an unconditional and nonwithdrawable income paid to every individual. The payments would be regular, that is, no less frequently than monthly; they would be of equal amounts, except that annual uprating would be expected; and the amount would not depend on employment status, household status, other income, wealth, or anything else. The only conditionality permitted would be the recipient's age. A standard amount might be paid to working age adults; less to younger adults; less again to children; and more to people over retirement age.

The debate about Basic Income is now global, and it has increased significantly in extent and depth since 2013. Whether my books and papers have been one of the causes of the increasing extent and depth of the debate in the UK and further afield is for others to judge, but they have certainly been symptoms of it. *Money for Everyone: Why We Need a Citizen's Income* (Torry, 2013) was the first general introduction to the subject for about twenty years, and might be described as answering the question 'Is Basic Income a good idea?' The following shorter book, *101 Reasons for a Citizen's Income: Arguments for Giving Everyone Some*

M. Torry, *Basic Income—What, Why, and How?*,
Exploring the Basic Income Guarantee,
https://doi.org/10.1007/978-3-031-14248-2_16

Money (Torry, 2015b), was on the same theme: for instance, arguing for desirability on the basis of administrative efficiency, employment incentives, financial security, lack of stigma, and so on. But the character of the debate was already changing, and the question of feasibility was becoming more urgent. So in 2016, I published *The Feasibility of Citizen's Income* (Torry, 2016c), and when in 2017 I was asked to update *Money for Everyone* for a second edition, we realised that the debate had changed to such an extent that the book had to be entirely rewritten, with far more of an emphasis on feasibility and implementation (Torry, 2018a). But for this author the question of feasibility has always been important: hence my journey in microsimulation.

The purpose of this chapter is to summarise the results of microsimulation research on Basic Income schemes undertaken by this author during the past fifteen years; to update the research; and to reflect on the journey taken by that research. The chapter explores the ways in which the contemporary policy context and constructive criticism of previous research projects have resulted in changes to the methods employed, and discusses ways in which the research has influenced the policy process. The increasingly lively debate on Basic Income has generated a wide variety of questions relating to Basic Income's feasibility, and the penultimate section of this chapter addresses some of the most pressing of those questions. A final section draws lessons from the research journey recounted here, and suggests avenues for future research activity.

There is now a substantial body of microsimulation research available related to Basic Income (Lansley & Reed, 2019; Martinelli, 2017a; 2017b; 2017c; Morgan et al., 2019; OECD, 2017; Reed & Lansley, 2016) and to such similar mechanisms as a Participation Income (Atkinson et al., 2017). This chapter draws comparisons with other microsimulation research on Basic Income, but does not discuss it in the depth that would be required for a thorough assessment of the field. This is first of all because that would constitute a separate study of its own, and secondly because an important purpose of this chapter is to explore how the policy context might affect and be affected by research methods, and this is better done by concentrating on a single author's research journey.

The debate about Basic Income is now global, but the focus of this chapter is entirely on the United Kingdom. While my interests are global (I was until recently the General Manager of the Basic Income Earth Network—BIEN: a global educational charity, and I remain its treasurer) (Basic Income Earth Network, 2022), all of my microsimulation research has related to the UK, mainly because for most of the past thirty-five years I was Director of the Citizen's Basic Income Trust, which is entirely focused on the UK's Basic Income debate. It is also because since I worked for the Department of Health and Social Security for two years forty-five years ago, administering means-tested benefits, it is the complexity of the UK's tax and benefits system of which I have some understanding, and for which I can confidently construct Basic Income schemes.

A question with which the reader might come to this chapter might understandably be: Why so many calculations that all look much the same? The answer is, that the research process has been an evolutionary one. As new critiques have been submitted, new questions have been asked, and new issues have emerged, changes have had to be made to the Basic Income schemes evaluated and to the methods used for evaluating them. Sometimes the distinctions are smaller ones (such as whether to order household incomes by original incomes or by disposable ones), and sometimes they have been rather more significant (for instance, whether to abolish existing means-tested benefits, or to leave them in place and recalculate them). It is always the context that has determined the next evolutionary step.

The research process outlined in the next section has been a journey, so it is that journey that we shall follow.

A Review of Earlier Empirical Work

The 2006 Project

In 2003 Holly Sutherland introduced me to POLIMOD, EUROMOD's predecessor, and in 2006 I used it to find the Income Tax rate that would be required to fund a Basic Income of £25 per week for working age adults (with £20 per week for 16 and 17 year olds, £35 for elderly people, and an increase in Child Benefit) if the Income Tax Personal Allowance was reduced to zero. The exercise found that a Basic Rate of Income Tax of 26% would be required. Table 16.1 shows resulting changes in mean disposable incomes for the different income deciles and the redistribution pattern that emerged: a version of a pattern that was to become somewhat familiar (Torry, 2006).

At the time, that was felt to answer the question as to whether it was possible to construct a revenue-neutral Basic Income—that is, one

Table 16.1 Percentage changes in mean disposable income by income decile

Disposable income decile	*1*	*2*	*3*	*4*	*5*	*6*	*7*	*8*	*9*	*10*
% increase in mean disposable income	26.17	14.78	9.51	5.70	1.34	−1.00	−2.63	−3.65	−4.40	−4.20

Source Torry (2006)

that could be paid for by adjusting Income Tax rates and thresholds—for which gains and losses would be in the right direction: but of course it did not. This became particularly clear when the Citizen's Income Trust's trustees submitted evidence on a revenue-neutral scheme to a parliamentary committee in 2006. One of the advantages often claimed for Basic Income is that it would release people from means-testing: so the scheme submitted in evidence abolished means-tested benefits, and the Income Tax rate required was calculated by combining figures from the national accounts with census data, rather than by using microsimulation (House of Commons Work and Pensions Committee, 2007). Unfortunately, the logic of the situation suggested that a revenue-neutral scheme that abolished means-tested benefits would be likely to impose sizeable losses on low-income households at the point of implementation, because although the Basic Incomes coming into a household would compensate for a loss of out-of-work benefits, particularly if Housing Benefit were to be left in payment, they would not be able to compensate for a reduction in the Income Tax Personal Allowance, an increase in tax rates, and the in-work means-tested benefits that households would no longer be receiving. Households previously receiving in-work benefits would find themselves much worse off. The 'national accounts' method was unable to provide evidence on the losses that households would suffer, so it was not able to prove that such losses would not occur, nor that they would be negligible if they did. It is therefore somewhat unfortunate that the 'national accounts' method for calculating the financial effects of a Basic Income scheme is still in use (Citizen's Income Trust, 2016a; Miller, 2017; Painter & Thoung, 2015).

The 2012 Project

It had clearly become essential to test Basic Income schemes that abolished means-tested benefits: so Torry (2012) tested an illustrative Basic Income scheme very similar to the one submitted to the select committee in 2006. The results for household losses can be found in Table 16.2.

This research revealed that a scheme that abolished means-tested benefits could generate large numbers of household net income losses at the point of implementation. However, just one scheme had been tested, and it could easily be objected that no more general conclusions could be drawn from that. So during the summer of 2013 a student volunteer, Chris Stapenhurst, tested a wide variety of Basic Income schemes that abolished means-tested benefits, altering in turn numerous variables of the schemes. He found that no scheme that he studied got anywhere near to abolishing the losses (Stapenhurst, 2014).

It is of course true that it is impossible to prove a negative because a previously untested example might be able to deliver a positive result. However, the logic of the situation facing in-work households with low disposable incomes suggests that such households would inevitably lose

Table 16.2 Gains and losses for an illustrative Basic Income scheme

	Results for individuals		*Results for households*	
Losses and gains	*No.*	*%*	*No.*	*%*
Loss > 15%	2392	4.18	1882	7.50
15% > loss > 10%	2302	4.02	679	2.71
10% > loss > 5%	6160	10.75	1914	7.63
5% > loss > 0	5532	9.66	4346	17.32
No loss or gain	19,747	34.48	1067	4.25
0 > gain > 5%	7350	12.83	6736	26.85
5% > gain > 10%	3647	6.37	3582	14.28
10% > gain > 15%	2358	4.11	1935	7.71
Gain > 15%	7788	13.60	2947	11.75
	57,276	100	25,088	100

Source Torry (2012)

Note This exercise and the calculations made in 2006 was carried out without applying the weights in the FRS survey data. See below for how the weights were used from 2014 onwards. The results obtained in 2012 would therefore have been accurate for the FRS sample (approximately 0.1% of the UK population) but less so for the population as a whole from any revenue-neutral Basic Income scheme that abolished means-tested benefits: so the search for a scheme that abolished means-tested benefits, and for which the losses would be non-existent or negligible for low-income households, ceased, at least for this author.

The 2014 Project

The 2014 project employed EUROMOD to research three different revenue-neutral Basic Income schemes. For all three schemes, National Insurance Contributions of 12% were charged on all earned income, and the Income Tax Personal Allowance was abolished (but not Old Age Personal Tax Allowance), and income thresholds were adjusted accordingly.

The method for testing this Basic Income scheme and all subsequent ones has been as follows: A new set of benefits is created in the UK country system in EUROMOD: a Citizen's Pension (CP) for over 65-year-olds, a Basic Income (CI) for adults aged between 25 and 64, and a Young adult's Basic Income (CIY) for adults aged between 20 and 24, and an Education age Basic Income (CIE) for anyone between 16 and 19 not in full-time education (they are named separately, but all of them are calculated in the same policy in EUROMOD (BCI)). In the definitions of constants, levels are set for these Basic Incomes, and all Personal Tax Allowances are set at zero or reduced. So that the additional taxable income is taxed at the basic rate, and not at the higher rate, the first tax threshold is altered (and so in 2019, for instance, it was set at £46,350). The National Insurance Contribution (NIC) Primary Earnings Threshold is set to zero or reduced, and in the NIC calculation the NIC rate above the Upper Earnings Limit is set to 12% (to match the rate below the limit). Child Benefit rates are increased by £20 per week or some other figure. As a transitional measure, and in the cause of an easy transition, the Education age Basic Income is not paid to a young person still in full-time education, in recognition of the fact that their main carer is receiving Child Benefit on their behalf. The Basic Income total is added to the benefits total and also to the means applied to each of the means-tested benefits. Simulations of the current tax and benefits system and of the Basic Income scheme generate two lists of household disposable incomes for the entire Family Resource Survey sample. These then generate a list of household gains (negative gains are losses), the gains are multiplied by the weighting figures supplied with the FRS survey results in order to scale up the survey sample to the entire population, and the total of the grossed up gains then gives the net cost of the scheme. To convert EUROMOD's monthly figures to annual figures the total is multiplied by 12. A process of trial and error adjusts the different Basic Income rates and the Income Tax rates until the net cost falls to no more than £2bn per annum. (For information on the household weights contained in the FRS data, see De Agostini, 2018: 53.) Household equivalised disposable incomes are then ordered (in earlier projects unequivalised original incomes were ordered), the bottom 20% are selected, the gains are calculated, and then the percentage gains. (It is the bottom 20% of the population of households, not the bottom 20% of the sample.) The percentage gains are then ordered and the households suffering losses of over 15%, over 10%, and over 5%, are selected. The weights attached to each of the relevant selected households are then added together to obtain the number of households in the whole population affected by such losses. The process is then repeated for all households.

The first scheme tested in 2014 was an updated version of the scheme submitted as evidence to the parliamentary committee in 2006. The updated version allocated Basic Incomes of £142.70 to individuals over 65, £71 to individuals over 25 and under 65, and £56.25 to every other individual (to match 2013 Income Support and Pension Credit rates), including children. Means-tested benefits (including Tax Credits, but not Housing Benefit or Council Tax Benefit) were abolished, as were the State Retirement Pension, Child Benefit, Incapacity Benefit, and contributory Unemployment Benefit. A funding gap of £20bn p.a. remained, which it was thought could be filled by restricting pension contribution tax relief to the basic rate of Income Tax and through administrative savings. Two further schemes were tested:

Alternative 1 retained the Basic State Pension, and paid a Basic Income for those over the state retirement age of £30 per week. Child Benefit was retained and a Child Basic Income was paid at £20 per week. The adult Basic Income rate remained at £71: the 2013 Income Support rate. All existing benefits were left in place, and the Basic Incomes were added to the means taken into account when means-tested benefits were calculated. Although the scheme generated usefully low household net disposable income losses at the point of implementation for both low-income households and for all households, even with Income Tax rates increased by 10 percentage points a funding gap of £24bn remained to be filled by restricting pension contribution tax relief to the basic rate of Income Tax and through administrative savings.

Alternative 2 was identical to alternative 1, except that the Basic Incomes for working age and young adults were reduced in value. It was found that if Income Tax rates were increased by 5 percentage points then the same funding gap remained to be filled as in alternative 1. The losses that would be experienced by all households were lower than for alternative 1 because Income Tax rates were lower.

The results are summarised in Table 16.3.

This project reinforced the view that abolishing means-tested benefits in the context of a Basic Income scheme that still left a funding gap to be filled was going to impose politically impossible net disposable income losses on low-income households: so from that point on I researched no further Basic Income schemes that abolished means-tested benefits, but only schemes that left in place the entire means-tested system, and that added each household's Basic Incomes to the means employed to calculate their means-tested benefits claims. The important question was now not whether it was possible to abolish means-tested benefits on the implementation of a Basic Income, but how many households could be taken off means-tested benefits by their Basic Incomes, and how many could be brought close to coming off them. For this task microsimulation was not only the perfect method: it was the only method.

The other possible response to the problem that it appeared to be inevitable that a revenue-neutral Basic Income scheme that abolished means-tested benefits would impose losses on low-income households was to suggest that the revenue neutrality condition should be abandoned, and that additional funding from outside the Income Tax system should be sought. There are of course numerous ways in which additional funding could be obtained: taxing appropriation of the commons, and in particular fossil fuels and land; a financial transaction tax; a tax on data; a tax on robots; consumption taxes; money creation (Torry, 2018a: 159–166); redirected subsidy funding; and the dividends on a permanent fund into which are paid royalties on resource extraction (Torry, 2016c: 43–49). All of these are possibilities. Whether any one of them on their own would reap sufficient additional revenue to fund a Basic Income of a useful amount must be open to question; whether they would be able to do so on a permanent basis would also be open to doubt; and whether they would impose net disposable income losses on low-income households would be an important factor to keep in mind. For instance, to fund Basic Incomes through consumption taxes could easily be detrimental to poorer households. The advantage of funding a Basic Income from within

Table 16.3 A summary of illustrative schemes tested in the 2014 project

For all three schemes, National Insurance Contributions are collected at 12% on all earned income	**Citizen's Income Trust 2013 illustrative scheme** (The 2006 scheme updated to 2013 values)	**Alternative 1**	**Alternative 2**
Relationship of Basic Income to means-tested benefits	Means-tested benefits are abolished except for Housing Benefit and Council Tax Benefit	Means-tested benefits are left in place and the Basic Income is taken into account when means-tested benefits are calculated	Means-tested benefits are left in place and the Basic Income is taken into account when means-tested benefits are calculated
Working age adult **CI amount** (ages 25–64)	£71	£71	£50
Young adult CI amount	£71	£71	£40
Income Tax, basic rate	20%	30%	25%
Income Tax, higher rate	40%	50%	45%
Income Tax, top rate	45%	50%	50%
Proportion of households in the lowest disposable income decile experiencing losses of over 10% at the point of implementation	21.12%	0.04%	0.08%
Proportion of all households experiencing losses of over 10% at the point of implementation	9.28%	5.38%	1.09%
Net cost of scheme*	£20bn	£24bn	£24bn

*Much of the additional cost would be met by restricting tax relief on pension contributions to the basic rate, and through administrative savings generated by the abolition of means-tested benefits (in the case of the 2013 illustrative scheme) or by many households leaving means-tested benefits as their Citizen's Incomes and additional earnings increased the means taken into account when their means-tested benefits were calculated (in the case of the two alternative schemes)

Source Torry (2014: 7)

the current benefits and Income Tax system is that the money gained from reducing tax allowances, increasing tax rates, and reducing means-tested benefits, would have to be used to fund Basic Incomes, because if the money were to be used for some other purpose then the scheme would be experienced as a cut in living standards: so only this funding method exhibits a degree of certainty that the revenue would be used to fund Basic Incomes. All of the other methods proposed for funding a Basic Income could result in the money being redirected to other government purposes and not ending up as Basic Incomes.

During the 2014 project a number of questions had to be both asked and answered, particularly in relation to the need to discover which households were 'low income' and which were not:

- In 2014, disposable incomes were ordered, rather than original incomes (that is, incomes before tax had been deducted and benefits added). Later studies ordered original incomes, and the most recent reverted to disposable incomes. The argument for using original incomes was that if disposable incomes are employed then in the two different situations of the current tax and benefits system and the Basic Income scheme, different participants will find themselves in the bottom decile or quintile, whereas if original incomes are used then the same participants will be in the bottom decile or quintile in both situations, meaning that the changed circumstances of the same participants are being evaluated. However, it is disposable income that determines whether or not a household might be in poverty: hence the recent reversion to ordering by disposable incomes.
- Whenever household net disposable incomes were used to order households so that households could be categorised into income deciles—that is, into the first tenth of households, the second tenth, and so on—a good range of income levels were found to be present in the lowest decile. However, if original incomes are used, then the range of incomes in the bottom decile becomes very narrow, because so many households have no original income and rely entirely on benefits of various kinds, and particularly on pensions. This means that when the switch was made to using original incomes to order households, it became essential to regard the bottom quintile, or 20%, of households as those with low incomes.

- For earlier schemes, for the purpose of reporting gains and losses total household disposable incomes were ordered. This is problematic. A household of two parents and three children with twice the disposable income of a household containing just one adult will not be as well off as that individual adult. More recent projects have employed equivalised disposable incomes—that is, household incomes adjusted for the composition of the household—in order to order households. How much difference this makes to those results that are dependent on the ordering of households is open to question. As we shall see later in this chapter, when EUROMOD employs equivalised incomes to order households into income deciles in order to generate a series of statistics, the results are remarkably similar for both the equivalised and the unequivalised household incomes.
- From 2014 onwards, household disposable incomes rather than individuals' disposable incomes have been compared. There are good arguments for both approaches. It is individuals who receive income, so gain or loss is an individual experience; and within a household income is not necessarily equitably shared, so the amounts that individuals receive might be more relevant than the amount that the household receives. However, we can assume that in most cases income is pooled within households, at least to some extent, so if one member gains and another loses then the household might be better off, and that might be a more significant factor than that one member of the household has suffered a loss in disposable income. Because households are of different sizes, an absolute gain or loss is not particularly relevant. However, percentage gains and losses are relevant, so this is the measure used.

The 2012 and 2014 projects can be seen to have established a number of aspects of a useful basis for further projects, and in particular the requirement for means-tested benefits to be left in place when illustrative Basic Income schemes were constructed, and also the advisability of revenue neutrality.

The 2015 Project

This project returned to the suggestion that the funding gaps discovered in the three schemes tested in 2014 should be filled by restriction of tax relief on pension contributions to the basic rate (Torry, 2014: 7; 2015a).

This would be problematic in two ways: first of all, an estimate has to be made as to how much revenue would be generated by restricting tax relief on pension contributions in this way (Citizen's Income Trust, 2013: 10; House of Commons Work and Pensions Committee, 2007: Ev 90); and secondly, and rather more importantly, there would be no guarantee that the additional revenue would be used to fund Basic Incomes. The net disposable incomes of some higher income households would be affected by the change, but no low-income households would be affected, and few households in the earnings mid-range: so the proceeds could easily be employed for any government purpose, and not necessarily for paying for Basic Incomes. It is for this reason that, following the publication of a paper by Donald Hirsch (2015) and subsequent correspondence, from the 2015 project onwards I have made a distinction between 'revenue neutrality' and 'strict revenue neutrality', and have required that illustrative Basic Income schemes should be strictly revenue neutral. 'Revenue neutral' means that no additional funding is required to pay for the Basic Incomes from beyond the benefits and Income Tax systems (which for this purpose includes National Insurance Contributions), whereas 'strictly revenue neutral' means that all funding for Basic Incomes should come from changes to the Income Tax Personal Allowance, changes to Income Tax thresholds and rates, changes to National Insurance Contribution thresholds and rates, and changes to means-tested benefits: and not from restricting tax relief on pensions contributions, or the restriction of any other allowance for which the proceeds could be used for other government purposes. All of the changes consistent with strict revenue neutrality would reduce household net disposable incomes for households across the income range, and those losses would have to be compensated by using the proceeds to pay for Basic Incomes. The revenue could not be directed to other purposes without making households worse off right across the income range.

Donald Hirsch's paper (2015) and further discussion resulted in a second requirement for financial feasibility: a severe restriction on permissible Income Tax rate rises. It might be argued that raising Income Tax rates substantially in order to pay for Basic Incomes would not be a problem if the net result would not be a loss in disposable income. However, this is not necessarily the case. Income Tax rate rises are a psychological matter and not simply a financial one. For the sake of political feasibility, it might therefore be wise to restrict Income Tax rate rises, and this is what I have done from the 2015 project onwards.

As well as strict revenue neutrality, and the restriction on Income Tax rate rises, the 2015 project was generally more specific in relation to what 'financially feasible' might mean in relation to a Basic Income illustrative scheme. The following set of criteria was established:

- Strict revenue neutrality (assumed to be within £2bn per annum of zero net cost).
- Income Tax rates not to rise more than 3 percentage points (adjustments to National Insurance Contributions earnings limits, and of National Insurance Contributions up to 12% of earnings, are permitted).
- No more than 2% of low-income households should suffer losses of over 5% of disposable income at the point of implementation.
- Any redistribution should be modest and should be from rich to poor.

The 2015 project introduced another innovation. As well as researching the possibility of a feasible strictly revenue-neutral Basic Income scheme, and finding that there was one, it also researched two possible implementation methods: all at once for the entire scheme, or starting with changing Child Benefit into a Child Basic Income, and then establishing a Basic Income for young adults and allowing them to keep it, with each new cohort of young adults being given a Basic Income and keeping it, and so on, enabling a complete scheme for the entire population to be rolled out gradually.

Torry (2015a) tested three illustrative schemes. All of them were strictly revenue neutral, all of them reduced the Income Tax Personal Allowance to zero, and all of them charged National Insurance Contributions at 12% on all earned income. The first and second schemes were similar to those tested in 2014: one abolished means-tested benefits, and the other retained and recalculated them. A third scheme, which I was requested to test, based Basic Income rates on the Minimum Income Standards published by the Joseph Rowntree Foundation (Hirsch, 2019). Results were as shown in Table 16.4.

There was clearly no way that schemes A or C were going to conform to the conditions set for financial feasibility: but there was a possibility that a scheme for lower Basic Incomes and that kept in place means-tested benefits might be able to do so. This required a new method. Before

Table 16.4 Three illustrative Basic Income schemes tested in 2015

	Scheme A	*Scheme B*	*Scheme C*
Relationship of Basic Income to means-tested benefits (All Basic Income amounts are per week)	Basic Incomes replace means-tested benefits except for Housing Benefit and Council Tax Benefit. Child Benefit and Basic State Pension are no longer paid	Means-tested benefits are left in place and Basic Incomes are taken into account when means-tested benefits are calculated. Basic State Pension and Child Benefit are still paid	Basic Incomes replace means-tested benefits except for Housing Benefit and Council Tax Benefit. Child Benefit and Basic State Pension are no longer paid
Citizen's Pension	£145.40	£30	£120
Working age adult Basic Income	£71.70	£50	£160
Young adult Basic Income	£56.80	£40	£120
Child Basic Income	£56.80	£20	£80
Income Tax rate increase required for strict revenue neutrality	5%	3%	28%
Income Tax, basic rate (on £0–42,010)	25%	23%	48%
Income Tax, higher rate (on £42,010–150,000)	45%	43%	68%
Income Tax, top rate (on £150,000–)	50%	48%	73%
Proportion of households in the lowest disposable income decile experiencing losses of over 10% at the point of implementation	28.03%	1.5% (and 4.37% with losses over 5%)	29.0%

(continued)

2015, I had chosen the illustrative scheme and then discovered its effects: for instance, the funding gap, or the Income Tax rates required to fund it. Now that both strict revenue neutrality and a restriction on Income Tax rates had been imposed, it was going to be essential to test a wide variety of different illustrative schemes to see if one could be found that would fit

Table 16.4 (continued)

	Scheme A	*Scheme B*	*Scheme C*
Proportion of all households experiencing losses of over 10% at the point of implementation	15.2%	1.24% (and 15.2% with losses over 5%)	30.2%
Administrative saving assumed	£4bn per annum	£1bn per annum	£4bn per annum
Net cost of scheme	£1.8bn per annum	−£1.9bn per annum: i.e. a saving of £1.9bn	−£0.47 per annum: i.e. a saving of £0.47bn

Source Torry (2015a)

the criteria. So such variables as the different Basic Income amounts for different age groups, and different Income Tax rates for different income bands, had to be varied in turn, each resulting scheme had to be coded into EUROMOD, the programme had to be run, and the results had to be tabulated, to see if the tests for feasibility had been passed. Three very clear conclusions could be drawn from this project.

First of all, and most importantly, a feasible scheme B was discovered. This meant that Basic Income would have been financially feasible in the UK in 2015. It only takes a single feasible illustrative scheme to prove that. (Strictly speaking, the scheme published as scheme B did not fulfil the requirement that no more than 2% of low-income households should experience household net disposable income losses of more than 5%. 4.37% was as close as I could get it. Only 1.5% suffered losses of over 10%.)

The scheme reduced all poverty indices, reduced the number of children in poverty by a quarter, reduced inequality, and because it made relatively few changes to the existing system, it could have been introduced quickly. What had become a familiar redistribution pattern, seen here in Fig. 16.1, would have been the result.

A second result, based on the high number of net household disposable income losses for scheme A, particularly for low-income households, confirmed conclusions drawn from Torry (2012, 2014): that a revenue-neutral Basic Income scheme that abolishes means-tested benefits would generate high numbers of substantial losses for low-income households.

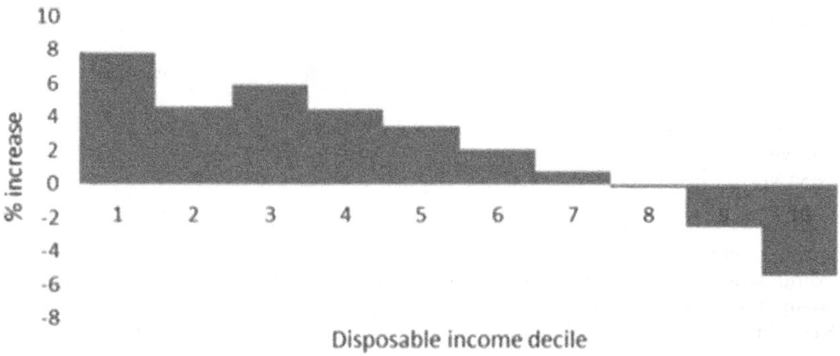

Fig. 16.1 % increase in disposable income on the implementation of scheme B by disposable income decile (*Source* Torry [2015a: 7])

A third result was not surprising, but the extent of the failure was interesting. The scheme based on published Minimum Income Standards for the levels of Basic Incomes, scheme C, required excessive Income Tax rates at the same time as generating very high numbers of significant losses for low-income households.

This third result had a significant afterlife. Torry (2015a) was perfectly clear that the scheme would be impossible to implement, and that the only feasible scheme was scheme B: but in a Westminster Hall parliamentary debate on Basic Income in 2016, a Member of Parliament suggested that the Citizen's Income Trust had said that an Income Tax rate of 48% would be required for a Basic Income. The Minister for Employment then questioned whether a scheme could be introduced that would avoid losses for low-income households, and whether the scheme would provide for people with disabilities. Scheme B was a clear answer to those questions. Ronnie Cowan MP, who had introduced the debate, did not have the information to hand that would have enabled him to respond that the paper from which the Member of Parliament had quoted figures had been clear that the scheme that required an Income Tax rate of 48% was infeasible, and that the paper included an entirely feasible scheme that was strictly revenue neutral, that required Income Tax rates to rise by only three percentage points, that would generate almost no losses for low-income households, and few losses for any households, and that would leave in place the means-tested benefits on which people with disabilities relied. The debate represented a low point for the integrity of the UK's parliamentary democracy (Citizen's Income Trust, 2016c).

The behaviour of the two Members of Parliament, one of whom was a minister, led the trustees of the Citizen's Basic Income Trust to debate how to prevent such abuse and avoidance of research results. They decided that as politicians could clearly not be trusted to treat research results with integrity, infeasible schemes would no longer be published. This is unfortunate, because the ethics of scientific research require negative results to be published as well as positive results: but it is difficult to see what other decision would have been possible.

As well as offering an 'all in one go' scheme, the 2015 working paper also offered a staged approach. It calculated that if Income Tax Personal Allowances were not changed, and National Insurance Contributions above the Upper Earnings Limit were paid at 6% rather than 2%, then increasing Child Benefit to £56.35 per week for every child would have required an increase in Income Tax rates of 4.5 percentage points, and to increase it to £40 per week for every child would have increased Income Tax rates by 2.5 percentage points. Losses for low-income households would have been negligible, and losses for all households sufficiently low.

The research went on to show that paying young adult Basic Incomes of amounts matching those for Child Benefit to everyone between their sixteenth and nineteenth birthdays would have required no increases in Income Tax rates and would have imposed negligible household disposable income losses if National Insurance Contributions above the Upper Earnings Limit had been increased by another 6 percentage points.

The 2016 Project

Torry (2016a) updated the figures for scheme B in Torry (2015a), offered a variety of additional evaluations, and studied the possibility of paying a Basic Income to a single-year cohort as a first step in rolling out such a Basic Income scheme to the entire working age population.

A significant disappearance at this point was the idea that administrative savings on the implementation of Basic Income could increase the amount of money available for the payment of Basic Incomes. Until 2015, estimates had been made of the savings that would accrue. An assumption was made that administration of Basic Income would cost 1% of the total paid out—the same proportion as for Child Benefit and the Basic State Pension—which would amount to somewhere between £2bn and £3bn per annum. As the Department for Work and Pensions' running costs are stated in the national accounts as £8bn, a saving of £4bn–£5bn was therefore assumed (Citizen's Income Trust, 2013: 8). From 2016 onwards, consistently with other poorly evidenced approximations, the suggestion that there would be administrative savings if a Basic Income were to be implemented disappeared. As only feasible Basic Income schemes that left means-tested benefits in place and took a lot of people off them or close to coming off them were being published, few administrative savings could be envisaged anyway.

A further change was that whereas previously Child Benefit, which paid more for the first child in a family than for subsequent children, was to have been replaced by a Child Basic Income paying the same amount for every child, Torry (2016a) retained and increased Child Benefit, thus preserving the difference in payment levels between the first child and the second and subsequent children. In the report that it published in 2015, the Royal Society of Arts similarly allocated a larger Child Basic Income for the first child of a family than for the second and subsequent children (Citizen's Income Trust, 2016a; Painter & Thoung, 2015: 22), which had the same effect as increasing each of the two Child Benefit rates by the same amount and removing the Child Benefit extension for over 16s still in full-time education. It might have been objected that this breaks the rule that every individual of the same age should receive the same Basic Income. We might respond to the objection as follows: Every Basic Income scheme envisages that Child Basic Incomes would be paid to the child's main carer. This means that children would not in fact receive their own Basic Incomes, and a main carer of children would be receiving a larger Basic Income than someone who was not the main carer of children because they would be receiving their own Basic Income and the Child Basic Incomes or Child Benefit allocated for their children. In this sense, the requirement that every one of the same age should receive the same Basic Income has already been breached: and to pay more for the first child of a family than for the second and subsequent children does not cause more of a breach than already exists, because all it does is adjust the already diverse amounts of Basic Income and/or Child Benefit received by the main carer of one or more children (Torry, 2016a: 3).

A further addition in 2016 was systematic calculation and reporting of the numbers of households taken off means-tested benefits, and also of the numbers brought to within £100 per month of coming off them in the case of most benefits, or within £50 per month of coming off them in the case of Pension Credit and Council Tax Benefit. The aim was to show that even if means-tested benefits were retained, a lot of households would no longer be receiving them, and a lot of households would be able to come off them if they found employment or additional employment of just two or three hours per week. These figures became a fixture in subsequent evaluations of illustrative Basic Income schemes alongside tables showing changes in poverty and inequality indices and graphs showing the redistribution pattern.

In relation to a gradual roll-out: Rather than calculating the cost and effects of an initial Basic Income for a three-year cohort, as the 2015 project had done, the 2016 project calculated the cost and effects of a Basic Income for a single-year cohort of sixteen-year-olds. Because this one-year cohort would not already have an Income Tax Personal Allowance that would need to be changed into a weekly or monthly cash payment, it could simply receive those payments rather than an Income Tax Personal Allowance by the simple mechanism of paying the Basic Income and then charging Income Tax on all earned income (Torry, 2016a).

Torry (2016a) had resulted in a Basic Income scheme that fulfilled all of the criteria, and it reduced inequality and most of the poverty indices: but unfortunately it increased poverty among elderly people. What had happened was that even though a Citizen's Pension had been paid on top of the Basic State Pension, and Pension Credit had been left in place, the removal of the Income Tax Personal Allowance had meant that some individuals who were over retirement age and were still employed or self-employed were finding themselves worse off. The problem was solved by reintroducing an Income Tax Personal Allowance of £5000 per annum for individuals over retirement age. This pushed the net cost of the scheme slightly over the £2bn per annum normally permitted to £2.79bn, but it did solve the problem, and it meant that 10.9% of elderly households were receiving the means-tested Pension Credit rather than 12.3%, and that the total cost of Pension Credit fell by 33% in relation to the existing system rather than by 22% for the unamended scheme.

Torry (2016b) also updated the research results for a Basic Income for 16 to 18-year-olds calculated in 2015, and found that out of various options for implementing and paying for such a Young Adult Basic Income, the most feasible would be to cease paying Child Benefit for anyone over the age of sixteen, to pay Basic Incomes to the three-year cohort, and to apply a BR (Basic Rate) tax code, which has the effect of reducing the Income Tax Personal Allowance to zero. It was found that more complex methods, for instance, involving changes to National Insurance Contributions for the three-year cohort, would save very little money, and would considerably complicate the administration. Suggestions were made as to how the net cost of £3.33bn per annum might be funded.

For the first time, the analysis contained a discussion of the difficulty of holding a genuine Basic Income pilot project in a more developed country. In a less developed country there is likely to be only a rudimentary existing benefits system, if any, and a rudimentary income tax system, if any. Establishing a Basic Income pilot project in such a context requires that the unconditional payments should be made to everyone in the chosen community or communities for the prescribed time period, and that the effects should then be evaluated, preferably in relation to control communities that have not received the Basic Incomes. In a more developed country, existing benefits and tax systems would need to be adjusted for the pilot community, because that is what would have to happen if a nationwide scheme were to be implemented. If that is not done, then the experiment will not be a genuine pilot project. The problem is that it is exceedingly difficult to alter complex tax and benefits systems just for pilot communities.

First of all, Torry (2016b) suggested that the 16–18 project would itself be a pilot project. It also suggested that a pilot project of this pilot project would be possible, because it would be relatively easy to pilot it in a single community or in several communities. This could be done by paying to every 16–18-year-old in the community the Basic Income, and allocating to each of them a BR tax code. The only complexity would relate to the decision as to whether Basic Incomes should be paid to individuals for whom Child Benefit was still being received, and their Child Benefit stopped, or whether Child Benefit should be retained for over 16s still in education, and the individuals concerned excluded from the pilot project.

If Torry (2016b) were being written today, then the suggestion would be made that if the number of young adults still in full-time education over the age of 16 continues to rise, then a pilot project for a 16–21 cohort might be more useful to evaluate than a 16–18 pilot project. The cost of a 16–18 pilot project in a single London borough with a population of 250,000 was calculated to be £13.8m per annum.

A further discussion of the possibility of holding something like a Basic Income pilot project appears later on in the chapter in response to a question that was asked.

The 2017 Project

The 2017 project was inspired by a consultation on the implementation of Basic Income held in 2016 by the Institute for Chartered Accountants of England and Wales. A report prepared for the consultation (Torry, 2016d) described and evaluated four different implementation methods, and a consultation was then held (Citizen's Income Trust, 2016b). The four implementation methods were as follows:

1. A Basic Income for every UK citizen, large enough to take every household off means-tested benefits (including Working Tax Credits, Child Tax Credits, and Universal Credit), and to ensure that no household with low earned income would suffer a financial loss at the point of implementation. The scheme would be implemented all in one go.
2. A Basic Income for every UK citizen, funded from within the current tax and benefits system. Current means-tested benefits would be left in place, and each household's means-tested benefits would be recalculated to take into account household members' Basic Incomes in the same way as earned income is taken into account. Again, implementation would be all in one go.
3. This scheme would start with an increase in Child Benefit. A Basic Income would then be paid to all 16-year-olds, and they would be allowed to keep it as they grew older, with each new cohort of 16-year-olds receiving the same Basic Income and being allowed to keep it.
4. Inviting volunteers among the pre-retired, between the age of 60 and the state pension age (Torry, 2016d: 6).

Torry (2014, 2015a) had already found the first method to be unlikely to be feasible without additional funding being available, and even then low-income households might find themselves worse off, so Torry (2017) did no work on this implementation method. The fourth method could not be evaluated because it would be impossible to know how many volunteers there would be. So the research evaluated the second and third options: the second being essentially the scheme evaluated in 2016, and the third a one-year version of the 2016 three-year proposal. The usual range of requirements was imposed on the schemes, the usual range of tests was applied, and, in response to an increasing number of questions being asked about the likely effects of Basic Income on employment market behaviour, for the first time marginal deduction rates were calculated:

> Would individuals be more or less likely to seek paid employment, or to seek additional earned income, if they were paid a Citizen's Basic Income? Factors often discussed in this context are the marginal effective tax rate (METR: also called the marginal tax rate, the marginal withdrawal rate, or the marginal deduction rate): a measure of the extent to which an employed individual's additional earned income fails to result in additional disposable income; and the participation tax rate (PTR): a measure of the extent to which an unemployed individual's new earned income fails to result in additional disposable income. While a wide variety of factors will determine whether an individual seeks paid employment, or seeks additional earned income, if a substantial rise in earned income results in only a small rise in disposable income then further employment market engagement is less likely to be forthcoming. Because the marginal effective tax rate and the participation tax rate are factors that can be measured, and other factors cannot be, these particular indicators might sometimes be given more prominence than they deserve: but because they can be measured, and because they are likely to be at least of some significance [(Collado, 2018)], this paper defines and calculates a variety of different marginal effective tax rates and participation tax rates. (Torry, 2017: 3)

The results relating to Income Tax rates, the levels of Basic Incomes, poverty and inequality indices, the numbers taken off various means-tested benefits, and so on, for option 2, an updated version of the 2016 scheme, were much the same as before. A new additional set of results in Torry (2017) gave the numbers of households on various benefits and within prescribed distances of coming off them for both the existing tax and benefits system and the Basic Income scheme, and the poverty and inequality indices for the existing system and the Basic Income scheme were also reported.

The main innovation in the working paper Torry (2017) was the reporting of calculations of two different sets of marginal deduction rates, as follows:

Marginal effective tax rates, method 1
EUROMOD's 'MTR' add-on calculates marginal effective tax rates (METRs) for all individuals who are earning an income. The add-on increases by 3 per cent the earned income of each working age adult in the household in turn and calculates the increase in the household disposable income that this generates. If y is an individual's original earned income, d the original household disposable income, and d' the final household disposable income, then the METR is given by (1 − ((d' − d)/0.03y)) × 100. I follow Makovec and Tammik (2017: 21–22) in removing from the list of METRs generated for the FRS sample any METRs with values over 150 per cent and any with negative values. The exercise is then repeated with earned income increased by 20 per cent, where the METR is given by (1 − ((d' − d)/0.2y)) × 100.

This method assumes that in every household every individual adult has complete knowledge of the household's financial resources, that all household members possess equal power in relation to household resources, and that each individual's employment motivation is a function of household disposable income.

Marginal effective tax rates and participation tax rates, method 2
A second method increases the earned income of every individual 16 years old and above by £200 per month, and calculates the change in that individual's disposable income. This method therefore generates results for individuals already in employment, and also for individuals not in employment. For someone not in employment who enters employment, (1 − the ratio between the change in disposable income and the new earned income) × 100 is the Participation Tax Rate (PTR); and for someone already in employment, (1 − the ratio between the change in disposable income and the change in earned income) × 100 is the Marginal Effective Tax Rate (METR). A high PTR represents an 'unemployment trap', and a high METR a 'poverty trap'. In relation both to individuals initially in employment and to those not, a household's benefits income is assumed to be received by the individual to which the payment is made rather than by the household as a whole; and the earnings of all adults in the household are increased at the same time (as opposed to method 1, which increases each earned income in turn). The calculation is the same for both the PTR and the METR: If d is the individual's original disposable income and d' is their final disposable income, then the PTR/METR is given by (1 − ((d'

> – d)/200)) × 100. £200 per month represents something between half a day a week and a day a week of additional employed hours at the National Living Wage, and so represents the kind of real-world employment market decision with which many individuals might be faced.
>
> This method does not assume equal knowledge or sharing of a household's financial resources within the household, but it does assume that each individual's motivation is a function of the payments that they receive. So if one member of a couple receives Working Tax Credits payments on behalf of the household, then they and not their partner will be assumed to be influenced by any decrease in that payment; and if the other member receives Child Benefit, then they and not their partner will be influenced by that.
>
> The reality in relation to household members' knowledge and sharing of household resources will generally lie somewhere between the two methods' assumptions for each household, with I suspect very few households at either end of the spectrum.
>
> (Method 2 is as follows: An additional calculation is added to the National Minimum Wage function (yem) in EUROMOD that adds £200 per month to the earned income of every individual over sixteen years of age. (The NMW parts of the policy are switched off.) The effect is to add £200 to the original income of every individual over the age of sixteen. EUROMOD is run to generate disposable income lists both before and after the change in earned income, for both the current tax and benefits system and for the illustrative Basic Income scheme. METRs/PTRs are then calculated, and for all of the individuals experiencing METRs/PTRs within the required range the weights provided in the FRS data are added together to give the total number of over 16s experiencing that range of METRs. These figures are then compared with the total number of over 16s in the population as represented by the total of the weights for every over 16 in the FRS data.) (Torry, 2017: 11)

A mistake was then made in the marginal deduction rate calculations for one stage of this pilot project. This was corrected in Torry (2018b).

The 2018 Project

Torry (2018b) first of all updated what had become the standard feasible Basic Income scheme, which from 2015 had been adjusted and retested to ensure that it fulfilled the now well-developed set of requirements for financial feasibility (although it still proved impossible to obtain less than 2% of household net disposable income losses of over 5% for low-income households: 2.67% was the figure for this iteration of the scheme). Secondly, it corrected the mistake that had been discovered in the marginal deduction rate calculations for the pilot project researched in Torry (2017). And thirdly, it responded to a question that had been asked about the effect of a Basic Income scheme on people with disabilities.

In relation to the updated results for the standard scheme, more detail was given in relation to marginal deduction rates, now corrected (Torry, 2018b: 12–16).

Figure 16.2 shows that household marginal effective tax rates, measured by method 1, change little on the implementation of the Basic Income scheme.

Method 2 is able to distinguish between waged and unwaged households. Figure 16.3 shows that waged households with the lowest incomes are now paying Income Tax and National Insurance Contributions on all earned income, so quite a lot of the individuals in them are finding themselves with marginal effective tax rate patterns similar to those for the households with higher incomes found in Fig. 16.4.

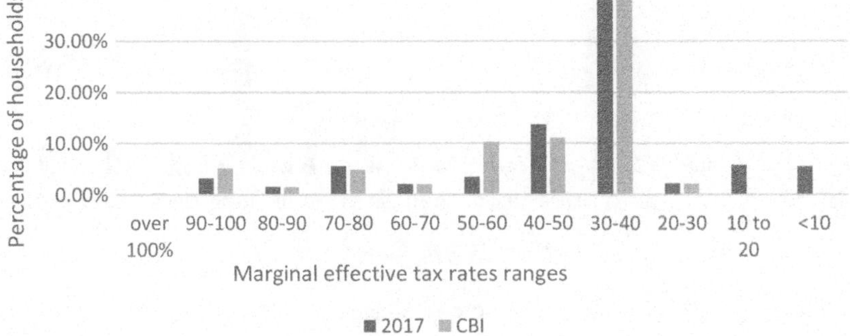

Fig. 16.2 Comparison of marginal effective tax rates, method 1, all waged households (*Source* Torry [2018b: 12])

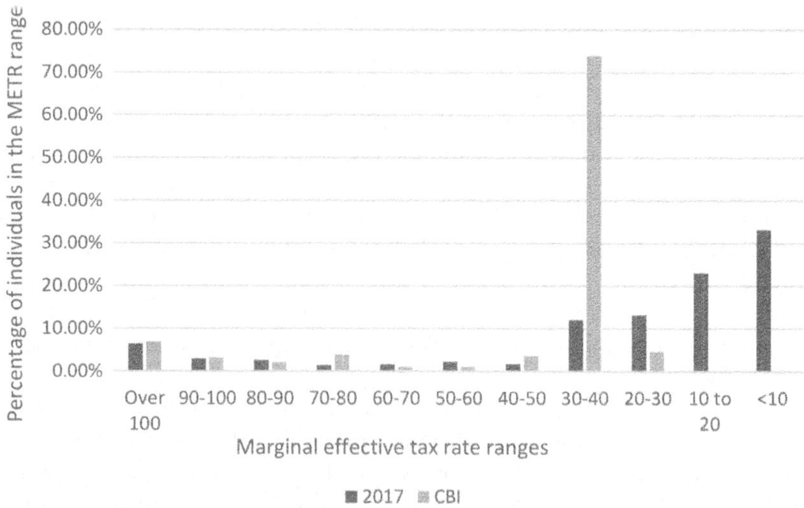

Fig. 16.3 Comparison of marginal effective tax rates, method 2, bottom quintile of waged households (*Source* Torry [2018b: 14])

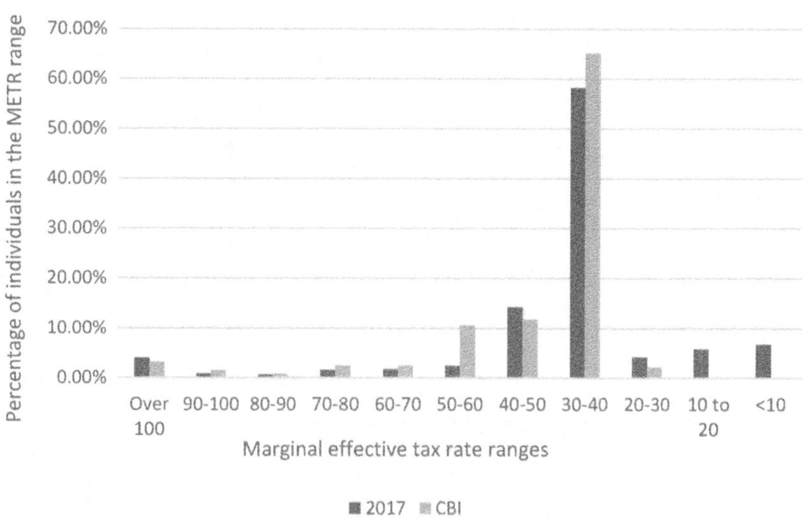

Fig. 16.4 Comparison of marginal effective tax rates, method 2, all waged households (*Source* Torry [2018b: 13])

Figure 16.5 shows the effect of the Basic Income scheme on the participation tax rates experienced by individuals in currently unwaged households if they find employment. The number of very high marginal deduction rates is reduced, and because Income Tax and National Insurance Contributions are now being paid on all earned income, marginal deduction rates for this group of individuals gravitate towards the 20–40% band.

In relation to the question as to how individuals with disabilities would fare in relation to the Basic Income scheme, a somewhat confused picture emerged (Torry, 2018b: 16). Table 16.5 provides the results.

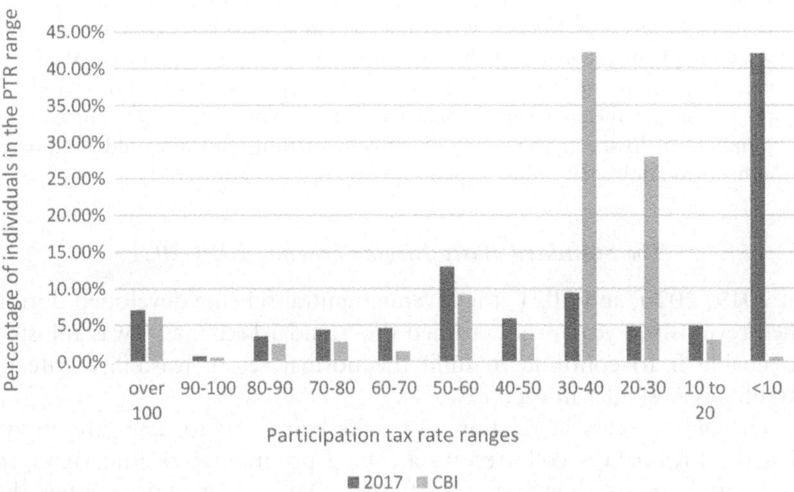

Fig. 16.5 Comparison of participation tax rates, method 2, all unwaged households (*Source* Torry [2018b: 15])

Table 16.5 Gains and losses for individuals with disabilities

Proportion of individuals with disabilities experiencing losses of over 10% at the point of implementation	8.20%
Proportion of individuals with disabilities experiencing losses of over 5% at the point of implementation	9.60%
Average gain for individuals with disabilities	£854 p.a.

Source Torry (2018b: 16)

On average, individuals with disabilities gain £845 p.a., but the complexity of the current benefits system for people with disabilities, compounded by the complex way in which the current benefits system relates to households containing members with disabilities, means that some individuals with disabilities would lose money. This does not necessarily mean that their households would do so.

A now familiar conclusion was drawn in relation to the updated Basic Income scheme:

> This simple scheme would substantially reduce poverty and inequality; it would remove large numbers of households from a variety of means-tested benefits; it would reduce means-tested benefit claim values, and the total costs of means-tested benefits; to the extent that marginal deduction rates affect employment market behaviour, it would provide additional employment market incentives, particularly for the large number of households no longer on means-tested benefits; it would avoid imposing significant numbers of losses at the point of implementation; and it would require almost no additional public expenditure. (Torry, 2018b: 16–17)

The Standard Basic Income Scheme, 2019–2021

In 2019, 2020, and 2021, the revenue-neutral scheme developed during the previous few years—now named the 'standard scheme'—was adjusted to enable it to continue to fulfil the normal set of feasibility criteria. Results were similar in each case.

The only caveats in relation to results being 'up to date' are always that the FRS data is collected via a rolling programme of interviews, so it is always to some extent out of date; that at that point neither the UK country system nor the FRS data enabled us to take account of the roll-out of Universal Credit, the UK Government's new means-tested benefit; and that because Council Tax Support was now localised, and each local authority could set its own regulations and taper rates, calculations relating to Council Tax Benefit might have provided less of a useful picture than calculations relating to other means-tested benefits.

The schemes tested in 2019, 2020, and 2021, were all funded from within the current tax and benefits system by reducing (either to zero or to a lower figure) the Income Tax Personal Allowance and the National Insurance Contributions Primary Earnings Threshold, charging National Insurance Contributions at 12% on all earned income, and increasing

Income Tax rates slightly. Current means-tested benefits were left in place, and each household's means-tested benefits were recalculated to take into account household members' Basic Incomes in the same way as earned income is taken into account. The list of requirements for financial feasibility was always as follows:

- as few changes as possible were to be made to the current tax and benefits system, consistent with the other aims in view;
- revenue neutrality (Hirsch, 2015), which I took to be a net cost or saving of no more than £2bn per annum;
- the avoidance of significant household net disposable income losses, particularly for low-income households (with at least an aim of ensuring that no more than 2% of low-income households should experience household net disposable income losses of more than 5%);
- Income Tax rates to rise by no more than 3 percentage points (Hirsch, 2015);
- reductions in inequality (measured by the Gini coefficient) and in all poverty indices;
- significant numbers of households to be taken off means-tested benefits, and even more to be brought within striking distance of coming off them.

Having set the criteria, the usual method for discovering a feasible Basic Income scheme was employed: that is, varying in turn the values of a wide variety of parameters of an illustrative scheme, testing each iteration by microsimulation to see whether it fitted the criteria, and continuing to test new iterations until a scheme that fitted the criteria was found. As with previous projects, no attempt was made to find an optimal scheme once a scheme that fitted the criteria had been discovered.

A Feasible Basic Income Scheme for 2021

The illustrative scheme that emerged from the usual research process in 2021 was as follows: The scheme is funded by reducing the Income Tax Personal Allowance from the projected £12,550 per annum to £2340 per annum; reducing to zero the various savings allowances; reducing the National Insurance Primary Earnings Threshold from the projected £185 per week to £45 per week; charging National Insurance Contributions at 12% on all earned income above the Primary Earnings Threshold; and setting Income Tax rates as shown in Table 16.6: the basic rate is raised from 20% to 22%, the higher rate from 40% to 43%, and the highest rate from 45% to 49%. Basic Incomes are taken into account in the same way as other income when means-tested benefits are calculated, except that in relation to Housing Benefit and Council Tax Benefit only half of each Basic Income is taken into account in order to reduce sufficiently the number of low-income household disposable income losses.

The significant difference between this Basic Income scheme and those published in 2019 and 2020 is the retention of a small Income Tax Personal Allowance and a small National Insurance Primary Earnings Threshold, which of course required a lower Basic Income to be paid. The rationale for this change is that to reduce the Income Tax Personal Allowance to zero would bring into income tax such teenage earnings as Saturday jobs and paper rounds, and other earned income of negligible amounts, all of which would be onerous to administer.

Table 16.7 shows how many households would suffer disposable income losses of over 10% and over 5%, and how many households in the lowest equivalised disposable income quintile would suffer losses of over 10% and over 5%.

(The OECD equivalisation method is used, which allocates 1 for the first adult in a household, 0.5 for a second person aged 14 or over, and 0.3 for children under 14 years old. The figures are added, and the household

Table 16.6 The illustrative Basic Income scheme

Basic Income levels, tax rates, and net cost of scheme	
Citizen's Pension per week (existing state pensions remain in payment)	£35
Working age adult Basic Income per week (25–65 years old)	£60
Young adult Basic Income per week (20–24 years old)	£50
Education age Basic Income per week (16–19 years old, but not young people still in full-time education)	£25
(Child Benefit is increased by £10 per week)	[£10]
Income Tax, basic rate (on £0–£50,250)	22%
Income Tax, higher rate (on £50,251–£150,000)	43%
Income Tax, top rate (on £150,000–)	49%
Net cost of scheme	£1.8bn p.a

Source Author's own calculations from the output files generated by UKMOD version A2.0+

Table 16.7 Household disposable income losses

Household disposable income losses over 10 and 5% for all households and for the lowest quintile	%
Proportion of all households experiencing losses of over 5% at the point of implementation	6.68
Proportion of all households experiencing losses of over 10% at the point of implementation	1.30
Proportion of households in the lowest equivalised disposable income quintile experiencing losses of over 5% at the point of implementation	1.91
Proportion of households in the lowest equivalised disposable income quintile experiencing losses of over 10% at the point of implementation	0.72

Source Author's own calculations from the output files generated by UKMOD version A2.0+

disposable income divided by the total to generate the equivalised income. Households are then ordered by their equivalised incomes and the losses experienced by households with the lowest 20% of equivalised disposable incomes are evaluated.)

Table 16.8 shows the changes in the numbers of households receiving means-tested benefits, and also the numbers of households brought within striking distance of coming off them.

Tables 16.9, 16.10, 16.11, and 16.12 show reductions in inequality and in poverty rates.

Tables 16.13 and 16.14, and Figs. 16.6 and 16.7, show the redistribution patterns that would result from the implementation of the Basic Income scheme, both in relation to incomes before housing costs and incomes after housing costs.

This is the kind of redistributive pattern that we might wish to see generated by a Basic Income scheme. Given that low-income households have a higher propensity to consume than higher income households, the additional income that lower income households would receive on average would increase demand in the economy. The scheme would also benefit the disposable incomes of mid-range income households. Only those with the highest incomes would experience average disposable income losses: but those losses should be well understood in the current circumstances, and also manageable.

Table 16.8 Reductions in numbers claiming means-tested benefits or within striking distance of coming off them, and the reductions in the total costs of the benefits and the average value of claims

Numbers of households claiming means-tested benefits or within striking distance of coming off them	*The existing scheme in 2021–2022 (%)*	*The Basic Income scheme (%)*
Percentage of households claiming any means-tested benefits	31.07	29.29
Percentage of households claiming more than £100 per month in means-tested benefits	26.82	23.61
Percentage of households claiming more than £200 per month in means-tested benefits	23.93	19.67
Reductions in total cost and average value of claims for means-tested benefits	*Reduction in total cost* (%)	*Reduction in average value of claim* (%)
All means-tested benefits	27.47	35.91

Source Author's own calculations from the output files generated by UKMOD version A2.0+

Table 16.9 Poverty indices for 2021–2022 for the Basic Income scheme (based on incomes before housing costs)

Poverty headcount by population group	*Poverty rates for current system*	*Poverty rates for Basic Income scheme (%)*	*Difference in poverty rates*	*Percentage reduction (%)*
All	16.33%	12.90	−3.42pp	21.00
Children	20.78%	16.11	−4.67pp	22.47
Adults	14.87%	11.58	−3.29pp	22.13
Adults economically active	6.29%	4.50	−1.79pp	28.46
Elderly	16.01%	13.61	−2.40pp	14.99
Fixed poverty line	£318.52			

Source UKMOD statistics presenter

Table 16.10 Poverty indices for 2021–2022 for the Basic Income scheme (based on incomes after housing costs)

Poverty headcount by population group	*Poverty rates for current system*	*Poverty rates for Basic Income scheme (%)*	*Difference in poverty rates*	*Percentage reduction (%)*
All	22.48%	18.92	−3.57pp	15.84
Children	30.05%	26.07	−3.98pp	13.24
Adults	20.94%	17.59	−3.35pp	16.00
Adults economically active	10.27%	8.67	−1.60pp	15.58
Elderly	18.82%	15.00	−3.82pp	20.30
Fixed poverty line	£277.83			

Source UKMOD statistics presenter

Table 16.11 Inequality indices for 2021–2022 household disposable incomes for the Basic Income scheme (based on incomes before housing costs)

Gini coefficient current system	*Gini coefficient for Basic Income scheme*	*Difference between the two Gini coefficients*	*S80/S20 ratio for current system*	*S80/S20 ratio for Basic Income scheme*	*Difference between the two S80/S20 ratios*
0.3140	0.3080	−0.0060	4.9617	4.7986	−0.1631

Source UKMOD statistics presenter

Table 16.12 Inequality indices for 2021–2022 household disposable incomes for the Basic Income scheme (based on incomes after housing costs)

Gini coefficient for current system	*Gini coefficient for Basic Income scheme*	*Difference between the two Gini coefficients*	*S80/S20 ratio for current system*	*S80/S20 ratio for Basic Income scheme*	*Difference between the two S80/S20 ratios*
0.3575	0.3508	−0.0067	6.8676	6.5756	−0.2920

Source UKMOD statistics presenter

Table 16.13 Percentage increase in mean equivalised household disposable income by equivalised household disposable income decile (based on incomes before housing costs)

	Current tax and benefits system, £ per week	*Basic Income scheme, £ per week*	*Difference, £ per week*	*Percentage increase (%)*
Decile 1	186.39	232.45	46.06	24.71
Decile 2	307.8	331.93	24.14	7.84
Decile 3	370.63	388.59	17.96	4.85
Decile 4	431.06	447.21	16.15	3.75
Decile 5	496.72	509.64	12.92	2.60
Decile 6	569.73	578.04	8.31	1.46
Decile 7	654.59	656.87	2.27	0.35
Decile 8	763.7	758.07	−5.63	−0.74
Decile 9	930.83	912.04	−18.79	−2.02
Decile 10	1527.89	1442.30	−85.59	−5.60

Source UKMOD statistics presenter

Table 16.14 Percentage increase in mean equivalised household disposable income by equivalised household disposable income decile (based on incomes after housing costs)

	Current tax and benefits system, £ per week	*Basic Income scheme, £ per week*	*Difference, £ per week*	*Percentage increase (%)*
Decile 1	85.62	129.15	43.53	50.84
Decile 2	231.11	255.28	24.17	10.46
Decile 3	292.38	310.03	17.65	6.04
Decile 4	353.98	369.94	15.96	4.51
Decile 5	424.76	439.23	14.47	3.41
Decile 6	502.97	511.82	8.85	1.76
Decile 7	588.27	590.39	2.11	0.36
Decile 8	695.9	690.44	−5.46	−0.78
Decile 9	855.84	836.85	−19	−2.22
Decile 10	1431.14	1346.69	−84.45	−5.90

Source UKMOD statistics presenter

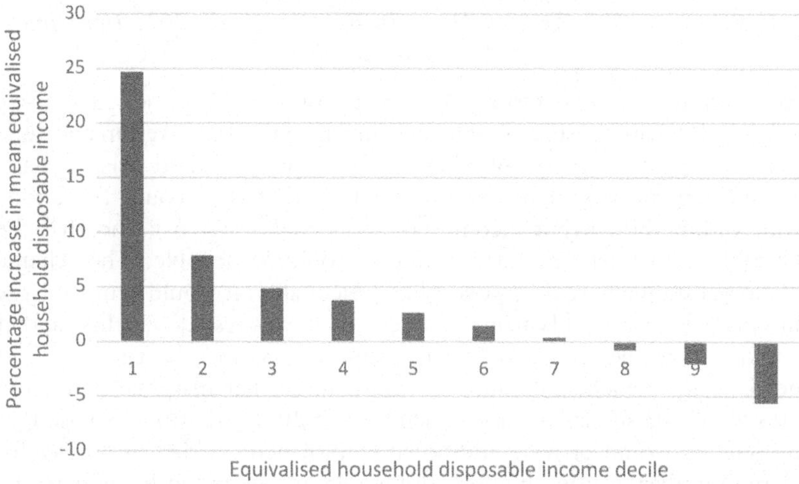

Fig. 16.6 Percentage increase in mean equivalised household disposable income by equivalised household disposable income decile (based on incomes before housing costs) (*Source* UKMOD statistics presenter)

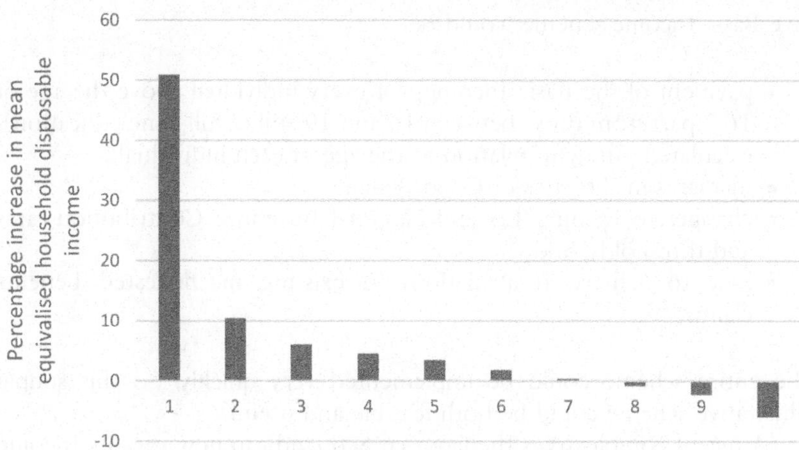

Fig. 16.7 Percentage increase in mean equivalised household disposable income by equivalised household disposable income decile (based on incomes after housing costs) (*Source* UKMOD statistics presenter)

Conclusions That We Can Draw in Relation to the 2021 Iteration of the Standard Scheme

To reiterate the conclusions drawn in previous analyses that have contained research results on schemes similar to this one: We can conclude that this updated version of what has become a standard feasible Basic Income scheme would be revenue neutral (that is, it could be funded from within the current income tax and benefits system); and that the increase in Income Tax rates required would be feasible. The scheme would substantially reduce poverty and inequality; it would remove large numbers of households from a variety of means-tested benefits; and it would reduce means-tested benefit claim values, and the total costs of means-tested benefits. Because we can assume that marginal deduction rates would be similar to those calculated in 2018, we can conclude that the scheme would provide additional employment market incentives for a large number of households no longer on means-tested benefits to the extent that marginal deduction rates affect employment market behaviour; and it would avoid imposing significant numbers of losses at the point of implementation.

Because the only changes required in order to implement this illustrative Basic Income scheme would be

- payment of the Basic Incomes for every individual above the age of 16 (apart from those between 16 and 19 still in full-time education), calculated purely in relation to the age of each individual,
- increases in the rates of Child Benefit,
- changes to Income Tax and National Insurance Contribution rates and thresholds, and
- easy to achieve recalculations in existing means-tested benefits claims,

the entire scheme could be implemented very quickly. So this simple illustrative scheme could be both feasible and useful.

(A recent complexity is the fact that Scotland can now vary its Income Tax rates slightly, and it can also vary and add Income Tax thresholds—and it does. For the purposes of this exercise, and for the sake of simplicity, Income Tax rates have been harmonised across the UK at 23, 43, and 48%, and the thresholds have been harmonised, even though for narrow bands of earnings this requires a change of 4 percentage points rather than 3 percentage points. It should not be assumed that this is what would happen if a Basic Income scheme were to be implemented.)

Responses to Questions

As well as communicating the results of the relevant iteration of what had become a standard approach to a feasible Basic Income scheme, each of the 2019, 2020, and 2021 working papers contained reports of microsimulation research exercises carried out to respond to questions that I had been asked. Here I list the conclusions of those research exercises. Full details can be found in the working papers (Torry, 2019, 2020, 2021).

Responses to Questions in 2019

> Would it be possible to raise the working age Basic Income from £63 per week (the level for working age adults for the 2018 project) to £70 per week?

Yes. Financial feasibility could have been achieved for a scheme that reduced the Income Tax Personal Allowance and the National Insurance Contributions Primary Earnings Threshold to zero, although at the cost of a far smaller increase in Child Benefit than for previous schemes: £5 per week rather than £20 per week. Predictably, this would mean the reduction in child poverty achieved by the £70 per week scheme would have been lower than that for the £65 per week scheme. Other indicators turned out to be fairly similar, except that there were generally higher numbers of household net disposable income losses in most of the loss categories. We can conclude that if for whatever reason a £70 per week Basic Income for working age adults was to be required, then a financially feasible scheme could be implemented.

> How much would it cost to run a pilot project for a whole community for a genuine Basic Income of £70 per week for working age adults?

This research project set out from the conclusions drawn earlier in this chapter about the difficulties of running a genuine pilot project in a country with a more developed economy and concluded that something similar to a pilot project would be possible if it was conducted along similar lines to the pilot project for the single year age cohort project by operationalising those changes that it would be possible to operationalise and not those that would not be.

The plan would therefore be to provide Basic Incomes for all adults over the age of 16 at the same levels as in the £70 per week project reported above. Everyone in employment would then be allocated a BR (Basic Rate) tax code. (A variety of possible consequences of doing this would need to be studied. For instance, in the normal course of events, if a BR tax code is applied throughout a tax year, then the Income Tax system will still assume that an Income Tax Personal Allowance should have been in place, and a tax refund will be issued. This would have to be prevented for the tax years relating to the pilot project. Similarly, how to handle earnings above the higher rate threshold and the top rate threshold would have to be discussed.)

Child Benefit would not be altered, Income Tax rates would not be altered, and the thresholds and rates for National Insurance Contributions would not be amended, as all of those changes would be too difficult to achieve for a single community. Every household on means-tested benefits would have their Basic Incomes added to the means employed in calculating benefit claims, so everyone's means-tested benefit claims would be reduced in value.

Microsimulation research showed that if the pilot project community population were to be 100,000, then the net cost would be £88m per annum; and if the pilot community population were to be 10,000, then the net cost would be £8.8m per annum. The significant assumption made in this calculation is that the financial profile of the pilot community matches in all respects the financial profile of the country as a whole. No household would be worse off with this scheme, because no National Insurance Contribution rates or Income Tax rates would have been increased. Hence the huge net cost of £57bn per annum if the scheme were to be rolled out nationwide. In that sense, the scheme is not financially feasible, so any pilot project of this nature would need to be evaluated in the knowledge that if the scheme were to be rolled out nationwide then Income Tax and National Insurance Contribution rates would have to change, imposing losses on some households.

All one can say about this project is that it is probably as close as it is possible to get to a genuine Basic Income pilot project in the UK, and that although rolling out the scheme nationwide would not be financially feasible, the pilot project would be.

> Would it be possible to construct a financially feasible Basic Income scheme that retained a small Income Tax Personal Allowance rather than reducing it to zero?

This question was answered in the affirmative by a microsimulation research exercise in 2019 that concluded that a scheme that retained an Income Tax Personal Allowance of £4000 per annum and that was based on a £50 per week working age Basic Income could be financially feasible, and it was that approach that was followed in relation to the Basic Income scheme researched in 2021 and discussed earlier in this chapter.

> Would it be possible to reduce the Income Tax rates required to fund a Basic Income scheme if the top rate of tax was raised to 70%?

This research exercise had to conclude that raising the total tax rate for the highest earners to 70% would not enable the other Income Tax rates to be reduced, and so would not change the general patterns of results for the schemes reported in this chapter. Raising the top total tax rate to 70% would unfortunately make almost no difference to the kind of Basic Income scheme that could be implemented.

> What is causing the losses for low-income households, and is it possible to reduce them?

This project hypothesised that one cause might have been the fact that a household's Basic Incomes had been added to the means used to assess means-tested benefits claims, and if the household was on a number of different means-tested benefits, then several benefits might have been withdrawn at the same time, which means that the value of the Basic Income might have been withdrawn more than once at the same time. To test whether this might have been at least part of the problem, a project that added only half of a household's Basic Incomes to the means used to calculate Housing Benefit was reported. The project discovered that this reduced household net disposable income losses. However, as we would also have expected, the total net cost of the scheme was higher, and the scheme was no longer strictly revenue neutral.

Whatever the problems that the UK Government's new Universal Credit has encountered, one of its aims is laudable: to bring means-tested benefits together into a single benefit so that individuals would suffer a single taper rate rather than risk facing more than one at the same time. It is unfortunate that the localisation of Council Tax Support has meant that households can suffer the withdrawal of Council Tax Support at the same time as Universal Credit is withdrawn, but it is still likely that for many households a single taper rate might apply, which would make it easier to avoid household net income losses on the implementation of a Basic Income.

Responses to Questions in 2020

In responses to questions that had been asked, the working paper published in 2020 reported that

- an Emergency Basic Income would not be administratively feasible in the UK because the country did not possess the database that would be required to administer it;
- a Recovery Basic Income scheme, with a working age adult Basic Income level of £196.59, would be able to be implemented once the required administrative infrastructure was in place;
- because of the scheme's considerable net cost of £237bn per annum, the Recovery Basic Income would have to be regarded as a short term economic stimulus measure rather than a permanent fixture;
- a permanent and useful Basic Income, as described earlier in this chapter, would be both feasible and useful once the coronavirus crisis had abated.

Responses to Questions in 2021

The 2021 research exercise evaluated a new iteration of what had become the standard Basic Income scheme, details of which appear earlier in this chapter. It also compared these results with two other options then under discussion: retention of the £20 uplift in the Universal Credit standard allowance and legacy benefits allowances implemented during the pandemic and now withdrawn; and an increase in Child Benefit.

The criteria by which illustrative Basic Income schemes are judged are as follows:

1. as few changes as possible to the current tax and benefits system, consistent with the other aims in view;
2. a net cost or saving of no more than £2bn per annum;
3. the avoidance of significant household net disposable income losses, particularly for low-income households, and in particular no more than 2% of low-income households should experience household net disposable income losses of more than 5%;
4. the basic rate of Income Tax to rise by no more than 2 percentage points, the higher rate by no more than 3 percentage points, and the top rate by no more than 4 percentage points (Hirsch, 2015);
5. reductions in inequality and in all poverty indices;
6. substantial numbers of households taken off means-tested benefits or brought within striking distance of coming off them.

Given that continuation of the current £20 per week increase in Universal Credit and legacy benefits rates, and an increase in Child Benefit of £9.27 per week, conformed to the first five of these criteria, we can legitimately claim that all three options are equally feasible.

However, differences were discovered.

- Continuation of the Universal Credit and legacy benefits rates increase, and an increase in Child Benefit, would be simple to administer (which is not to say that Universal Credit or the legacy benefits are simple to administer: they are not). If a Basic Income scheme were to be implemented then a new database would be required containing every legal resident's name, contact details, date of birth, and bank account details. This would not be difficult to construct if the political will to do so were present (Citizen's Basic Income Trust, 2020a, 2020b; Torry, 2021), and it would only need to be done once. Ongoing administration of a Basic Income would be radically simple; and every household taken off means-tested benefits would represent a reduction in the administrative burden both for the Government and for themselves.

- Means-tested benefits impose on their claimants sanctions regimes, bureaucratic intrusion, complexity and stigma. A continuation of higher Universal Credit and legacy benefit rates would mean more people on means-tested benefits, and not fewer, because earned incomes would have to be higher to take households off them. Because Child Benefit is not taken into account when means-tested benefits are calculated, an increase in Child Benefit would make no difference to the number of households on means-tested benefits. It is only the Basic Income scheme that would reduce the number of households on means-tested benefits; that would bring a higher number of households within striking distance of coming off them; and in addition would reduce significantly the average value of means-tested benefit claims and their total cost.
- The higher the amount of means-tested benefits received by a household, the more additional earned income is required to escape from the high marginal deduction rates imposed by means-tested benefits, so the lower the employment incentive. The continuation of increased Universal Credit and legacy benefit rates would impose higher marginal deduction rates on more households; an increase in Child Benefit would make no difference; and the Basic Income would take a significant number of households off means-tested benefits and bring more families within striking distance of coming off them. Every household taken off means-tested benefits by the Basic Income scheme would experience an immediate increase in employment incentive (Collado, 2018).
- The Basic Income scheme would cause a larger reduction in inequality (in relation to both of the metrics employed) than either the Child Benefit increase or the continuation of the increase in Universal Credit and legacy benefits, and would cause a far larger reduction in poverty in relation to all of the indices. (The patterns of poverty reduction, inequality reduction, and gains and losses, are not dissimilar for the Child Benefit increase and the continuation of the increase in Universal Credit and legacy benefits increase, except that the Child Benefit increase would deliver a larger reduction in child poverty.)

Table 16.15 Comparison of the three options' effects on income security

Quantity of totally secure income per month for working age adults	*Individual*	*Couple*	*Couple with two children*
Continuation of the Universal Credit and legacy benefits increase	0	0	£152.32*
Child Benefit increase	0	0	£232.66*
Basic Income scheme	£260**	£520**	£758.99***

*Child Benefit; **Basic Income; ***Basic Income and Child Benefit

- Most importantly in the current circumstances, as measured by the quantity of income that is totally secure (and so only unconditional benefits, and benefits such as the Basic State Pension that are effectively unconditional once they are in payment), the Basic Income scheme would offer a far larger increase in income security than either of the other two options, as shown in Table 16.15.

Taking all of these factors together, it is clear that all of the advantages are with the Basic Income scheme: so if the UK Government wishes to maintain household incomes in the current circumstances, then the clear choice must be to implement the kind of Basic Income scheme outlined in this chapter. As there might be a delay in constructing the required database, it is clear from the discussion above that an interim measure ought to be an increase in Child Benefit rather than the return of the increase in Universal Credit and legacy benefits.

Conclusions

A number of lessons have been learnt during the process of discovering feasible Basic Income schemes and responding to questions by using POLIMOD and EUROMOD during the past fifteen or so years:

1. To be able to show financial feasibility, very strict requirements must be listed before research begins. Other researchers either set somewhat vague conditions (for instance, 'affordable', allowing schemes with sizeable funding gaps to be regarded as feasible (Lansley &

Reed, 2019; Reed & Lansley, 2016), or they do not set initial conditions but rather evaluate a wide range of schemes and then debate their effects and feasibilities (Martinelli, 2017a, 2017b, 2017c; OECD, 2017). The scientific approach is to set a clear hypothesis—for instance: that there is an illustrative Basic Income scheme that fits a long list of rigorous criteria—and then to look for such a scheme. If such a scheme is found, then the hypothesis has been proved correct.

2. Lessons have been learnt in relation to the set of requirements:

   - Strict revenue neutrality—that is, funding the Basic Income by adjusting the Income Tax Personal Allowance, Income Tax rates, means-tested benefits, and National Insurance Contribution rates and allowances—is essential for the financial feasibility of a scheme. Any other assumption—for instance, that a funding gap could be filled by restricting tax relief on pension contributions, by consumption taxes, and so on—leaves an illustrative scheme open to the charge that it would not be financially feasible, simply because any revenue collected from reducing tax relief on pension contributions, by charging consumption taxes, or by any other mechanism, could be directed elsewhere. Only funding methods that leave gaps in household disposable incomes that have to be filled by Basic Incomes can be permitted.
   - It is essential to ensure that as few changes as possible are made to the current tax and benefits structure. Making the small number of changes envisaged in this chapter makes life difficult enough. The levels of Basic Incomes already constitute a list of variables that can be varied. Every change made to the structure of the tax and benefits system adds another variable that can be varied as all of the variables are altered in turn. If evaluating a scheme using a microsimulation programme is beginning to prove too complicated to manage, then it is likely that administration of such a scheme would also be difficult to manage.
   - It is essential that household net disposable income losses should be kept to a minimum, especially for low-income households. I am aware that a significant gap in the argument of this chapter is a discussion of precisely how low the number

of losses over 5%, 10%, and 15% need to be, for households in general, and for low-income households in particular. Out of the three schemes tested in Torry (2015a) it was clear that two of them produced unsustainable losses and the other one sustainable losses: but neither 'unsustainable' nor 'sustainable' were closely defined. In 2015, a condition was set that 'No more than 2 per cent of low-income households should suffer losses of over 5 per cent of disposable income at the point of implementation': but this condition has not been rigorously applied since then; for most illustrative schemes researched between 2015 and 2019 the figure has been around 4%; and the only scheme that has fulfilled the condition has been the one reported in this chapter that retains a small Income Tax Personal Allowance (see Table 16.7 earlier in this chapter). There is clearly a debate to be had about the acceptable number of household net disposable income losses on the implementation of a Basic Income scheme.

- Absolutely essential conditions for feasibility must be a reduction in inequality, measured by the Gini coefficient (and potentially by other measures as well), and a reduction in every poverty index. When in Torry (2016a) an illustrative scheme was found to increase elderly poverty, it was essential to put that right.
- It is also essential that Income Tax rate rises should be kept to 3 percentage points. Anything above that is likely to be psychologically and therefore politically infeasible.

3. There are financially feasible Basic Income schemes available. This is perhaps the most important outcome of the research behind the various papers.
4. There are at least two viable ways to implement a Basic Income scheme: all at once; or starting with a single age cohort.
5. There are at least two viable ways to hold a pilot project: in a single community for its entire population; and in a single community for a particular age cohort.
6. A significant gap in the research relates to employment market behaviour. The research results on marginal deduction rates reported here have their interest, but it is not clear precisely

how relevant marginal deduction rates are to changing employment market behaviour. What is required is extending a static microsimulation model with explicit modelling of employment market behaviour: although the risk with that is that employment market models are based on significant assumptions, and to combine such a model with such a static microsimulation programme as EUROMOD/UKMOD, which works only with real-world data and real-world tax and benefits regulations, would turn a programme that operates without relying on significant assumptions into a combination that relies on them.

7. Related to that requirement: Static microsimulation offers useful evaluation of illustrative Basic Income schemes, but only of the 'morning-after' variety. In real life, receiving a Basic Income, and experiencing related changes to employment patterns, would together change individual and household disposable incomes, Income Tax and National Insurance Contribution payments, and means-tested benefits, in turn generating more employment market behaviour change, and so on. A dynamic approach is required to model the complex dynamic processes constituted by employment market behaviour change and changing disposable incomes, means-tested benefits, and taxes, with and without a Basic Income. How 'feasible' might then be defined in relation to a Basic Income scheme would become a question somewhat different from the way in which 'feasible' has been defined in this chapter.
8. Equally useful from the point of view of this particular researcher—and even more useful in the longer term—would be a computer algorithm that could automate the process of testing Basic Income schemes. As things stand, conditions are set, an initial scheme is established, variables are set, the EUROMOD programme is run, columns are extracted from output files and placed on different sheets of a spreadsheet workbook, calculations are done, and the results are tabulated to see if the scheme fits the requirements. If it does not, then a variable is altered, EUROMOD is run, and so on. It is a tedious process. While it is possible for users to construct their own algorithms to automate this process in relation to their specific research questions, I look forward to the day when a generic tool can be constructed within EUROMOD that will enable the researcher to vary a wide variety of parameters at the same time and

automatically find not simply a single illustrative scheme that fits the requirements, but the one that *best* fits the requirements.

This chapter records what has been a fascinating journey in microsimulation. Some might think that a contradiction in terms. I do not. This is partly because the pursuit of illustrative schemes that are feasible in relation to a rigorous set of criteria is satisfying when a feasible scheme is found (although deeply frustrating when it is not). Seeking and discovering illustrative Basic Incomes that are 'affordable' (carefully defined), that are 'adequate' (that is, they provide a useful solid financial floor on which households can build), and that 'secure the advantages on which Basic Income is sold' is not so much a 'trilemma' (Martinelli, 2018) but a challenge. Some of us find the challenge an invigorating one.

But far more importantly, the journey in microsimulation recorded here has a fascination because this is research that might matter. There are plenty of reasons for wanting to see a Basic Income implemented (Torry, 2013, 2015b, 2018a), and because only a feasible scheme could be implemented, the pursuit of feasibility across a broad front is an essential research process (Torry, 2016c). Microsimulation is the only tool adequate for the task of proving financial feasibility. Its use and its development are therefore essential to the now global Basic Income debate. The UK has been a world leader in this field. Now every other country needs microsimulation researchers committed to the task of exploring the feasibility of illustrative Basic Income schemes, simply because Basic Income is an idea whose time might have come, and whenever the policy process factors align to enable the idea to be considered as a serious policy option, good quality research on feasible Basic Income schemes needs to be available.

Acknowledgements This chapter is constructed from material drawn from three working papers published by the Institute for Social and Economic Research at the University of Essex (Torry, 2019, 2020, 2021). Most of the chapter is drawn from the 2019 working paper, but detailed evaluation of an illustrative Basic Income scheme is drawn from the 2021 paper, and the final sections draw on both the 2020 and 2021 working papers (Torry, 2019, 2020, 2021). Permission to publish material from the working papers is gratefully acknowledged.

I am most grateful to Holly Sutherland, Matteo Richiardi, Alari Paulus, Cara McGenn, Iva Tasseva, Paola De Agostini, and all those from the Institute for Social and Economic Research who have given me considerable assistance with microsimulation research and the writing of working papers during the past fifteen years.

In relation to this chapter, I am particularly grateful to Alari Paulus for the trouble that he took to review the content of the long 2019 working paper and to make many useful suggestions for its improvement.

The results presented here are based on UKMOD version A2.0+ and EUROMOD version I1.0+ and previous versions. UKMOD and EUROMOD are maintained, developed, and managed by the Institute for Social and Economic Research (ISER) at the University of Essex in collaboration with national teams from the EU member states. The process of extending and updating UKMOD is financially supported by the Nuffield Foundation, based on the annual update of the UK component of EUROMOD funded by the European Union Programme for Employment and Social Innovation 'EaSI' (2014–2020). The UK Family Resources Survey data was made available by the Department for Work and Pensions via the UK Data Archive.

The results and their interpretation are the author's responsibility. UKMOD delivers static microsimulation results, and does not account for possible behavioural responses nor for general equilibrium effects. Opinions expressed in this chapter are not necessarily those of the Institute for Social and Economic Research.

References

Atkinson, A. B., Leventi, C., Nolan, B., Sutherland, H., & Tasseva, I. (2017). *Reducing poverty and inequality through tax-benefit reform and the minimum wage: The UK as a case-study* (EUROMOD Working Paper EM 13/17). Colchester: Institute for Social and Economic Research, University of Essex. Retrieved March 27, 2022, from https://www.euromod.ac.uk/sites/default/files/working-papers/em13-17.pdf

Basic Income Earth Network. (2022). *Basic Income*. Retrieved March 27, 2022, from https://basicincome.org

Citizen's Basic Income Trust. (2020a). *Coronavirus and the next time it happens*. London: Citizen's Basic Income Trust. Retrieved March 27, 2022, from https://citizensincome.org/news/coronavirus-and-the-next-time-it-happens/

Citizen's Basic Income Trust. (2020b). *Getting Basic Income done*. London: Citizen's Basic Income Trust. Retrieved March 27, 2022, from https://citizensincome.org/news/getting-basic-income-done/

Citizen's Income Trust. (2013). *Citizen's Income: A brief introduction*. Citizen's Income Trust.

Citizen's Income Trust. (2016a). Review of Anthony Painter and Chris Thoung, *Report: Creative citizen, creative state—The principled and pragmatic case for a Universal Basic Income*. London: Royal Society of Arts. *Citizen's Income Newsletter*, issue 2 for 2016: 20–21. London: Citizen's Income Trust. Retrieved March 27, 2022, from http://citizensincome.org/research-analysis/the-royal-society-of-arts-report-on-citizens-income/

Citizen's Income Trust. (2016b). *ICAEW report on implementing Citizen's Income*. London: Citizen's Income Trust. Retrieved March 27, 2022, from http://citizensincome.org/news/icaew-report-on-implementing-citizens-income/

Citizen's Income Trust. (2016c). Members of Parliament debate Citizen's Income. *Citizen's Income Newsletter*, issue 3 for 2016: 9. London: Citizen's Income Trust. Retrieved March 27, 2022, from https://citizensincome.org/news/members-of-parliament-debate-citizens-income/

Collado, D. (2018). *Financial work incentives and the long-term unemployed: The case of Belgium* (EUROMOD Working Paper EM1/18). Colchester: Institute for Social and Economic Research, University of Essex. Retrieved March 27, 2022, from https://www.iser.essex.ac.uk/research/publications/working-papers/euromod/em1-18

De Agostini, P. (2018). *EUROMOD country report United Kingdom 2015–2018*. Colchester: Institute for Social and Economic Research, University of Essex. Retrieved March 27, 2022, from https://www.euromod.ac.uk/sites/default/files/country-reports/year9/Y9_CR_UK_Final.pdf

Hirsch, D. (2015). *Could a 'Citizen's Income' work?* York: Joseph Rowntree Foundation. Retrieved March 27, 2022, from https://www.jrf.org.uk/sites/default/files/jrf/migrated/files/citizens-income-full.pdf

Hirsch, D. (2019). *A minimum Income standard for the United Kingdom in 2019*. York: Joseph Rowntree Foundation. Retrieved March 27, 2022, from https://www.jrf.org.uk/report/minimum-income-standard-uk-2019

House of Commons Work and Pensions Committee. (2007). *Benefit simplification: The seventh report of session 2006–7*. HC 463 (Vol. 2). London: The Stationery Office. Retrieved March 27, 2022, from www.publications.parliament.uk/pa/cm200607/cmselect/cmworpen/463/463ii.pdf

Lansley, S., & Reed, H. (2019). *Basic Income for all: From desirability to feasibility*. London: Compass. Retrieved March 27, 2022, from http://www.compassonline.org.uk/basic-income-for-all/

Makovec, M., & Tammik, M. (2017). *Baseline results from the EU28 EUROMOD: 2011–2016* (EUROMOD Working Paper EM17/14). Colchester: Institute for Social and Economic Research, University of Essex. Retrieved March 27, 2022, from https://www.iser.essex.ac.uk/research/publications/working-papers/euromod/em6-17

Martinelli, L. (2017a). *The fiscal and distributional implications of alternative Universal Basic Income schemes in the UK*. Bath: Institute for Policy Research. Retrieved March 27, 2022, from https://www.bath.ac.uk/publications/the-fiscal-and-distributional-implications-of-alternative-universal-basic-income-schemes-in-the-uk/

Martinelli, L. (2017b). *Exploring the distributional and work incentive effects of plausible illustrative Basic Income schemes*. Bath: Institute for Policy Research. Retrieved March 27, 2022, from https://www.bath.ac.uk/publications/exploring-the-distributional-work-incentive-effects-of-plausible-illustrative-basic-income-schemes/

Martinelli, L. (2017c). *Assessing the case for a Universal Basic Income in the UK*. Bath: Institute for Policy Research. Retrieved March 27, 2022, from https://www.bath.ac.uk/publications/assessing-the-case-for-a-universal-basic-income-in-the-uk/

Martinelli, L. (2018). *Which countries would benefit most and which face the greatest fiscal challenges from implementing basic income?* Retrieved March 27, 2022, from https://www.iser.essex.ac.uk/files/misoc/events/FOSS18/Luke_Martinelli.pdf

Miller, A. (2017). *A Basic Income handbook*. Luath Press.

Morgan, G., Reed, H., & Torry, M. (2019). Analysis of the financial effects of Basic Income. In M. Torry (Ed.), *The Palgrave international handbook of Basic Income* (pp. 191–211). Palgrave Macmillan.

OECD. (2017). *Basic Income as a policy option: Can it add up?* Paris: OECD. Retrieved March 27, 2022, from www.oecd.org/employment/emp/Basic-Income-Policy-Option-2017.pdf

Painter, A., & Thoung, C. (2015). *Report: Creative citizen, creative state—The principled and pragmatic case for a Universal Basic Income*. London: Royal Society of Arts. Retrieved March 27, 2022, from https://www.thersa.org/discover/publications-and-articles/reports/basic-income

Reed, H., & Lansley, S. (2016). *Universal Basic Income: An idea whose time has come?* London: Compass. Retrieved March 27, 2022, from http://www.compassonline.org.uk/publications/universal-basic-income-an-idea-whose-time-has-come/

Stapenhurst, C. (2014). Experiments in EUROMOD. *Citizen's Income Newsletter*, issue 3 for 2014: 11–17. London: Citizen's Income Trust. Retrieved March 27, 2022, from https://citizensincome.org/wp-content/uploads/2016/02/CIT_Newsletter_2014_Issue_3.pdf

Torry, M. (2006). *A Citizen's Income: A recipe for change*. A Compass Think-piece. London: Compass. Retrieved March 27, 2022, from https://www.compassonline.org.uk/publications/a-citizens-income-a-recipe-for-change/

Torry, M. (2012). Research note: A Citizen's Income scheme's winners and losers. *Citizen's Income Newsletter*, issue 3 for 2012: 2–4. London: Citizen's

Income Trust. Retrieved March 27, 2022, from https://citizensincome.org/wp-content/uploads/2016/02/CIT_Newsletter_2012_Issue_3.pdf

Torry, M. (2013). *Money for everyone: Why we need a Citizen's Income*. Policy Press.

Torry, M. (2014). *Research note: A feasible way to implement a Citizen's Income* (EUROMOD Working Paper EM17/14). Colchester: Institute for Social and Economic Research, University of Essex. Retrieved March 27, 2022, from https://www.iser.essex.ac.uk/research/publications/working-papers/euromod/em17-14

Torry, M. (2015a). *Two feasible ways to implement a revenue neutral Citizen's Income scheme* (EUROMOD Working Paper EM6/15). Colchester: Institute for Social and Economic Research, University of Essex. Retrieved March 27, 2022, from https://www.iser.essex.ac.uk/research/publications/working-papers/euromod/em6-15

Torry, M. (2015b). *101 reasons for a Citizen's Income: Arguments for giving everyone some money*. Policy Press.

Torry, M. (2016a). *An evaluation of a strictly revenue neutral Citizen's Income scheme* (EUROMOD Working Paper EM5/16). Colchester: Institute for Social and Economic Research, University of Essex. Retrieved March 27, 2022, from https://www.iser.essex.ac.uk/research/publications/working-papers/euromod/em5-16

Torry, M. (2016b). *Citizen's Income schemes: An amendment, and a pilot project—Addendum to EUROMOD working paper EM5/16* (EUROMOD Working Paper EM5/16a). Colchester: Institute for Social and Economic Research, University of Essex. Retrieved March 27, 2022, from https://www.iser.essex.ac.uk/research/publications/working-papers/euromod/em5-16a

Torry, M. (2016c). *The feasibility of Citizen's Income*. Palgrave Macmillan.

Torry, M. (2016d). *How might we implement a Citizen's Income*. London: ICAEW. Retrieved March 27, 2022, from www.icaew.com/-/media/corporate/files/technical/sustainability/outside-insights/citizens-income-web---final.ashx?la=en

Torry, M. (2017). *A variety of indicators evaluated for two implementation methods for a Citizen's Basic Income* (EUROMOD Working Paper EM 12/17). Colchester: Institute for Social and Economic Research, University of Essex. Retrieved March 27, 2022, from https://www.iser.essex.ac.uk/research/publications/working-papers/euromod/em12-17

Torry, M. (2018a). *Why we need a Citizen's Basic Income: The desirability, feasibility and implementation of an unconditional income*. Policy Press.

Torry, M. (2018b). *An update, a correction, and an extension, of an evaluation of an illustrative citizen's Basic Income scheme* (EUROMOD Working Paper EM 12/17a). Colchester: Institute for Social and Economic Research, University of Essex. Retrieved March 27, 2022, from https://www.iser.essex.ac.uk/research/publications/working-papers/euromod/em12-17a

Torry, M. (2019). *Static microsimulation research on citizen's Basic Income for the UK: A personal summary and further reflections* (Institute for Social and Economic Research Working Paper EM13/19). Colchester: Institute for Social and Economic Research, University of Essex. Retrieved March 27, 2022, from https://www.iser.essex.ac.uk/research/publications/working-papers/euromod/em13-19.pdf

Torry, M. (2020). *Evaluation of a Recovery Basic Income, and of a sustainable revenue neutral Citizen's Basic Income, with an appendix relating to different universal credit roll-out scenarios* (Institute for Social and Economic Research Working Paper EM7/20). Colchester: Institute for Social and Economic Research, University of Essex. Retrieved March 27, 2022, from https://www.iser.essex.ac.uk/research/publications/working-papers/euromod/em7-20.pdf

Torry, M. (2021). *Three income maintenance options for 2021.* Centre for Microsimulation and Policy Analysis Report. Colchester: Institute for Social and Economic Research, University of Essex. Retrieved March 27, 2022, from https://www.microsimulation.ac.uk/publications/publication-526555/

Index

M. Torry, *Basic Income—What, Why, and How?*, Exploring the Basic Income Guarantee,
https://doi.org/10.1007/978-3-031-14248-2

P

The manufacturer's authorised representative in the EU is Springer Nature Customer Service Centre GmbH, Europaplatz 3, 69115 Heidelberg, Germany. If you have any concerns regarding our products, please contact ProductSafety@springernature.com

Printed and bound by CPI Group (UK) Ltd, Croydon, CR0 4YY
28/09/2026
02224072-0016